Hamza Kaïdi
in collaboration with
Nadjm Oud-Dine Bammate
and El Hachemi Tidjani

Mecca and Medinah today

Sponsored by
the Organisation of
the Islamic Conference

¦¦¦ les éditions j.a.

*M*ecca is the focal point towards which Muslims all over the world turn to pray five times a day. Each year, millions of faithful go there on a pilgrimage. Thus Mecca is the point of convergence of the entire Islamic community.

To go to Mecca is an act of faith prescribed by religion, and the most ardent wish of every Muslim. All meet there as equals in the plain white garnment of the pilgrim.

Mecca is thus universal and at the same time a specific place on the map, with a long history of its own, a place to be discovered and to be remembered by all who go there. This book, "Mecca and Medinah today", is both a guide for the pilgrim and a general introduction to the Muslim faith for those who wish to understand this religion better, to become better acquainted with Muslims in general and to find out more about their beliefs. The pilgrimage is so essential to Islam that to know more about it is to become more familiar with the whole religion.

Though the pilgrimage is a ritual obligation for all those who are in a position to carry it out, the Koran stresses the fact on a number of occasions that none must feel obliged to accomplish a task beyond his or her particular capacity and endurance. He who cannot undertake the pilgrimage for reasons of ill-health, out of poverty or for any other valid reason is not in a state of sin if he does not go to the Holy City. He is forgiven in advance. The pilgrimage has to be the accomplishment of a vow rather than a painful duty for the pilgrim or for his family. That is why all doctors of Islamic law are unanimous in declaring that the pilgrim must be in a financial position to provide for his loved ones in his absence and to pay for his journey and his stay in Mecca without having recourse to illegitimate means.

Such rules are in keeping with those verses of the Koran which state that "God does not burden any man beyond his capacities". For this reason, the giving of alms or offerings, or fasting, can take the place of the pilgrimage. For this reason also, the custom of sending a relation in one's place under certain circumstances has evolved; it is tolerated but not recommended.

The "Niyah", in other words the intention avowed by the would-be pilgrim, is considered the most essential ingredient in each individual's commitment to making the pilgrimage.

The vow, taken serenely, in private, with the concomittent determination to see it through, is what gives the pilgrimage that will follow its true impact. It is the vow that underlines the meaning of the cry "Labbayaka" — "I am with Thee" or "Here I am in Thy presence".

In the first part of this work, we shall attempt to show what motivates the pilgrim; in the second part, we shall describe the pilgrimage rite by rite, without forgetting also to supply a good deal of practical information.

les éditions j.a.

TRANSLATOR'S NOTE

The spelling of Arabic words in English is approximative, and there is no one correct spelling, universally accepted by all official sources, of the various Islamic terms. For example, there are at least four different ways of spelling the title of the Muslim sacred text: Coran, Koran, Kuran and Qu'oran. All can be regarded as correct since each is used in a number of approved texts such as the Encyclopedia of Islam, the book of Pilgrimage issued by the Mosque in London, the Encyclopaedia Britannica, etc.

The most common interchangeable spellings involve the use of the s or the c (as in 'Ishà/Icha), the o and the u (as in Muhammed, Mohammed or Muhammad), the e or the i (as in Hegira/Hijrah), the q or the k (as in Qibla and Kibla), the i or the y (as in Sa'i), the use of dj or j (as in Djihad and Jihad), the omission or inclusion of the al in the prefix "al" (as in Thu-l-Hijjah/ Thu-al-Hijjah), the ending of words in a or in ah (as in Ka'ba or Ka'bah) or the ending of words with an e or the leaving out of the e (as in Mutawiff and Mutawiffe).

When confronted by a variety of spellings, I have endeavoured to select the spelling most familiar to an English-speaking reader (Koran instead of Qu'ran, Abraham, instead of Ibraheem), or those whose spelling is surely easier for the non-Arab to understand and, eventually, to approximate the pronunciation. It is, for example, easier to guess at the sound of a word written Hajj, rather than that of one written Hadjdj.

Summary   The Pilgrimage

Invocations (Ad'iya)

the pilgrimage

the pillars of Islam

■ The pilgrimage is one of the five pillars (or *Arkān, Rokn* in the singular) of the Muslim religion, the other four being the profession of faith (*As-Shahāda*), prayer (*Aŝ-Ŝalāt*), fasting during the whole of the month of Ramadan (*As-Sawm*), and the official giving of alms (*Az-Zakat*).

The profession of faith

The profession of faith is the first condition required of the adherent to the Muslim faith. This adherence of an individual or a group is not automatic. It must be freely undertaken and is regarded as genuine only if it is preceded by a long period of reflection, sometimes over many years. It is a belief inherited from one's social background, inculcated from childhood, stressed during adolescence and definitively accepted as an adult.

Though the profession of faith is a choice, an attitude, it takes on its full force only when the individual proclaims it in words and expresses his faith by his actions, his way of life within society and even the way he eats and dresses.

Prayer

Prayer purifies the body. If one considers that man consists of a material shape, thoughts and a soul, one can understand how prayer can purify the individual by drawing him out of himself and his personal problems towards other things, such as the causes underlying the creation of the world and the living creatures that people it and above all the primary cause: God, in whom the soul recognizes its Creator, its Benefactor, its Master and the Master of the Universe, its Guide and its Supreme Arbitrator, Wisest of the wise by definition, whose Omnipotence can at any moment change the course of our destiny.

GREAT DATES OF ISLAM

Towards 1950 BC : The Prophet Abraham, father of the three monotheistic religions (Judaism, Christianity and Islam), restores the Ka'bah.
Towards 570 AD : Birth of the Prophet Muhammed.
Towards 610 : Beginning of the Revelation of the Koran.
622 : Emigration of the Prophet and his companions from Mecca to Yathrib, which will later be known as Medinah, Beginning of the Islamic era.
11/1/630 (20th Ramadan of the year 8 H*) : Peaceful entry of Mecca by the Muslims.
8/6/632 : Death of the Prophet Muhammed.
632 - 634 : Caliphate of Abu Bakr.
634 - 640 : Islamization of Syria and Palestine.
634 - 644 : Caliphate of 'Umar Ibn al-Khattab.
634 - 641 : Islamization of Mesopotamia (Iraq).
639 - 642 : Islamization of Egypt.
642 - 647 : Islamization of Libya.
637 - 650 : Islamization of Persia.
644 - 656 : Caliphate of 'Uthman Ibn 'Affan.
647 - 698 : Islamization of North Africa.
656 - 661 : Caliphate of 'Ali Ibn Abi Talib.

Previous pages:
Two of the seven minarets
of the Great Mosque of Mecca
seem to dominate the modern city.

There is nothing surprising in the fact that this effort of contemplation of the grandiose phenomena of nature, neglected by most men whose senses and sensibility have grown dull from habit, that this inner contemplation of the Divinity should be the best way of making individuals more conscious of the divine hand that inspires our behaviour in the least detail and our most secret intentions. "He holds the keys to the mysteries (of the universe) which He alone knows. He knows that which is hidden deep in the ground and in the depths of the oceans. There is not a molecule buried in the darkness of the earth, a green or a dry twig, that are not listed in the ledger that is set out [of Creation]."

Koran, VI - 59.

In this light, prayer has the priceless quality of calming down a person's passions, of helping him to master his baser instincts, of developing in him a feeling of gratitude towards Divine Mercy, towards paternal and maternal love, making him more understanding not only of those who share the same beliefs as himself but of all human beings in general.

"Recite that which has been revealed to you of the Book. Accomplish your prayer. Prayer turneth away from turpitude and from evil. To invoke God is a capital duty. God knoweth all your acts"

Koran, XXIX - 45.

There are several forms of prayer in Islam:
1. The compulsory Coranic prayer (*Ŝalāt*) at set hours, five times daily, either recited collectively (the faithful praying behind a chosen *Imam*) or individually.
2. Optional prayer (*Natawil*).
3. Prayer of request (*Du'a*) or invocation (*Zikr*).

Prayer generates piety, modesty and human solidarity. It is always preceded by indispensable measures of bodily hygiene and spiritual preparation, such as ablutions (the ritual washing of certain parts of the

---

661 : Triumph of the Umayyads of Mu'awiyah, who had proclaimed himself Caliph in 661. Damascus becomes the capital of the Muslim empire.
661 - 750 : Umayyad dynasty.
711 - 718 : Islamization of the greater part of the Iberian peninsula.
750 - 1258 : Abbassid dynasty. Capital : Baghdad.
812 to 1258 : Progressive decentralization of the power of the Baghdad caliphate. Emancipation of the provinces. Creations of the Umayyad caliphate at Cordoba (756) and of the Fatimid caliphate at Cairo (969).
1096 - 1291 : The eight Crusades are launched by Christian Europe in its endeavour to get hold of Jerusalem and the Tomb of Christ.
Rise of the Hafŝi in Tunisia (1228 - 1574).
Rise of the Zianides in Algeria (1237 - 1555).
Rise of the Merinides in Morocco (1269 - 1465).
1258 : Sack of Baghdad by the Mongols and end of the Abbassid caliphate.
1250 - 1517 : The Mamelukes in Egypt and in Syria.
1260 : Victory of the Mamelukes against the Mongols in Palestine. Egypt becomes the centre of the Muslim world.
1453 : The Ottomans take Constantinople.
1492 : Fall of the last Muslim kingdom in Spain.

---

* H : Hijrah

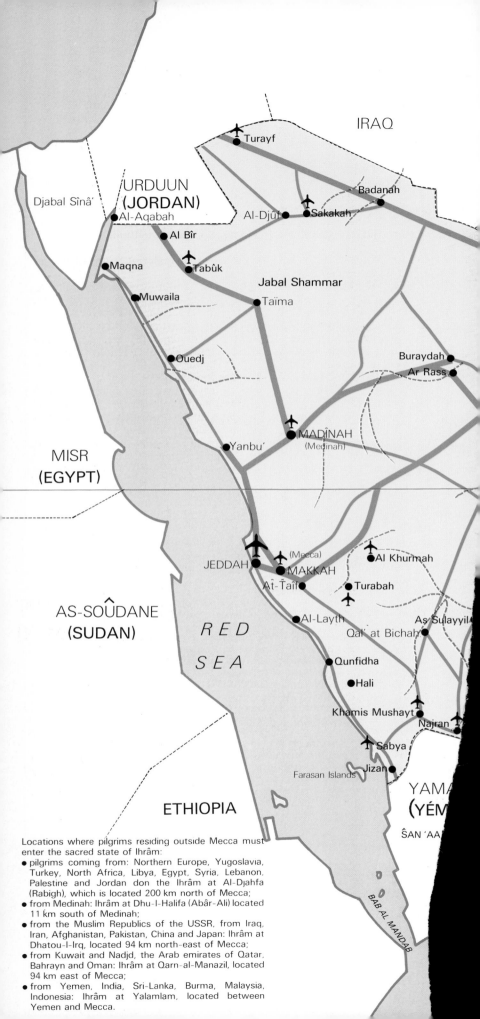

IRAQ

URDUUN
(JORDAN)

Djabal Sînâ'

Al-Aqabah
Turayf
Badanah
Al-Djûf
Sakakah
Al Bîr
Maqna
Tabûk
Jabal Shammar
Muwaila
Taïma
Ouedj
Buraydah
Ar Rass

MISR
(EGYPT)

Yanbu'
MADÎNAH
(Medinah)

JEDDAH
(Mecca)
MAKKAH
Al Khurmah
Aî-Ṭaîf
Turabah

AS-SOÛDANE
(SUDAN)

RED

SEA
Al-Layth
As Sulayyil
Qal' at Bichah

Qunfidha

Hali

Khamis Mushayt
Najran

Sabya
Farasan Islands
Jizan
YAMA
(YÉM

ETHIOPIA
ŜAN 'AA

BAB AL MANDAB

Locations where pilgrims residing outside Mecca must
enter the sacred state of Ihrâm:
• pilgrims coming from: Northern Europe, Yugoslavia,
Turkey, North Africa, Libya, Egypt, Syria, Lebanon,
Palestine and Jordan don the Ihrâm at Al-Djahfa
(Rabigh), which is located 200 km north of Mecca;
• from Medinah: Ihrâm at Dhu-I-Halifa (Abâr-Ali) located
11 km south of Medinah;
• from the Muslim Republics of the USSR, from Iraq,
Iran, Afghanistan, Pakistan, China and Japan: Ihrâm at
Dhatou-I-Irq, located 94 km north-east of Mecca;
• from Kuwait and Nadjd, the Arab emirates of Qatar,
Bahrayn and Oman: Ihrâm at Qarn-al-Manazil, located
94 km east of Mecca;
• from Yemen, India, Sri-Lanka, Burma, Malaysia,
Indonesia: Ihrâm at Yalamlam, located between
Yemen and Mecca.

AL-ARABIYAH AS-SAOÛDIYAH
(SAUDI ARABIA)

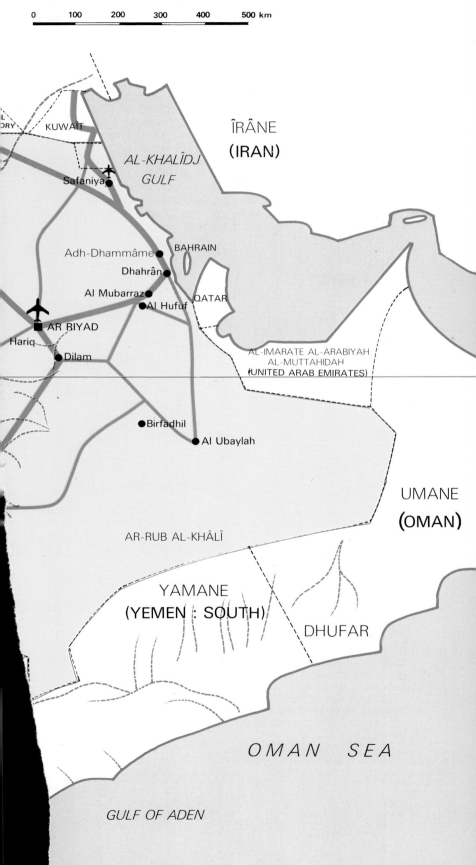

0   100   200   300   400   500 km

ÎRÂNE
(IRAN)

KUWAIT

AL-KHALÎDJ
GULF

Safaniya

Adh-Dhammâme   BAHRAIN

Dhahrân

Al Mubarraz   QATAR

Al Hufuf

AR RIYAD

Hariq

Dilam

AL-IMARATE AL-ARABIYAH
AL-MUTTAHIDAH
(UNITED ARAB EMIRATES)

Birfadhil

Al Ubaylah

UMANE
(OMAN)

AR-RUB AL-KHÂLÎ

YAMANE
(YEMEN : SOUTH)

DHUFAR

OMAN   SEA

GULF OF ADEN

body accompanied by the recitation of certain sacred formulas). The person officiating is not invariably an official *Imam*, but one who can be chosen by the congregation or who appoints himself. There is no clergy in Islam. However, except in special circumstances, the hours of the canonical prayers cannot depend on the changing moods of an individual or a group. They are, on the contrary, fixed according to the different phases of the rotation of the Earth on its axis and around the sun: dawn, beginning of the afternoon, end of the afternoon, dusk, night, these hours vary by several hours according to the seasons.

Fasting

The month of Ramadan is the month of fasting. This month, which is determined according to the lunar calendar, is more flexible than the rigidly set solar calendar. The month of fasting thus is mobile and falls in varying seasons of the year.

The fast prescribes total abstinence from food and sex for 11 to 18 hours daily (depending on the season) throughout the month of Ramadan. Its severity is unique to the Muslim religion but its merits are numerous: amongst them, we can point out the advantage of giving the various sexual, nervous and digestive functions a rest, of teaching individuals to master their impulses and to come to terms with hunger, while also teaching them to understand what it means to be a starving indigent.

The legal alms that must be bestowed come to 2.5 % of a person's income, his merchandise, his real estate or his livestock. Fasting is a kind of tithe on those "goods" which are the pleasures of the body, constantly tempted by wordly attractions.

In fast, the term *Az-Zakat* has no

THE 'UMRAH

■ *The 'Umrah, or Lesser Pilgrimage, is the visiting of the Holy Places of Mecca with a view to accomplishing an individual pilgrimage. These rites are slightly abridged compared to those of the Collective Pilgrimage, or* Hajj.
*The 'Umrah is not an obligation (*Fard*), but a Tradition which is almost compulsory for those who have the means to accomplish it. Its nature varies slightly from one theological school (*Hadh 'Hab*) to the next. The Hanbalites and the Shafe'ites regard it as compulsory (*Fard*).*
The Malikites and the Hanifites acknowledge it as a Tradition, the accomplishment of which is warmly recommended.
Its conditions are identical to those of the Hajj. *To perform it, one must be :*
1. a Muslim,
2. an adult,
3. free (the notion of responsibility is underlined by this condition),
4. sound of mind,
5. in a position to accomplish it both physically and materially.
*The 'Umrah is not confined to any one set time (*Meeqāt Zamanee*). It can be carried out at any moment of the year, though the Hanifites exclude the five principal days of the* Hajj *: the day of the standing at 'Arafat, the day of the Feast of the Sacrifice, and the three days of the Tashreeq which are spent at Mina. According to the Hanifites, the 'Umrah cannot be accomplished between the 9th and the 13th Thu-l-Hijjah.*

real equivalent in English and the use of expressions such as "legal almsgiving" or "tithe" is not really adequate to convey what it entails.

Legal alms-giving

One must not give alms to beggars or to poor persons only out of compassion for them, but also out of religious duty, exactly as one acquits oneself of prayer. Alms are the rightful reward of all unhappy victims of slavery, of the homeless, of those who are fighting for God and of poverty-stricken travellers. It is the duty of the State to force the well-off members of its community to pay up this legal offering of alms, just as it collects income tax and other taxes. Yet if a faithful Muslim wants his soul to be purified, he must make it a point of honour to fairly assess his earnings and his yearly expenditure and to set aside the correct sum (particularly in this day and age, when most Islamic governments no longer collect the tihte). This he must do every lunar year, employing the sum to do good: for example to pay for the education of a poor orphan, to pay the hospital expenses of someone who cannot afford to do so, to buy clothing for a poor family, etc.

It is essential to go over the other pillars of Islam in order to situate the fifth pillar, the pilgrimage, within its context.

The pilgrimage

There are two different kinds of pilgrimage:
— the *Hajj*, a yearly pilgrimage at set dates, known as the greater pilgrimage or collective pilgrimage.
— the *'Umrah*, known as the lesser or individual pilgrimage. (See below). ☐

The rites of 'Umrah *are :*
1. The Ihram. *As for the* Hajj, *the pilgrim must enter upon the sacred state at a specific* Meeqât. *He must make a declaration of intent to perform the pilgrimage at this given spot (see chapter on* Ihram*).*
Meccans or pilgrims who have come for the Hajj *and are therefore already at Mecca must leave the sacred territory of the* Haram *in order to enter the sacred state. They must go to* Attan'eem, *which is located about three miles from Mecca. It must be pointed out that the* 'Umrah *is not related to a specific assignation of place.*
2. The Tawaf, *or circumambulation around the* Ka'bah.
3. The journey between the hillocks of Aŝ-Ŝafa *and* Al-Marwah.
4. The shaving of the beard and the symbolic cutting of the hair at the closing of these rites. Once this last rite is accomplished, the pilgrim can leave the sacred state, don his ordinary clothing and resume normal activities.
The prohibitions during Ihram *are the same for* 'Umrah *as for* Hajj *(see chapter on this subject).*
The 'Umrah *can be accomplished at the same time as the* Hajj, *and can be performed jointly with the Greater Pilgrimage (*Qiran *and* Tamattu'*), or else it can be performed just after the* Hajj, *according to the* Ifrad *formula.*
The 'Umrah *does not include the other rites of the* Hajj, *the standing at* 'Arafat, *the stopover at* Muzdalifah, *the sojourn at* Mina, *etc.*

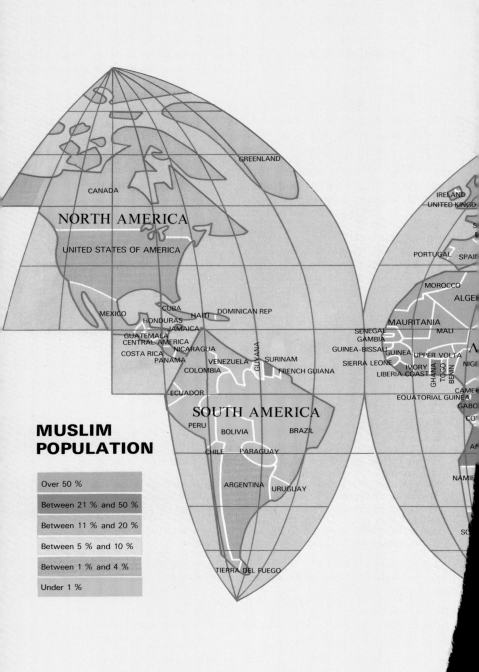

GREENLAND

CANADA

NORTH AMERICA

UNITED STATES OF AMERICA

IRELAND
UNITED KINGD

PORTUGAL   SPAII

MOROCCO

ALGE

MEXICO   CUBA   HAITI   DOMINICAN REP
HONDURAS
GUATEMALA   JAMAICA
CENTRAL AMERICA
COSTA RICA   NICARAGUA
PANAMA
COLOMBIA
ECUADOR

VENEZUELA   SURINAM
GUYANA
FRENCH GUIANA

MAURITANIA

SENEGAL   MALI
GAMBIA
GUINEA-BISSAU   GUINEA   UPPER VOLTA
SIERRA LEONE   IVORY   NIGE
LIBERIA   COAST
GHANA   TOGO   BENIN

CAME
EQUATORIAL GUINEA
GABO
CO

A

SOUTH AMERICA

PERU   BOLIVIA   BRAZIL

CHILE   PARAGUAY

ARGENTINA   URUGUAY

NAMIE

SC

TIERRA DEL FUEGO

MUSLIM
POPULATION

| Over 50 % |
| Between 21 % and 50 % |
| Between 11 % and 20 % |
| Between 5 % and 10 % |
| Between 1 % and 4 % |
| Under 1 % |

ISLAM IN THE WORLD TODAY

SWEDEN
RWAY
FINLAND
NORWAY
EUROPE
ARK
ANDS
G.D.M. POLAND WHITE RUSSIA
CZECHOSLOVAKIA
AUSTRIA UKRAINE
HUNGARY
ROMANIA
YUGOSLAVIA
ITALY
ALBANIA BULGARIA AZERBAIJAN
GREECE TURKEY
JISIA
SYRIA
YA
JORDAN
IRAQ
EGYPT
SAUDI
ARABIA UAE
SUDAN
RAL
EPUBLIC
ETHIOPIA
YEMEN SOUTH YEMEN
UGANDA
NDA
NDI
KENYA SOMALIA
TANZANIA
BIA
BWE
MOZAMBIQUE
MADAGASCAR
AZILAND
HO

UNION OF SOVIET SOCIALIST REPUBLICS
ESTONIA MARIYA
LITHUANIA MORDOV
UDMURT
KAZAKHSTAN
CRIMEA
UZBEKISTAN
TURKEMENIYA
MONGOLIA
SINKIANG
AFGHANISTAN
ASIA
CHINA
KASHMIR
TIBET
NORTH KOREA
PAKISTAN NEPAL BHUTAN
JAPAN
SOUTH KOREA
OMAN
BANGLADESH
LAOS
TAIWAN
INDIA
BURMA
PHILIPPINES
THAILAND
KAMPUCHEA
BRUNEI IRIAN JAYA
MALAYSIA
KALIMANTAN
PAPUA NEW GUINEA
INDONESIA
TIMOR
AUSTRALIA
IRAN

TASMANIA

17

the pilgrimage

■ The pilgrimage is compulsory once in the lifetime of every adult Muslim, man or woman, who is in a position to undertake the journey, in accordance with the divine proclamation: "To go on the pilgrimage (*Hajj*) to the House is a duty towards God for whomsoever is able to accomplish it". The Prophet Muhammed (peace be upon him) also declared: "God has prescribed unto you a pilgrimage, therefore accomplish it."
A certain number of conditions must be met to go on the pilgrimage to Mecca. They are the following:
1. One must be a Muslim.
2. One must have reached puberty. The embarking on a pilgrimage to Mecca by a child is not considered necessary and does not dispense him from having to accomplish it in his adult years.
3. One must be free. The notion of individual responsibility is obvious in this condition.
4. One must be sound of mind and in full possession of one's mental faculties.
5. One must be in a physical and material position to accomplish the pilgrimage. The would-be pilgrim must be in a position to bear the strain placed upon him by the journey and by the fulfilment of the prescribed rites.
6. If one is prevented for reasons of health, one can send another person in one's place, provided that person has already accomplished the pilgrimage on his own behalf. One must also be in a position to pay for the cost of the journey and the stay, as well as for the upkeep of one's family during one's absence'with money earned by honest means.
7. Furthermore, women must be accompanied by a close relative (husband, father, son, brother) or a trusted woman friend even if she is not a relative. A husband cannot prevent his wife from going on the pilgrimage. If he tries to, the wife has the right to forego his consent.
The *Hajj* pilgrimage takes place at set dates, in accordance with the divine words: "The pilgrimage takes place in the known months."
These months are :
— the month of *Shawwal*, or 10th month of the Muslim lunar calendar (the month following *Ramadan*),
— the month of *Thu-l-Qa'dah* (11th month of the Muslim calendar),
— the beginning of the month of *Thu-l-Hijjah* (12th month of the Muslim calendar).
The pilgrim can go to the Holy Places from the 1st *Shawwal* on and enter the state of *Ihrām* from that date in view of the pilgrimage. But it is only from the 9th month *Thu-l-Hijjah* on that he can accomplish the principle rites of the pilgrimage. His presence is therefore not compulsory except between the 8th and the 12th *Thu-l-Hijjah*.
If a pilgrim is prevented from getting there earlier, he can even arrive as late as the 9th, but if he is not present in the valley of 'Arafāt for the rite of standing (*Wuqūf*) before the dawn of the 10th *Thu-l-Hijjah*, his greater pilgrimage will be invalidated and he will only be able to carry out the lesser pilgrimage.

The rites
of the
greater pilgrimage

The rites of the pilgrimage must be accomplished at fixed times and in set places.
From the 1st Shawwal to the 8th Thu-l-Hijjah:
1. *Al-Ihrām* (or entering upon the sacred state) at the *Meeqāt* or assignation of time and place.
2. *Tawaf al-Qudoom* or circumambulation of arrival.
3. *Sa'y Bayn Aŝ-Ŝafā Wa Al-Marwah* or procession between Aŝ-Ŝafā and Al-Marwah.
On the 8th Thu-l-Hijjah:
4. Departure for Minā (*Tarwiyah*), night at Minā.
On the 9th Thu-l-Hijjah:
5. Departure for 'Arafāt, *Wuqūf* (standing) in this valley, an essential rite (*Rokn*, or pillar) if the pilgrimage is to be valid.
6. *Al-Ifādah* or unfurling. Departure from 'Arafat to Muzdalifah after nightfall. Reciting of the *Maghrib* and the *al-'Ishā* prayers upon arrival at Muzdlalifah and

gathering of between forty-nine and seventy pebbles for the lapidation of the pillars symbolizing Satan at Minā in the course of the following days. These pillars did not exist at the time of the Prophet. They were added in order to clearly mark the spots where the pilgrims were to hurl their stones. They have the added advantage of preventing stones from being thrown in all directions and wounding other pilgrims. Night spent at Muzdalifah.

10th Thu-l-Hijjah:
7. Standing at dawn before *al-Mash'ar al-Harām* (sacred oratory). Departure for Minā before dawn.
8. Arrival at Minā. The hurling of seven pebbles at the pillar of Al-'Aqabah or Great Pillar (symbolizing Satan).
9. Optional immolation of a head of livestock (*Na'hr*).
10. Shaving of the head or symbolic cutting of the hair. Partial lifting of the state of *Ihrām*.
11. Departure for the *Harām ash-Shareef* (the Great Sanctuary) at Mecca, with a view to accomplisching the *Tawaf al-Ifādah* (circumambulation of the total lifting of the sacred state).
12. Return to Minā. Night spent at Minā.

11th Thu-l-Hijjah:
13. Lapidation of the three pillars of Satan in the course of the afternoon. Night spent at Minā.

12th Thu-l-Hijjah:
14. Day spent at Minā. Lapidation of the three pillars. It is now permitted to return to Mecca.

13th Thu-l-Hijjah;
15. Last day at Minā for those who wish to continue the *Tashreeq* to the end. End of the stay and return to Mecca. End of the pilgrimage.
16. *Tawaf al-Wadā'*, or circumambulation of Farewell (before leaving Mecca).

Importance of the rites

The rite of the pilgrimage fall into three different categories according to their degree of importance.

1. *Al-Arkan* (singular: *Rokn*) or pillars, or again basic rites, without which the *Hajj* would not be valid. The pilgrim cannot leave the *Ihrām* or sacred state before he has accomplished all of them. The omission of one of these rites invalidates the pilgrimage.
2. *Al-Wajib* or duty. The rites in this category are compulsory, but the non-observance of one of them would not make the pilgrimage null and void. Nonetheless, in the case of an involuntary or voluntary omission of one of these rites, the pilgrim must sacrifice a head of livestock (camel, cow, sheep or goat) to atone for it. It should also be pointed out that the voluntary omission of one of these rites is regarded as a fault.
3. The rites concerning the *Sunnah*, or acts, gestures, attitudes and words of the Prophet Muhammed (may he rest in peace) as chronicled in Tradition. The validity of the pilgrimage does not depend on the accomplishment of these rites and their non-observance does not entail the sacrifice of an animal in atonement. But the pilgrim cannot attain perfection if he omits them and it is therefore preferable for him to include them in the pilgrimage.

The obligatory nature of each act of pilgrimage varies from one school to another. A succession of charts classifying the principal rites according to their importance for each of the four major Islamic schools will help the reader to see at a glance the degree of importance attached to each rite by the school he adheres to.

All the commandments, all the prescriptions, all the prophecies and the rules laid down by the Koran saw the light of day in Arabia and most particularly in Mecca and Medinah. Muhammed, the Messenger of the Revelation, was born in Mecca and lived in that town for 53 years. He spent the last ten years of his life at Medinah, where he died aged 63. The two cities were also the seat of events which consolidated the foundations of the new religion and led to the fantastic expansion of the Arabs to the East, all the way to China, to the West, right up to the Atlantic, and to the North as far as Poitiers in France. □

Pilgrims crowding round the Ka'bah,
whose protective covering
has been lifted.

Abraham and the pilgrimage

■ For a genuine understanding of what the pilgrimage to Mecca is about, we must dwell at greater length on the figure of Abraham as he appears in the pages of the Koran. After all, the halt and the prayer at the *Maqām Ibraheem*, or station of Abraham, is one of the most crucial moments of the pilgrimage and many of the other rites accomplished by the pilgrims are directly connected with the actions performed by Abraham or the members of his family, as for example the rebuilding of the *Ka'bah*, the presence at 'Arafāt, the commemoration of the sacrifice, the stoning of the idols and the rush of Hājir between the hills aŝ-Ŝafā and al-Marwah in a desperate search for water to save her dying child.

Hājir and the Zamzam spring

Going a little further back in history, we come to the year 2500 BC, when Mecca was but a desert valley overlooked by two hills known as Aŝ-Ŝafā and Al-Marwah. It was here that the Zamzam spring started gushing at the feet of Ismāel, son of Abraham and Hājir (also known as Agar). If one goes even further back in time, one finds Adam and Eve on the hill that overlooks the vast plain of 'Arafāt, after they had been expelled from Paradise.

It is only natural for the people of this area to commemorate the memory of Hājir, their remote ancestor, and her moment of panic when she saw her child suffering from thirst. They celebrate her rush from one hill to the other in the attempt to see, from the top, a caravan passing which might save the life of Ismāel. She made the journey seven times and climbed the hills eight times, but her reward was even better than a rescue caravan; it was a spring of water spouting from the ground at the feet of her child. It gushed so strongly that the boy was all wet with its spray.

No, it was not a mirage but a miracle! This spring became the celebrated Zamzam well, where pilgrims now quench their thirst.

The rebirth of Bakkah

No sooner had the caravans heard of the event that a village of tents sprang up around the Zamzam well, once the initial scepticism had dissipated. The village grew and, little by little, mud and stone houses replaced the tents, which is how Bakkah (the ancient name for Makkah or Mecca) was born anew. It had disappeared several centuries earlier after a natural cataclysm, the sequels of the Deluge according to some. "Truly the first temple established for the people was that of Bakkah, a holy place that gives guidance to all beings." *Koran III, 96.*

Abraham and his elder son, Ismāel, guided by the Divine Revelation, rediscovered the foundations of the ancient temple built by the father of humanity, Adam, and used them for the rebuilding of the Ka'bah.

It is extremely likely that, originally, the Temple was a shelter or hut inside which our very first ancestors adored their Creator. Subsequently, as the population grew, the shelter became too small and people therefore worshipped out of doors. Thus Mecca amid its hills, today worn down to the hillocks of Aŝ-Ŝafā and Al-Marwah, has been a historic shrine and place of pilgrimage for thousands of years and not just since 610 AD with the apparition of Islam. The two hillocks delineate the path borrowed by Hājir in her search for water, the Zamzam spring gushing at the foot of the infant Ismāel, the Ka'bah or Temple of God restored by Abraham but founded and built by Adam.

The immolation

The immolation consecrates the final part of the pilgrimage and puts an end to the state of sacralization. It constitutes a commemoration of the sacrifice of Abraham, a sacrifice hailed by the Jews and the Christians as well as by the Muslims. The Jews claim that it was the Prophet Isaac who had to be sacrificed, while the Muslims maintain that is was Ismāel.

The Bible mentions Isaac as the victim's name: "And he said: Take your one and only son, your beloved Isaac, and go forth unto the country of Morija, and offer him unto God as sacrifice on the hill that I shall name unto you." *Genesis*: 22,2 cf., also Infra, 22, 12.

In fact, Isaac was never an only son since he was the younger brother of Ismāel. Whereas Ismāel was an only son for fourteen years, since Abraham was 86 at the time of his birth and 100 at the time of the birth of Isaac. (cf. supra: 16, 26 and 21,5).

When the same sacrifice is described in the Koran, neither of the brothers are mentioned by their names. What truly matters in the story is not the identity of the son but the actual test to which God puts Abraham, who is the real hero of the tale. It was the father who was ordered by God in a dream to immolate his son, the person he loved most in the world.

"And he said, 'Verily, I repair to my Lord who will guide me: O Lord give me a son, of the righteous.' We announced to him a youth of meekness. And when he became a full-grown youth, his father said to him, 'My son, I have seen in a dream that I should sacrifice thee; therefore, consider what thou seest right.'

"He said, 'My father, do what thou art bidden; of the patient, if God please, shalt thou find me.'

"And when they had surrendered them to the will of God, he laid him down upon his forehead:

"We cried unto him, 'O Abraham! Now hast thou satisfied the vision'. See how we recompense the righteous. This was indeed a decisive test. And we ransomed his son with a costly victim, and we left this for him among posterity. Peace be on Abraham!

"Thus do we reward the well-doers, for he was of our believing servants. And we announced Isaac to him — a righteous Prophet — And on him and on Isaac we bestowed our blessing. And among their offspring were well-doers, and others, to their own hurt undoubted sinners."

Koran, XXXVII, 100 - 113.

The trials of Abraham

This text shows that the announcement of the birth of Isaac (son of Sarah) was made only after the trial and that therefore it must certainly have been Ismāel (son of Hajir), the eldest, who was to be immolated. This conclusion is confirmed by a tradition of the Prophet which has him saying: "I am the son of the two sacrificial victims," by which he must have meant his father, 'Abd Allah, who was almost immolated in fulfilment of a vow made to God in pre-Islamic days, and Ismaeel, his distant ancestor.

Nonetheless, the Koran does not attach much importance to the identity of Abraham's victim, for both were equal in the eyes of God. The Ancient Testament specifies that it was Isaac, but the Koran regards both sons of Abraham with equal respect and thus interchangeable, as it regards all prophets whatever generation they belong to.

The sacrifice described above is reminiscent of another trial to which Abraham was subjected at the beginning of his prophetic mission; he was sentenced to burn at the stake by the Babylonians, whose idolatry he opposed, but was saved by a miracle: "We said, 'O fire, grow thou cold and harmless for Abraham' "

Koran, XXI, 69.

From his earliest youth, this model servant of God dedicated his life to the sublimation of his individual and social behaviour, to preaching to his relations, his friends and all his fellow-men a way of life more in keeping with the healthy laws of nature, those laws decreed by the Creator of Nature with a view to facilitating the passage of men from the ephemeral life of this world to the eternal life of the next world, while being happy in both.

When Abraham was advanced in years, he felt the need to hand over the flame of prophecy to a younger man, who would carry on his mission. God did not disappoint him and gave him a son. But just as that son was reaching man's estate Abraham was asked to sacrifice him. The great prophet, father of a long line of prophets, was thus sorely tried twice over: both on his behalf and on that of his young son.

The stoning or lapidation

The lapidation is an integral part of pilgrimage, and is the corollary of the immolation, though it precedes it in time. This is how the origin of the stoning is reported in the popular legend from which the practice sprang up: angered by Abraham's fidelity towards God, Satan — the sworn enemy of the human race — resolved to persuade the Prophet not to immolate his son, in other words to disobey God. He therefore appeared before Abraham on several occasions and in human guise, using false arguments of every kind to dissuade the prophet. Tiring of his presence, Abraham finally resorted to force to get rid of him. As he had no stick and could find no large stone, he gathered a handful of pebbles which he hurled at the face of the meddlesome stranger, who disappeared. The devil reappeared seven times and each time the prophet hurled yet another handful of pebbles at him. Changing tactics, Satan tried to corrupt Hājir instead, playing on her feelings in an attempt to make her dissuade her husband. But Hājir was also a faithful servant of God, and she too reacted like Abraham, hurling pebbles at Satan seven times over. At last, Satan turned to the child. Putting on the most debonair of his masks, he tried to touch the boy's heart and to turn him against his father, accusing Abraham of being an unloving father and a cruel man to want to immolate Isaac not really in order to obey God but because of some foolish dream or vision. But once again Satan did not get his way; though Ismaeel was only fourteen, he too hurled stones at Satan seven times over.

This then is the meaning of the lapidation which is practised by pilgrims when they hurl pebbles at the three pillars symbolizing Satan. They are perpetrating the gestures of Abraham, Hājir and Ismāel. □

*Pilgrims quenching their thirst
at the Zamzam well.*

THE WORLD AT THE BIRTH

■ *At the time of the birth of Islam, Japan was trying with the greatest difficulty to set up a federation of kingdoms which had for a long time been opposed to one another. The equilibrium of this federation was constantly threatened by the latent antagonism between the decadent conservatives and the younger generation, impregnated with the Chinese culture and the Buddhism of India.*

In China, the influence of Confucius was receding before that of Buddha, the Indian sage two generations his junior. China's military might had grown to such an extent that it now controlled the silk route, to the detriment of its Japanese and Korean neighbours. It was soon destined to enter a period of civil war that lasted for four centuries however, from the end of the VIth century to the Xth century. India on the other hand went through a long period of economic prosperity — from the IVth to the begining of the VIth century, under the celebrated Gupta dynasty.

Persia was in the throes of an internal crisis brought on by several factors: the Armenian and Aramaean minorities were causing trouble; the Yemen was struggling to free itself from the Persian yoke; the collaboration of the Arab Lakhmides, vassals of Iraq, posed a threat, as did the castes within Persia itself, especially the warlike Iranian aristocracy which thirsted after the destruction of Byzantium, already vanquished by them in Syria and Palestine. Egypt, vanquished by Rome in 30 BC, had been under the domination of the Eastern Empire since 395 AD, and had been christianized at the time of Constantine. The country was collapsing under the strain of the disastrous religious quarrels between the Appollinarian Monophysites and the Sectarian Nestorians. As far as the local Coptic population was concerned, all it wanted was to get rid of its foreign masters, the Graeco-Roman colonialists who squabbled so bitterly about the true nature of Christ.

Arabia, almost forgotten by contemporary historians just as it was by their Graeco-Roman predecessors, is nonetheless well worth taking into closer consideration.

Located at one of the crossroads of the world, the vast peninsula had entertained commercial, military and cultural ties with Persia since the days of Antiquity, both through the Arab-Persian gulf and through Mesopotamia, which had always been inhabited by Semitic populations: Akkadians, Chaldeans, Babylonians, Assyrians and finally the Lakhmid Arabs, also known as the Manadhirah.

Though they were the vassals of the Persians, these Iraqi Arabs enjoyed genuine autonomy. Their kingdom of Hira *lasted from 195 to 605 AD, and numbered twenty-five sovereigns, amongst them the famous* Manadhirah *(plural of* Mundhir: *five kings bore this name), the five* Nu'man, *the three* Imru'u-l-Qays, *the three* 'Amr, *etc.*

Greater Syria (Syria, Palestine, the Lebanon, Jordan) were the domain of the Ghassanid Arabs, who were more or less the subjects of the Byzantine suzerainty. Their reign lasted from 292 to 636 AD, and numbered no less than forty-two monarchs.

Allies of the Greeks whenever a danger threatened their empire, they enjoyed the rest of the time an autonomy equal to and often greater than that of their brothers, the Lakkhmid Arabs who were allied to the Persians. Needless to say, given their respective alliances, they fought against one another each time the Persians and the Byzantines settled their differences on the battlefield.

The Arabs of Ghassane gave birth to two remarkable leaders: Odenath (in Arabic, Udhayna), *king of Palmyra (in Arabic:* Tadmor) *victor*

OF ISLAM

over the Persians. The Roman emperor, Gallien (218-268) was forced to recognize him "Emperor of the East". He also was a great patron of the arts and of literature. He was assassinated at Homs and his wife, Zenobia (in Arabic: Zanubiya, synonym or diminutive of Zaynab) succeeded him, acting as regent on behalf of their son. But she was such an intelligent and cultured woman, and so brilliant at politics and diplomacy, that she chose to become queen in her own right and took over full control of the throne. Her power spread to Greater Syria, to Mesopotamia and to parts of Egypt. She encouraged thinkers, artists, poets and especially military strategists, which soon gave umbrage to the Roman might.

The Emperor Aurelian (214-275) personally took command of the armies sent to Syria, vanquished the Arab army and took Zenobia and her suite back to Rome with him, as this captives. One of the queen's freed slaves avenged her by murdering the emperor.

The least well-known of the pre-Islamic Arab States is that of Petra (in Arabic: al-Batra) in what is today Jordan. It was the realm of the Nabatean Arabs, who resisted Persian and Roman attempts to vassalize them for over four centuries before accepting to submit themselves to the Roman emperor Trajan (106 AD). This act of submission was, however, provisional for the kingdom of Petra soon took back its independence.

In the vth Century AD, the kingdom of Kinda succeeded in the domination of the najd and the Hijaz tribes, though it never managed to achieve unification among them.

The most celebrated of the Arab states is, without a doubt, the kingdom of Saba (Sheba) which came into being in Yemen and which lasted throughout the ixth to the iimd Century BC. Its most famous monarch was queen Balqis (incorrectly spelt with a k: Balkis). Her meeting with King Solomon (970-931 BC) is described in the Koran (xxvii, 20-45). As for the people and the State of Saba, the Holy Book speaks of them in Chapter xxxiv, 15-19.

A second dynasty followed that of Saba: that of Tubba, also called Himyar, the first name being synonymous with "king", like the word "pharaoh" in Egypt, "Shah" in Persia or "Negus" in Ethiopia. The Himyarites ruled from 381 BC to 529 AD, which was when the Yemen was occupied by the Ethiopians who, in turn, were supplanted by the Persians in 601. The country became independent once more with the advent of Islam (630).

It was at the time of the Saba and the Himyarites that successive waves of Yemeni Arabs swept across Egypt, Libya and North Africa for several generations, settling there after pushing back towards the south the original black inhabitants. These mass immigrations were doubtless set off by economic motives, and their impact was reinforced by other waves of Arabs from Syria, who were also of Yemenite origins.

As can be seen from the above, the Arabs were the legitimate heirs of the Akkadians, the Babylonians, the Chaldeans, the Assyrians, the Hyksos or Amalecites (the shepherd kings who founded the 15th and 16th pharaonic dynasties) and the Arameans; they were in Iraq, in Syria, in the Nadjd and especially in the Yemen, the torchbearers of the illustrious civilizations of Mesopotamia and Egypt.

the Ka'bah and the Black Stone

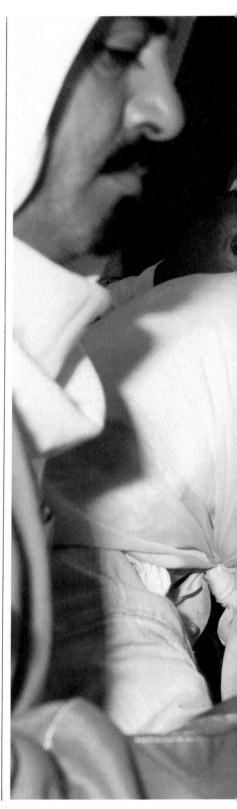

■ It would doubtless be useful to dispel here a few of the misunderstandings that have arisen around the Ka'bah and the Black Stone. The first is a great cubic structure, about 15 metres high and 12 by 13 metres square. It is covered by an immense piece of black drapery (*Kiswah*) which has verses from the Koran embroidered in gold thread all around its hem. The *Kiswah* is renewed every year on the occasion of the Great Pilgrimage.

In the time of Abraham and during the centuries that followed, the Ka'bah served as a temple, whereas now its interior remains unused. From time to time, a monarch, a head of State, a minister or a scholar, all belonging to the Muslim faith, are allowed to go inside the Ka'bah. This is regarded as a great privilege and a blessing.

The sacred centre of Islam

The Ka'bah is the sacred centre of Islam, as are its immediate surroundings.

As for the Black Stone, it is an oval-shaped stone about 18 centimetres in diameter ; it rests within a mesh of silver wire, some of which go right through it in order to prevent it from ever crumbling. It is set in the angle of the Ka'bah which is between the side known as *al-Multazam* and the Yemenite angle (thus called because it faces the Yemen), which is at the far end of the same side, in other words on the side opposite to that of the *Hijr Ismāel* (the enclosure of Ismaeel) that was once inside the Ka'bah and which is now outside, protected by a semi-circular wall about one and a half metres high, about the same height from the ground as the Black Stone.

The origins of this stone are not clear. According to some, it was extrated from the soil by Ismāel, on the mountain of Abu Qubays. He is meant to have given it to his father Abraham, that it might be placed at one of the angles of the Ka'bah that they were rebuilding. According to another version, it was the archangel Jibreel (Gabriel) who

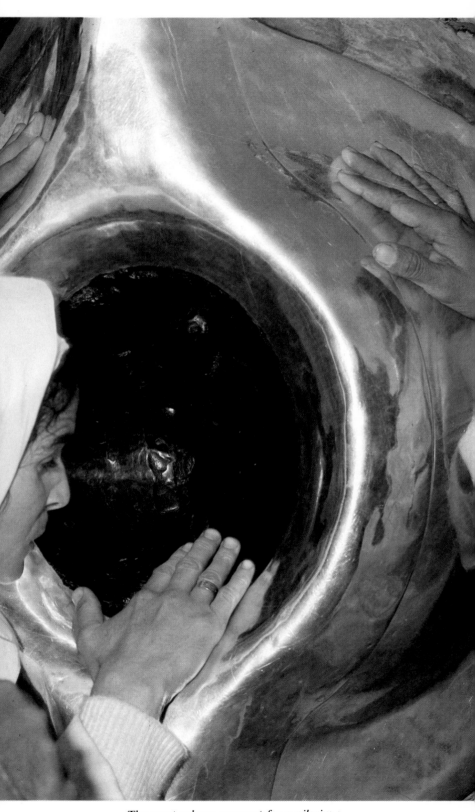

The most solemn moment for a pilgrim :
touching the Black Stone.
Not all pilgrims can get this close
and they are only required
to hail it from a distance.

brought it to Adam in Paradise. The first man then kept it and transmitted it after the Deluge to Noah's descendants, which is how it came into Abraham's hands.

There is one incontrovertible piece of historical evidence concerning the Black Stone, though it has nothing to do with the actual origin or nature of the stone. When the Ka'bah was restored in 605 AD, the stone was removed during reconstruction work and when the time came to put it back in its place a violent quarrel ensued. Each of the clans wanted the honour of replacing the stone, so much so that several tribal leaders had already unsheathed their sword, ready to fight for the privilege. It was decided *in extremis* to ask the first man who entered the sacred precinct to decide on the matter. It so happened that the first man was Muhammed, much to the relief of the men who were arguing. "Providence be praised that it should be *Al-Ameen*!" they all cried out, for that was what they called the future Prophet, who was only 35 years old at the time. *Al-Ameen*, "he who can be trusted" would become a prophet only five years later.

Muhammed asked them to bring a rug, in which he placed the holy relic. He asked the representatives of each Qureishite tribe to clasp the hem of the cloth and to lift it to the chosen spot. He thereupon placed the Black Stone with his own hands against the angle and sealed it in ; this act was indeed premonitory, considering the great mission with which he was soon to be entrusted.

At that time, no-one realized that paganism was about to breathe its last and that the replacing of the Holy Stone heralded the definitive return to the pure monotheism of Abraham that *Al-Ameen* was to reinstate forever.

Since the birth of Islam, the holy relic has been removed and replaced on the following occasions :
1. After the restoration of the Ka'bah, half destroyed by the

WOMEN AND THE BIRTH OF ISLAM

■ *The role played by women in the birth of Islam is quite a remarkable one.*
First of all, that of Khdîjah, daughter of Kuwaylid, first wife of the Prophet, to whom he remained faithful until her death. A most unusual and exceptional person, she was the first to embrace Islam. It was she who managed to put the Prophet's heart at rest after his deeply disturbing encounter with the archangel Jibreel (Gabriel) in the Hira grotto. It was also she who persuaded him that he had a genuine mission and that the revelation was authentic, taking him to consult one of her cousins, a blind sage nearly a hundred of years old. This wise old man, Waragah Ibn Nawfal, convinced Muhammed that his visitor was none other than the Messenger of the All-Powerful Being, and that he, Muhammed, had been selected to be one of the Prophets.
Khdîjah (peace be upon her) made over her entire fortune and all her worldly belongings to Islam.
Islam's first martyr was also a woman. Her name was Sumayyah, daughter of Khayyat, and her husband too was to be a martyr (both died in 615 AD), as was her son, Ammar Ibn Yacir, who fought with the fourth Caliph, Ali Ibn Abi Talib, at the battle of Siffeen (in 657 AD).
Once again it was a woman who gave the best example of fidelity to

the Hira grotto

catapults of the Umayyad commander Al-Hajāj Ibn Yusuf when he fought against the anti-Caliph 'Abd Allah Ibn Az-Zubayr and his partisans, who had taken refuge inside the sanctuary in 693 and were desperately resisting the assault of the troops of the second Umayyad Caliph, Yazid Ibn Mu'āwiyah.
2. When the Ka'bah was reinforced with sheets of silver, after cracks were discovered in its walls in 757, under the Abbassid Caliph Al-Mansur.
3. When it was stolen by the Shi'ite Qarmat revolutionaries in 938 ; the Black Stone was kept by them for eight years.* ☐

* As reported in an anonymous Arabic manuscript quoted by N. Desvergers in *Arabia* (Paris, 1847), p. 12.
21 years according to Mohammed Hamidullah, *France-Islam*, n° 98-99, in the sections "Practices of Religious Life", p. 78.
22 years according to Ali Tantawi: Min Nafahat Al-Haram (Dar al-Fikr, Damascus 1379/1960, p. 232).

■ There is one place at Mecca which will be mentioned in these pages though it is not a part of the rites of pilgrimage. The *Ghār* (grotto) *Hirā* is located about 20 metres from the top of the hill that bears the same name : *Jabal Hirā*, about 5 kilometres north-east of the capital of Islam. It was in this secluded spot that the Prophet, fleeing the polytheism of his compatriots, was in the habit of seeking refuge for the three years preceding his mission. Here it was that he would meditate on the differences among the religions that he had seen practised at the Hijaz and in the areas of Greater Syria which are now called Jordan, Palestine and Syria. He would also ponder on the social and economic aspects of life in his native town of Mecca, an important Arabian city for thousands of years, and also upon the destiny of mankind in general and the great metaphysical problems.

It was in this grotto that the Prophet was overcome to receive the

her faith: Umm Habiba Ramlah, daughter of Abu Sufian, the political and military leader of Mecca ans sworn enemy of Islam for over twenty years. This heroine, along with her husband, was one of the first Muslim immigrants to leave for Abyssinia. Her husband, attracted by the money of his hosts, became an apostate and left the faith. His wife, who had a small daughter, instantly left her renegade husband just as she had broken off relations with her pagan father. Unaided and all alone in her exile, in the most dreadful material conditions, she never succumbed to despair and finally became the wife of the Prophet.
In the 8th year of the Hijrah (630 AD) her father, though he was the arch-enemy of the Prophet, was allowed to enter Medinah to visit his daughter. But she refused to let him sit down on the Prophet's modest rug, thus showing her preference for her faith above and beyond the ties of blood.
Umm Habiba died in 664 AD at Medinah.
Abu Sufian finally became converted and became one of Islam's staunchest supporters. He gave up all his worldly possessions for his faith and lost an eye in the battle of At-Ta'if (629 AD) during the Prophet's lifetime. He lost the other eye at the famous battle of Al-Yarmuk in Palestine, which he fought against the Byzantines after the Prophet's death.

visit of the archangel Jibreel and the revelation of the first five verses of *Surah* (group of chapters) known as *al-'Alaq*, sometimes translated as "clot of blood"(Pesle and Tidjani, H. Boubakeur).

These five short verses contain the essence of the new faith: they teach the existence of one, all-powerful Deity.

They read as follows: "In the Name of God, the Compassionate, the Merciful, recite thou, in the name of thy Lord who created. Who created man from clots of blood. Recite thou! For thy Lord is the most Beneficient, Who hath taught the use of the pen, hath taught Man that which he knoweth not."
Koran, XCVI, 1 - 5.

Mount Hirā has been called *Jabal an-Nur* (the Hill of Light) for the past fourteen centuries.

Though the climb is exceedingly arduous, many a rugged pilgrim climbs to the top. As for the grotto itself, it has grown considerably narrower over the centuries than it was in Muhammed's day, and only one person at a time can enter it, kneeling to do so.   □

---

the house of Al-Arqam

■ Another place of a more modest sort played an extremely important role in the implantation of Islam in the pagan city that was Mecca at the time of Muhammed's prophetic mission; it is the house of Al-Arqam, also called "the house of Islam".

Al-Arqam, son of 'Abd Manaf, became converted to Islam at the age of 17. Al Arqam, who belonged to a wealthy family, turned his house (next to the hill of Aŝ-Ŝafā, at the time well outside the sacred precinct) into a centre for the propagation of the new faith; it became the seat of the Prophet, who spent almost all his time there. It was to this house that the future second Caliph, 'Umar Ibn al-Khattab, came to be converted to Islam and to abjure paganism, the same 'Umar who had once sworn to the Meccans that the would kill the Prophet.

The meetings at the house of Al-Arqam were long held in secret because of the ever-growing threat posed by the polytheists. 'Umar discovered the address through his sister, who had become converted before him. He went to her house to force her to forswear Islam and to make her revert to the idolatrous faith of her ancestors. He insulted her, struck her hard and almost killed her husband, also a convert to Islam. Nevertheless, 'Umar insisted on knowing first what had motivated his sister and his brother-in-law when they had embraced the new religion. Though her face was streaming with blood, his sister managed to recite beginning of the Ṭā-Hā (*Koran*, XX, 1-8): "Not to sadden thee have we sent down this Koran to thee, but as a warning for him who feareth; It is a missive from Him who hath made the earth and the lofty heavens! The God of mercy sitteth on his Trone: his, whatsoever is in the heavens and whatsoever is in the earth, and whatsoever is between them both, and whatsoever is beneath the humid soil! Thou needest not raise thy voice for He knoweth the secret whisper, and the yet more hidden. God! There is no God but He! Most excellent his Titles!"

Deeply moved, the rough 'Umar asked in a low voice who had transmitted these magnificent words. "The man you wanted to kill, whom you swore to get rid of!" replied his sister. "Where can I find him?" asked 'Umar. His sister sensed that a great change had come over him, and for this reason she dared to answer: "You will find the Prophet of God in the house of Al-Arqam. Go there, and may God guide you towards the faith!"   □

At Mecca, the faithful
rest on their arrival.

life of the Prophet Muhammed

■ It is in a simple light that we propose to take a look at this life which began in the stony, sunbaked plain of Mecca, hemmed in by its red and brown volcanic hills.

Youth of the Prophet

According to the Arabian custom which refers to a man's lineage as well as to is clan, Muhammed's full name was Abu-l-Qassim Muhammed Ibn-'Abdullah Ibn 'Abd al-Muttalib Ibn Hashim, son of 'Abdullah who died shortly before his child's birth, and member of the important Hashim family from Mecca, which was a sub-division of the Qureishites clan. He was born toward the year 570 in Mecca; his mother, Amina, died when he was only six years old, and he was an orphan from that time onward, as it is stated in the Koran. He was taken in first by his grandfather, 'Abd al-Muttalib, who died several years later, then by his paternal uncle, Abu Tālib.

He was entrusted to the care of a nurse called Halima, who became like a second mother to him. The boy spent his early years as a humble shepherd, leading a nomadic existence in the hilly region around Mecca. Later on, he started accompanying the caravans from Mecca that were headed north towards Syria or south towards Yemen. It was on these voyages that he began to reveal his considerable qualities of fairness and honesty. He looked after the affairs of a widow, Khdîja, whom he eventually married. This union, which lasted until Khdîja's death (towards 619), turned out to be a particularly happy one. The Prophet trusted his wife and told her of his revelations; she was the first to believe in his mission and to become converted to Islam.

Until he was past forty, Muhammed's life was uneventful. The bustling, commercial city where he lived was a lively place, and almost all its

A SUBLIME GOAL

■ *The French poet, Lamartine, has beautifully described Muhammed's dual role as prophet and legislator in a little-known work entitled* A History of Turkey, *published in 1854 :*

"Never has a man proposed, either of his own free will or upon orders from above, so noble a goal... If a man's genius is measured according to the greatness of his design, the limited nature of the means at his disposal and the immensity of the results achieved, then Muhammed was great in a way that no modern figure can hope to emulate. The most celebrated among them have done no more than win a few victories, pass a few laws or create an empire. When and if they actually accomplished something, it was usually swept away after their death. Muhammed's ideas set whole armies in motion, affected legislations, empires, peoples, dynasties, millions of people in an area covering one third of the inhabited surface of the globe. But he accomplished more than that: he also stirred up new ideas, beliefs and souls. On the sake of one book, whose every word has become a law, he created a spiritual nationality that embraces people of every colour and language. The indelible character of this Muslim faith resides in a hatred of false idols and a passion for the one and only, immaterial deity... Philosopher, orator, apostle, legislator, warrior, conqueror of ideas, restorer of rational dogma, of a cult without images, founder of twenty worldly empires and one spiritual empire, such is Muhammed. According to every standard by which human greatness can be measured, what man was ever greater?".

male inhabitants had been warriors at some time or another; but the future Prophet had, from the start, been a contemplative, retiring and peace-loving sort of man. Forty years of age was looked upon as nearing old age in those days, and at any rate no age at which to start embarking on any new adventures. Nevertheless, it was at this point in his life that Muhammed had his first Revelation, and his whole existence was revolutionized in the process. A new life was about to start for him.

Around the year 610, Muhammed was in the habit of withdrawing to the mountains on the outskirts of Mecca at regular intervals, in order to meditate and to pray. This was a common practice among pious individuals who needed complete solitude to concentrate on spiritual matters. Men who did this were honoured; they were known as *hanīfs*. But one night, when Muhammed was on Mount Hirā, the word of God was revealed to him by the archangel Jibreel, who appeared to him on the horizon and kept on repeating to him "Read!". Muhammed's first reaction was one of awe at the magnitude of the event. He told his wife how a being made of light had seized him and had ordered him to repeat and to preach the sacred words. Khdīja would later describe her husband's anxious doubts concerning the authenticity of the vision. He was afraid of becoming one of those mad seers who preached on the market-place of Mecca. For a while, he felt an inner void and "the Revelation ceased to manifest itself to him." Yet he continued to feel deeply disturbed. Eventually, the being made of light appeared to him once again and this time the order it gave was clear and imperious.

Muhammed began to preach in 613. His sermons consisted of startling rythmic exhortations, full of powerful metaphors and comparisons proclaiming that God, the Creator and the Judge of the whole Universe, was all-powerful, but that he was also a God of Mercy who showered upon the world tokens of His Glory and His Grace. God, Muhammed explained, is transcendental. He is closer to each man "than his own jugular vein is" as the Koran puts it. Everybody is therefore morally responsible to his Maker. There are no intermediaries who can intercede between God and each human being. The essence of the Revelation rests in this absolute confrontation between he who prays and the Supreme Being before whom he prosternates himself. Muhammed was renewing with a very ancient tradition of monotheism, which he injected with a new life.

What recur over and over again in the Revelations of the Koran are references to the parables of Abraham, of Moses, of Jesus and other prophets, who thus make up an unbroken chain of messengers transmitting the same fundamental message to humanity. The major difference was that the sacred texts were now set down in the Arabic language.

Reactions at Mecca

For several years, Muhammed's preaching did not extend beyond a small circle of his friends and relatives. All of them instantly accepted his message and adhered to the new faith. Gradually, however, Muhammed's teachings spread and a certain amount of opposition sprang up in a portion of the community which felt threatened and challenged by the new Prophet's message. Some people wrongly imagine that Muhammed started out by preaching to the nomadic desert tribes. Right from the start, his words were addressed to all mankind. He wanted to be heard by all those who had ears to hear, and to be understood by all those who had the faculty of understanding. Mecca was, in fact, the first place where Muhammed delivered his sermons. It could only exist as a merchant city, since the rock-strewn valley that surrounded it offered little opportunity for a thriving agriculture. A market town, essentially urban in outlook, Mecca was ruled by an oligarchy made up of the wealthiest merchants, especially those belonging to the most ancient, highly-respectable families.

Furthermore Mecca had for centuries been a place of pilgrimage where Arab idolators came to revere their tribal divinities in the Ka'bah, the Black Stone.

The rulers of Mecca construed Muhammed's message as an attack of their prerogatives and on the mercantile habits of the city's inhabitants. At first, the townfolk's hostility to the Prophet's ideas took the form of derision, but it soon degenerated into downright hostility. Persecutions followed and, by 615, the situation was so tense that the Prophet advised the most vulnerable among his followers to seek refuge in the Christian country of Ethiopia. These public trials and tribulations were followed by ordeals of a more personal nature: in 619, the Prophet's "year of mourning", his wife Khîdja and his uncle Abu Țālib died. By now, it had become clear that the Prophet would have to seek aid and shelter elsewhere. He therefore got in touch with the citizens of Yathrib, which was later renamed "Madīnatu-n-Nabī" — the City of the Prophet, in other words Medinah.

The years at Medinah

Unlike Mecca, Yathrib was not a commercial centre but an agricultural oasis whose principal crop was dates.

Hostile factions had been struggling for power in Yathrib for so long that the situation had grown hopelessly entangled and the inhabitants had decided to have resort to a neutral, outside arbitrator. Muhammed was the leader of a new spiritual community whose principles extended well beyond all tribal considerations, and this fact seemed to make him the ideal referee. The end result of the secret negociations that took place was an agreement called the 'Aqabah Pact. The Prophet's disciples swore an oath of allegiance to the pact and set off for Yathrib in small groups with the intention of settling there. It was at this stage that the citizens of Mecca attempted to assassinate Muhammed, who had remained almost alone

in his home town. But he managed to escape and, after taking refuge on Jabal-ath-Thawr for a while, he too made his way to Yathrib.

The year 622 heralded the beginning of the Islamic era, properly speaking; for it was in the course of that year that Islam officially took shape as a doctrine , a religious faith, an organized community and a way of life, all in one. The year 622 was a turning-point for Muhammed too, for it was the year in which he set down his principles of government in a charter which was, in effect, the first Islamic constitution. The charter has been carefully preserved until the present day, and it shows remarkable political insight and shrewdness.

One of the first steps taken by Muhammed was aimed at facilitating the integration of the Islamic refugees within the tight-knit Yathrib community. To do this, he devised a system of juridical fraternity between the Meccan imigrants and natives from Medinah known as *Ansār* (helpers, or rescuers). This amounted to an extension of the ancient principle of legal adoption, or the regarding of strangers as blood brothers by their hosts in the name of hospitality.

If Mecca and its temple of Abraham were destined to be the heart of Islam, Medinah could only be a temporary solution at best. Furthermore, given their control over the trade routes, the citizens of Mecca were in a position to apply considerable economic pressure on the refugees and on their hosts. The new imigrants at Medinah, who had had to leave their wordly belongings in Mecca, were suffering from poverty despite the assistance of those who had taken them in. Gradually, they found themselves drawn into war with the citizens of Mecca. It started with a skirmish here and a raid there. The first important victory won by the followers of Muhammed took place at Badr in 624. Though outnumbered, they won a battle against their foes. The inhabitants of Mecca, eager by now to avenge their dead, built up an army of three thousand men. The soldiers of Islam who were lacking in discipline, suffered a setback at Uhud, and

One aspect of the Muslim faith :
pilgrims touching one
of the walls of the Ka'bah.

Muhammed himself was wounded. But the citizens of Mecca were not able to press their advantage. In March 627, the army was ready to set off again. Unlike at Uhud, Muslim tactics had become principally defensive and they were digging trenches now, a most unusual practice in Arabia around this time. The coalition of their enemies had grown so weary that the Meccan army was easily defeated and finally dispersed.

The return to Mecca

Once again, Muhammed had the initiative. He made good use of it to negociate with the people of Mecca, who were battle-weary and who knew by this time that the Muslims were determined to make of their city the final destination of the pilgrimage, and that this pilgrimage to Mecca was to be the corner-stone of the new religion. When Muhammed and his companions set out on the pilgrimage, their non-violent march was halted by an armed group on the outskirts of Mecca. Certain conditions were postulated: the Muslims were to go back to Medinah without being allowed to visit the temple at Mecca; but they would be allowed to return the following year on condition that their visit did not exceed three days. A ten-year truce was agreed upon and, in case of disagreement, a third party would be called upon to settle the conflict and to enforce neutrality.

This agreement, known as the Hudaibiya pact, forced the Muslims to make certain concessions that were bitterly criticized by some of Muhammed's followers. But it reveals to an astonishing degree how fair and far-sighted the Prophet really was, however much he believed in the rightness of his cause and in the truth of his Revelation. Once again, he struck a balance - or *mizan* - between his faith and his reason, between the sacred and the political, the *din* and the *dunya*.

The Hudaibiya pact achieved its purpose, for it forced the people of Mecca to acknowledge the legal existence of the Muslims, whom they had started off by dimissing with derision and by chasing out of their city. It also gave Muhammed the opportunity to consolidate his community, which achievement alone was worth making a few short-term concessions.

The date of the pilgrimage which had been agreed upon was 629. After it had been accomplished, the Muslims left Mecca whose citizens could not fail to be impressed by the sight of the new community's strength, unity and moderation. The time had grown ripe for taking a final decision. The opportunity presented itself when the truce betweem Muslims and Meccans came to an end in 630. That year, the Muslims marched on the city, which put up only token resistance. Nearly all the inhabitants of Mecca became converted to Islam. Muhammed's patience, his willingness to run a certain number of risks and his moderation had paid off at last. His moderation manifested itself also in the hour of victory, for he did not harm the population of Mecca and declared a general amnesty, though he had all the idols of the Ka'bah destroyed and decreed that the temple should from then on be used exclusively by Muslims.

A number of Islamic missions were sent out during the years 630-631, as well as several military expeditions. These years also saw the rapid, though usually peaceful, spread of Islam throughout Arabia. The administration of the territories which recognized Islam as the supreme authority had to be completely reorganized accordingly. Alms-giving, or *Zakat*, became a legal institution that was to remain one of the "pillars" of Islam.

The brotherhood of Muslims replaced the old ties that had existed between nations, clans and tribes. Paganism was abolished and the Muslim community was based on the principle of equality. The new social system also gave women the right of ownership and inheritance while, for the first time, husbands had to acknowledge certain duties towards their wives.

In 632, Muhammed in person led the pilgrimage that was to become known as the "Farewell Pilgrimage" because it was his last. The Farewell Pilgrimage, which we have already described in some detail, was a final recapitulation, a collective examination of the work accomplished so far. Its principle themes were the Oneness of God and of the community, the brotherhood of men above and beyond all wordly and provisional distinctions, the rights of women and the abolition of usury. It consecrated the triumph of Islam over polytheism. On this occasion.

When Muhammed returned to Medinah, he was gravely ill with a fever. He spent his final hours with his youngest wife, 'Ayesha, and died in that same year (632). A mosque was built on the site of the humble dwelling where he had died and been buried, in other words 'Ayesha's room. It has since that time become a place to which Muslims go after the pilgrimage to Mecca. According to tradition, the newly-elected Caliph, Abu Bakr, announced the Prophet's death in the following words: "If you worship Muhammed, know that he is dead. If you worship God alone, know that He lives and does not die ."

Muhammed died as he had lived ever since the beginning of his mission, a wholly sincere man whose mission came before every personal consideration, a man whose inspiration never once failed him, yet whose sense of justice and whose political vision remained steady to the end. The great inner strength that his Revelation lent him never flagged. His message had not once been merely abstract and philosophical; the prophet lived his teachings fully, was always the first to give the example and to demonstrate their rightness, their truth and their strength. It is because Muhammed practised what he preached both on a spiritual and on a day to day basis that his teachings have retained their vigour intact right till the present time, and why they are so enthusiastically taken up by the youth of each successive generation. □

IN THIS XVTH CENTURY OF ISLAM

■ *The Islamic era began with the emigration in 622 AD of the Prophet Muhammed and his followers from Mecca, where he had suffered persecution, to Medinah where he was made welcome. This was the Hijrah. Muslims date the beginning of their history and their new calendar from this moment. Theirs being a lunar calendar, the year 1980 is the first year of the XVth century for Islam.*
The opening of a new century represents, for the community as a whole and for each Muslim member, a time of reckoning, an opportunity to reflect at greater length on the significance of belonging to Islam today, what responsibilities this entails, particularly as far as the Islamic community's relations with the outside world are concerned.
This first year of the XVth Century is a time for reflection and reappraisal that will enable every Muslim to reaffirm his faith and his ideals, to proclaim his faith in all sincerity since nothing more is required when a non-Muslim wishes to convert himself to Islam.
"There is no God but Allah and Muhammed is His Prophet" are the only words that need be spoken. What do the words "Muhammed is His Prophet" really mean?
Muhammed is not the author of the Koran. All Muslims reject such a suggestion as blasphemous. The Koran was revealed to Muhammed by God in the precise and literal form that has come down to us today. The Prophet is simply the messenger who transmitted God's words.

40

Invocation of the pilgrims
on the hill of Aŝ-Ŝafa,
point of departure for the procession.

THE MAJOR ISLAMIC DYNASTIES

Spread and chronology

This chart cannot hope to capture the political complexity characteristic of several periods in Islam's history. A large section of Central Asia, China, South-East Asia and Black Africa are not included in it.

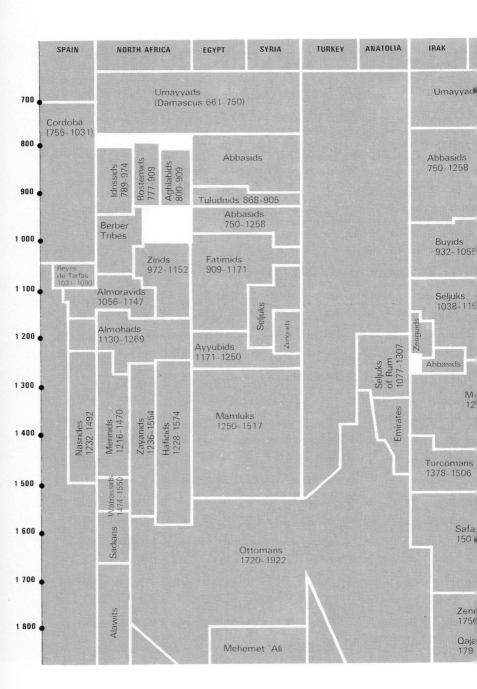

SPAIN	NORTH AFRICA	EGYPT	SYRIA	TURKEY	ANATOLIA	IRAK	

700 — Umayyads (Damascus 661-750) — Umayyad

Cordoba (755-1031)

800 — Abbasids — Abbasids 750-1258

Idrissids 789-974 / Rostemids 777-909 / Aghlabids 800-909

900 — Tuludnids 868-905

Berber Tribes — Abbasids 750-1258

1 000 — Buyids 932-105

Reyes de Tarfas 1031-1090 — Zirids 972-1152 — Fatimids 909-1171

1 100 — Almoravids 1056-1147 — Seljuks — Seljuks 1038-11

1 200 — Almohads 1130-1269 — Ayyubids 1171-1250 — Seljuks — Zenguids — Zenguids — Abbasids

Seljuks of Rum 1077-1307

1 300 — M 12

Nasrides 1232-1492 / Merinids 1216-1470 / Zayanids 1236-1554 / Hafcids 1228-1574 — Mamluks 1250-1517 — Emirates

1 400 — Turcomans 1378-1506

1 500 — Watrassids 1474-1550

1 600 — Sadians — Ottomans 1720-1922 — Safa 150

1 700

1 800 — Alawits — Zen 175 — Qaja 179

Mehemet 'Ali

42

social aspect of the pilgrimage

■ There is a social side to the pilgrimage which, when studied more closely, does not seem in any way more profane than the spiritual one.

It is indeed an unusual sight to see two million pilgrims from five different continents, from almost every country in the world, carrying the passports of a hundred different nationalities, belonging to the yellow, the black and the white races, all mingling together in total symbiosis.

Men and women of all ages, of every size, of completely different appearance, are engaged here in the accomplishment of the rites, forgetting their country and even their own language, since the prayers and the invocations are recited in the language of the Koran.

Transcending all fashions in costume, the white cloth (*Izàr*) of the sacred garnment, seems to anticipate the moment when all men will stand before their master, on the day of the Resurrection and the Last Judgement.

This reunion spells true brotherhood amongst peoples. Men and women of all races perform identical gestures, strike up the same attitudes, recite the sames verses of the Koran, the same invocations, repeat several times a day the same ablutions to purify their bodies and make a tremendous effort to penetrate the Greatness of God.

Of course, men are fallible, and it is therefore inevitable that even in Mecca one should hear sharp exchanges or even see persons quarrelling. But the pilgrim is far too preoccupied by the demands made upon him by his faith and by the potent religious and historical reality of the place to take any interest in such an event, having neither the time nor the curiosity to get involved or to ask the protagonists to mend their ways.

At any rate, a disagreement is soon dissipated in the great surge of faith all around, drowned out by the clamour of the invocations being recited everywhere. These great waves of faith sweep everything in their path in a movement towards the divine Majesty, supreme arbitrator of all creatures and of creation. □

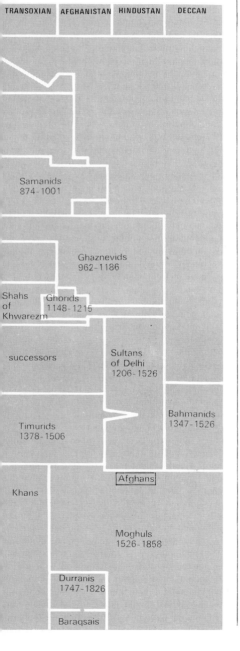

TRANSOXIAN   AFGHANISTAN   HINDUSTAN   DECCAN

Samanids
874-1001

Ghaznevids
962-1186

Shahs of Khwarezm

Ghorids
1148-1215

successors

Sultans
of Delhi
1206-1526

Bahmanids
1347-1526

Timurids
1378-1506

Afghans

Khans

Moghuls
1526-1858

Durranis
1747-1826

Baraqsais

the pilgrimage rite by rite

Al-Irhām
(entering into the sacred state)

■ *Ihrām* is the ritual of entering into the sacred state with a view to accomplishing the *Hajj*, the *'Umrah* or a combination of both pilgrimages. *Ihrām* is linked to assignments (*Mawāqeet, Meeqat* in the singular) of time and place.

The time Meeqāt

The *Ihrām* for the *Hajj* is linked both to a time and a place *Meeqāt*. The pilgrim can enter the state of *Ihrām* only at appointed times for the collective pilgrimage: from the 1st Shawwal (feast day which spells the end of the *Ramadan* or *Eid al-Fiṯr*) to the dawn of the 10th Thu-l-Hijjah (feast of the sacrifice or *Eid al-Aḍ'hā*). The *Hajj* of the pilgrim who enters *Ihrām* before or after these dates is not retained in his favour, though he can accomplish an *'Umrah* if he wishes.

The place Meeqāt

The *Meeqāt* of place is the location where the pilgrim must enter *Irhām* for the *Hajj* or for the *'Umrah*. This place, which depends on the pilgrim's point of arrival, must not be crossed whatever the means of transportation utilized until the pilgrim has accomplished the rites of entering *Ihrām*. Pilgrims coming from Syria, Egypt or North Africa must begin their *Ihrām* at Rabigh (200 km from Mecca). Pilgrims coming from Medinah must enter the state of *Ihrām* at Thu-al-Huleifah (Abar 'Ali), 11 kilometres south of Medinah. Pilgrims coming from Iraq must enter the state of *Ihrām* at That al-'Irq, 94 kilometres north-east of Mecca. Pilgrims coming from Kuwait and Saudi Arabia enter the state of *Ihrām* at Qarn al-Manazel, near As-Sayl (94 km east of Mecca) and those coming from Yemen and India at Yalamlam, south of Mecca.

These assignments of place were set out by the Prophet (peace be upon him) in person, and they were later confirmed by the *Rashidīn* or "Enlightened" Caliphs.

If pilgrims go to the Holy Places by land, they will have no difficulty whatsoever in entering their *Ihrām* at the appointed spot, but they will have a lot more trouble doing so if they go by sea or air.

Those who go by ship must enter the state of *Ihrām* while still at sea, shortly before the ship docks at Jeddah harbour. Those who go by air are well-advised to enter the state of *Ihrām* before their departure or else at the last stop-over before landing at Jeddah airport, from whence they go onto Mecca. The rites that accompany the entry into the state of *Ihrām*, such as prayers and ablutions, are impossible to carry out during a flight.

Pilgrims who wish to visit Medinah and the Prophet's tomb (peace be upon him) before they embark on the pilgrimage, must enter the state of *Ihrām* at the *Meeqāt* that has been appointed to the inhabitants of Medinah (Abar 'Ali), or else just before leaving the "city of the Prophet" if they are flying on to Mecca via Jeddah. Mecca itself does not have an airport.

The different kinds of Ihrām

There are three different forms of *Ihrām* for the *Hajj*.

First of all, the *Al-Ifrād* or intention of performing the *Hajj* alone, apart from the *'Umrah* (which is accomplished after the *Hajj*). The pilgrim enters the sacred state at the suitable *Mawāqeet* of time and place. On his arrival at Mecca, the pilgrim must accomplish:

— the optional circumambulation on arrival, or *Tawaf al-Qudoom,*

— the walk between Aŝ-Ŝafā and Al-Marwah (which the pilgrim can carry out later),

— all the rites of pilgrimage, while remaining in the full sacred state until the stoning of Al-'Aqabah. After the optional immolation of a victim, the pilgrim shaves his head, or at least cuts off a few symbolic locks of hair (women, naturally, perform only the second part of this ritual), and enters a state of partial *Ihrām*. All prohibitions relating to the sacred state are lifted with the exception of sexual relations, which are permitted only after the *Tawāf al-Ifādah* (circumambulation or unfurling) which spells the end of the state of *Ihrām*.

Secondly the *Tamattu'*. The pilgrim expresses at the *Meeqāt* his intention of performing the *'Umrah* alone. Immediately upon his arrival at Mecca, he performs his rites: the *Tawaf* or circumambulation around the Ka'bah, the *Sa'y* or walk between Aŝ-Ŝafā and Al-Marwah, and the cutting off of a lock of hair. Once his *'Umrah* is finished, he leaves the sacred state. All prohibitions are lifted. He can dress as he wishes, wear perfume and enjoy all the pleasures allowed him by his religion until the 8th Thu-l-Hijjah, known as the day of *Tarwiyah*. On this date, he dons the *Ihrām* robes once again, but without having to go to a specific *Meeqāt* of place; instead, he enters the sacred state in his dwelling or in the *Harām*, like the inhabitants of Mecca. He then proceeds to accomplish all the rites of the *Hajj*.

Those who take advantage of this somewhat easier approach, which shortens the times of the sacred state of *Ihrām*, must nonetheless immolate a ram at Minā on the day of the *Na'hr* (sacrifice) or during the course of the three days that follow. If they abstain from the sacrifice, they must fast instead for three days during the pilgrimage and for seven more days after they return to their homes. Only those pilgrims who live in the city of Mecca itself are exempted from this offering.

Thirdly, the *Qirān* or junction of the *'Umrah* and the *Hajj*. The greater and the lesser pilgrimages are undertaken together, without a break in the sacred state of *Ihram* as there is in the *Tamattu'*.

At the *Meeqāt*, the pilgrim expresses his intention of accomplishing the *Hajj* and the *'Umrah*. He carries out the rites of *'Umrah* as soon as he arrives in Mecca, then waits for the appointed time for the accomplishment of the *Hajj*, without leaving the sacred state of *Ihrām*. The pilgrim who adopts this plan must also sacrifice a ram.

The change of form of Ihrām (going from the *Ifrad* to the *Tamattu'*

or vice-versa) is permitted if there is a good reason, as long as the *Ṭawaf al-Qudoom* (or circumambulation upon arrival) has not been performed. It is not allowed after that time.

In Islam, the intention (*Niyah*) which must precede the action is what commits the pilgrim to the pilgrimage. Through the *Niyah*, the individual expresses his faith, his devotion and his submission to God, in order to obtain His forgiveness and His blessing.

This commitment, which will turn the individual into a pilgrim, must be made at the *Meeqāt*. The pilgrim will have previously performed his ablutions or *Ghosl* at his own dwelling. He will then remove his ordinary clothes to don, for as long as his *Ihrām* lasts, only two lengths of white cloth without seams, the *Izār* and the *Ridā*, each about two metres long. The first will serve as a loincloth and be wound round the waist; the second must cover the whole torso except for the right shoulder. The only shoes which are permitted are unstitched sandals (*Naʿl*) that leave the heel and the toes uncovered. A belt with pockets is permitted as long as it is unstitched; it is used to fasten the loin-cloth and to keep documents and money.

Naturally, this garb is compulsory only for men. Women must wear clothing that covers the whole body except for their face and hands, which must remain uncovered.

Women can therefore wear their usual clothing and footwear as long as these are clean and decent. They can be of any colour.

Once the bodily *Ihrām* has been accomplished, the pilgrim can then make his declaration of intent; whether he wishes to perform the *Hajj*, the *'Umrah*, or both at the same time, he must pronounce the following verbal address to his Creator:

"ALLĀHŪMA INNI AHRAMTU LAKA BEL HAJJ (or BEL'UMRATI or BEL HAJJ WAL UMRATI). FATAQABBALHU (or FATAQABBALHA, or FATAQABBALHUMA) MINNI."

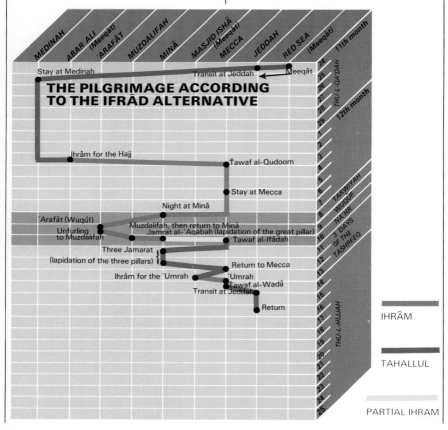

THE PILGRIMAGE ACCORDING TO THE IFRĀD ALTERNATIVE

"O God, I intend to make *Hajj* (or *'Umrah*, or *Hajj* and *'Umrah*). I beg you to receive it from me."

He reinforces his commitment by saying a prayer consisting of two *raka'at** (genuflections), preferably reciting in the first, after the ritual *Fātihah* (opening), the surah *al-Kāfiroon* (the miscreants):

"O unbelievers!
I shall not adore that which you adore!
You shall not adore that which I adore!
I cannot adore that which you adore!
And you need not adore that which I adore.
Keep to your religion as I keep to mine."

The selecting of this surah must be a way of showing one's determination to resist the temptations and to express one's steadfast opposition to both internal and external siren-calls.

In the second *raka'ah* the pilgrim can read after the *Fātihah* the surah *al-Ikhlās* (pure faith):

"Proclaim He is God the One,
God the Invoked,
He is without child and was not fathered,
None can equal Him."

It is not compulsory to select these two surah. Each pilgrim can select other surah to recite in accordance with his knowledge.

Once these rites are performed, the pilgrim only has to pronounce the *Talbyah* formula prayer, or answer to the divine call, to enter the sacred state of *Ihrām* fully:

"LABBAYKA ALLĀHŪMA, LAB-BAYK
LABBAYKA LA SHAREEKA, LAB-BAYK
INNA-AL HAMDA, WA-N-NI'MATA LAKA WA-L-MULK,
LA CHARIKA LAK."

---

* *Prayer unit made up of various movements and positions, amongst them the inclination (Roukou').*

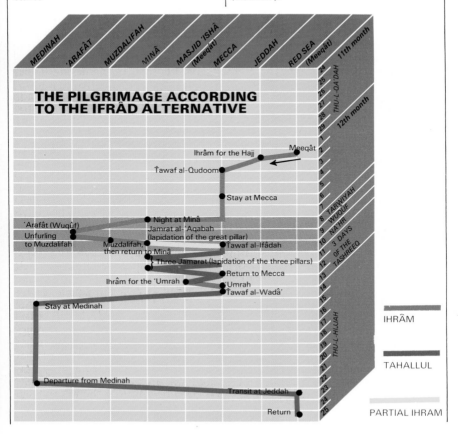

THE PILGRIMAGE ACCORDING TO THE IFRÂD ALTERNATIVE

"I am here, O God, I am here. I am here, Thou art without companion, I am here!

Praise and blessings are Thine, and Dominion!

Thou art without companion!"

The pilgrim must repeat this formula countless time, alone or in a group; it is in uttering it that he enters the sacred state and he must go on repeating it until the day of *Na'hr* (sacrifice), the 10th Thu-l-Hijjah, after the stoning of the Great Pillar or *Jamrat al-'Aqabah*. The *Talbyah* is compulsory only on the collective pilgrimage. He who accomplishes the *'Umrah* is dispensed from it.

For as long as he is in the sacred state, the pilgrim is forbidden to do the following things :

1. To wear sewn garnments if he is a man. Only the wearing of the *Ihrām* cloth, or *Izār*, and *Ridā*, and of sandals that leave the heel and the toes bare (*Na'l*) is permitted. It is allowed to change the *Izār*.

2. To wear jewellery (rings and wedding-band included). Again, women are dispensed from this prohibition.

3. To cover one's head (male pilgrims only), though the use of a sun-shade is allowed.

4. To wear perfume. It is allowed to wash the body as long as the soap utilized is unscented.

5. To cut the fingernails.

6. To remove more than three hairs from the body by whatever means (pluckings, shaving or merely shortening the hair). It is allowed to shave or to cut the hair only when an illness makes it necessary (a skin rash, for example) or if one has to get rid of lice. But if such is the case, the removal of hair must be compensated for by the immolation of an animal. Hair which falls out of its own accord is not regarded as an infringement of this rule.

7. Sexual relations, flirting, kissing or becoming engaged are strictly prohibited. The sexual act during *Ihrām* automatically invalidates the pilgrimage.

8. The slaying of all land animals is forbidden, with the exception of harmful animals and insects (such as flies, mosquitoes, fleas and bedbugs, etc.) or animals that can endanger life (snakes, scorpions, etc.). Fishing and hunting at sea are permitted however.

9. It is forbidden to cut trees or any green plants or in any way destroy the greenery of the sacred territory. Only the plucking of dried-up grass is permitted.

10. It is forbidden to commit any acts of violence, to quarrel or to enter into litigation with anybody whatsoever.

Atonement

Any forbidden action which has been committed either deliberately or accidentally, out of ignorance or out of necessity (illness for example) requires atonement of the fault either in the form of an animal sacrifice, or by fasting or by an offering. The same thing applies to any act of oversight.

The cutting of hair or nails, the use of head-covering, the wearing of sewn garnments entail the immolation of a ram or, failing this, a fast of three days or the providing of food for six persons in need.

The hunting of game must be atoned for by the sacrifice of a head of livestock or by the offering of foodstuff worth the cost of the animal.

The use of perfume requires no act of atonement unless it was intentional.

Sexual acts, flirtation, etc. sully the pilgrimage. The pilgrim who gives himself over to the pleasure of the senses while in a state of complete *Ihrām*, in other words before the stoning of the pillar of Al-'Aqabah at Minā on the 10th Thu-l-Hijjah, must sacrifice a camel or a bovine and start his pilgrimage all over again at a subsequent date.

If these actions occur after the partial lifting of the *Ihrām*, in other words after the Al-'Aqabah stoning but before the *Tawaf al-Ifādah* (circumambulation of the lifting of the sacred state), the pilgrimage is not made null and void, though a fault has been committed; the pilgrimage is not invalidated, but the pilgrim must atone by sacrificing a ram. □

the Ṭawaf
(circumambulation)

■ The *Ṭawaf*, or circumambulation, is the circling round the Ka'bah seven times, keeping the house of God to one's left as one does so (going counter-clockwise).

The first circling must start from the Yemenite angle which precedes the angle where the Black Stone is embedded and must end, the seventh time round, at exactly the same spot. The *Ṭawaf* must be undertaken only when the pilgrim is perfectly clean (*Ṭaharah*) and has previously performed his ablutions. A woman who is menstruating must not perform the *Ṭawaf*. Before setting off, the pilgrim must make his declaration of intent to perform the circumambulation. This act is a condition of the accomplishment of the rite, which may otherwise be nullified.

The prayer formula which is commonly used is as follows:

"ALLĀHŪMMA INNI OUREEDU ṬAWĀFA BAYTIKA-L-HARAM FA YASSIRHOU LI, WA TAQABBALHŪ MINNEE, SAB'ATA ASHWĀTIN, LI-L-LAHE TA'ĀLA."
"In the Name of God, the Compassionate, the Merciful. O God, I desire to perform *Ṭawaf* aroud Thy House, the Holy. Make it easy for me, and receive from me the seven circuits."

The pilgrim must then kiss the Black Stone or make a gesture of simulated touching, saying:

"BI-SMI-L-LAH ALLĀHŪ AKBAR WA LI-L-LĀHI-L AL-HAMD"
"In the name of God! God is most Great!
And unto God, Praise!"

During the circuit, the pilgrim invokes God in personal terms and according to his individual inspiration, or else he recites invocations specifically intended for this purpose (see the chapter on *Ad'iya* or invocations).

Each time he passes in front of the *Rokn al-Yamani* (the Yemenite angle) which is located before the Black Stone, the pilgrim will try to touch the uncovered portion of this angle or at least will hail it by a gesture. Then, between the two angles (the Yemenite angle and that of the Black Stone), he will address

the Lord with this verse from the Koran:

"RABBANA ĀTINĀ FI-DDUNIA HASSANATAN WA FI AL-ĀKHIRATI HASSANAH WA QINĀ 'ADHAB ANNĀR"
"Our Lord, grant us good in this world,
And good in the hereafter,
And save us from the torments of the Fire."

There are four different kinds of Ṭawaf. The rules and the method of doing them are identical. Only the moment at which they are carried out varies.

The different kinds of Tawaf

The *Ṭawaf al-Qudoom* (circumambulation upon arrival), also known as the *Ṭawaf at-Tahiyyah* (the circling of greeting) is the official way of greeting the Ka'bah, replacing the usual prayer (*Ṣalat*) of two genuflections (*Raka'atayn*) which is performed upon entering an ordinary mosque. This *Ṭawaf* is recommended though not compulsory.

The *Ṭawaf al-Ifādah*, also known as the *Ṭawaf az-Ziyyarah* or circling of the visit is compulsory. It is a pillar of the pilgrimage and if it is omitted the *Hajj* is nullified. It can only take place after the *Wuqūf*, or the rite of standing at 'Arafat.

This *Ṭawaf* can be performed on the Day of the Sacrifice (10th Thu-l-Hijjah). From the first hour of this day according to the Shafe'ites and the Hanbalites, and from dawn of that day according to the Malikites and the Hanifites. There is no deadline for its performance according to the Hanifites, the Hanbalites and the Shafe'ites, but the Malikites limit it to the month of Thu-l-Hijjah.

Generally-speaking, however, this *Ṭawaf* is performed on the day of the sacrifice, after the stoning of the *Great Pillar*, the immolation of the victim (*Na'hr*), the shaving of the head or the cutting of the hair partially lifting the sacred state. The pilgrim momentarily leaves Minā to go the Harām in Mecca. He leaves the sacred state with this circling, then returns to Minā to complete his stay. It must be noted that a woman who is menstruating at this time cannot perform this *Tawaf* any more than the other circlings. She must wait until the end of her period in order to perform it, after taking a complete bath (*Ghosl*). Only then can she fully lift the sacred state of *Ihrām*.

The *Tawaf al-Wadā'*, also known as the *Tawaf aŝ-Ŝadr* (the circling of farewell or of departure) is the one in which the pilgrim bids farewell to the Ka'bah before leaving Mecca for Medinah or for his home. He performs this *Tawaf* during his last visit to the Holy Mosque, which he must finally leave walking backwards as a sign of veneration (this gesture is obligatory, recommended or optional, according to the different theological schools).

This *Tawaf* is regarded as a duty (*Wajib*) by the Hanbalites, the Hanifites and the Shafe'ites. The *Hajj* pilgrim must make an offering of atonement if he does not perform this *Tawaf*.

According to the Malikites, this *Tawaf* is a *Sunna* (tradition of the Prophet) and its omission does not entail a sacrifice.

The *Tawaf Attaîawwu'* or superogatory circling can be performed at any time by the pilgrims.

After performing any circumambulation the pilgrim must say a prayer of two genuflections at the Place of Abraham (or Ibraheem), which is a few feet away from the *Matâf*, the space where the circling is performed, facing the *Multazam'* (side of the Ka'bah right after the angle in which the Black Stone is set, and on which opens the Ka'bah's only door). □

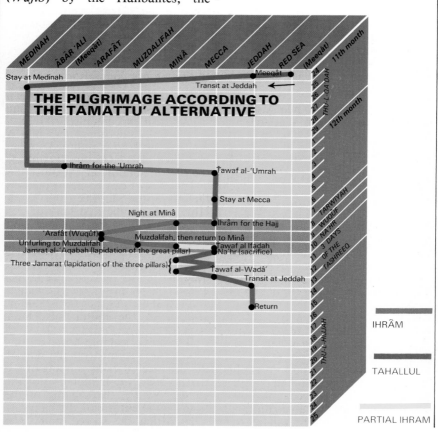

the Sa'y
(procession)

■ The *Sa'y* is the rite of going seven times between the hillocks of Aŝ-Ŝafā and Al-Marwah.

Each one-way journey counts as a length (*Shawt*) out of the seven to be performed. The *Sa'y* must absolutely begin on the hillock of Aŝ-ŝafa and thus must end at Al-Marwah.

The *Sa'y* is regarded by the Malikite, Shafe'ite and Hanbalite schools as one of the pillars of the *Hajj* and the *'Umrah*. According to these three schools, the leaving out of the *Sa'y* makes the pilgrimage null and void. The Hanifites regard it as a duty and claim that the *Hajj* pilgrim who has not been able to perform the rite of *Sa'y* has not invalidated his pilgrimage, but that he must immolate a sacrificial victim instead.

To perform the *Sa'y*, one does not need to be in a state of *Ťaharah* (purity, cleanliness) as one does for the *Ťawaf* or for the prayer. A menstruating woman can therefore perform it.

Those pilgrims who have opted for the *Tamattu'* (*'Umrah* preceding the *Hajj*) must carry out the procession as soon as they have accomplished their *Ťawaf* at Mecca. They cannot leave the sacred state until they have accomplished these two rites, followed by the symbolic cutting of the hair. This last rite is usually carried out as one leaves the *Mas'à* (procession gallery). The prohibitions of the *Ihrām* are then lifted for the pilgrims until they enter the sacred state once more for the *Hajj*, on the 8th Thu-l-Hijjah, which is the day of departure for Minā (*Tarwiyah*). These pilgrims must perform a second *Ťawaf* and one more *Sa'y* from the 10th Thu-l-Hijjah onwards.

The pilgrims who have adopted the *Qirān* formula are allowed to accomplish only one *Sa'y* for the *Hajj* and the *'Umrah*. They can accomplish it either upon their arrival at Mecca, if they are doing the *Ťawaf al-Qudoom*, or on their return from Minā for the *Ťawaf al-Ifādah*.

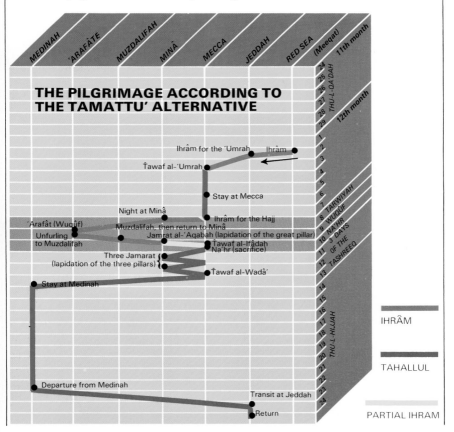

THE PILGRIMAGE ACCORDING TO THE TAMATTU' ALTERNATIVE

the Tarwiyah
(day for making provisions in water)

Those who have opted for the *Ifrād* formula will have the same choices in the matter of the *Sa'y*, but if they do the *'Umrah* after the *Hajj* they will have to perform one more *Ṭawaf* and one more *Sa'y* for the *'Umrah*.

The *Sa'y* must always be accomplished after the *Ṭawaf*. When the pilgrim has finished his circumambulation, he traditionally drinks from the *Zamzam well* and splashes his body and clothing with its water, then heads for Aŝ-Ŝafā. Upon his arrival, he recites the following:

"I begin where God and his Messenger began. Aŝ-Ŝafā and Al-Marwah are rites prescribed by God. So if those who make Pilgrimage to the House, or make *'Umrah*, go around them both, it is allowed to them. And if anyone obeyeth his own impulse to good, God is Grateful, All-Knowing."

The Niyah

Turning towards the Ka'bah, the pilgrim expresses the *Niyah*, or declaration of intent to perform the rite of *Sa'y*. He then climbs the hillock of Aŝ-Ŝafā and says:

"ALLĀHU AKBAR, ALLAHU AKBAR, ALLĀHU AKBAR, WA LI-L-LAHI-L-HAMD"
"God is most Great, God is most Great, God is most Great! And unto God, Praise!"

The pilgrim then starts on the walk. Upon his arrival in the hollow of the valley between the two hillocks, he accelerates his pace at the spot marked by a green post, then slows down again at a second green post. Once he has reached Al-Marwah, which he also climbs, he turns back in the direction of Aŝ-Ŝafā. His walk, or Procession, ends at Al-Marwah after the seventh of the journeys. □

■ On the 8th Thu-l-Hijjah, the day before the decisive date of the *Hajj*, pilgrims leave Mecca at sunrise to go to Minā. This day is called *Yawm Attarwiyah*, or "day for making provisions in water"; for it was on this day that, in the old days, pilgrims prepared the water supplies which were to last them through their stay at 'Arafāt. They would then leave Mecca and set off for the valley of Minā at sunrise, spending the rest of the day and the following night at Minā. The next day, they would leave Minā at sunrise and set off for 'Arafāt where they were to perform the *Wuqūf*, or rite of standing.

This stop-over at Minā is looked upon as a duty by the Hanifites, and as a Tradition (non compulsory) by the three other schools. In this day and age, few pilgrims perform this rite because of the practical difficulties which it poses for the *Mutawwifeen* (pilgrim guides). Most pilgrims now go directly from Mecca to 'Arafāt on the 8th or even the 9th Thu-l-Hijjah.

It must be recalled that those pilgrims who have opted for the *Tamattu'* formula and who have therefore left the sacred state after performing the *Ṭawaf* and the *Sa'y* must take on *Ihrām* once again before they leave for Minā or for 'Arafāt. □

'Arafāt

■ The gathering of all the *Hajj* pilgrims on the 9th Thu-l-Hijjah at 'Arafāt is known as the *Wuqūf* (litterally, the standing).

The *Wuqūf* at 'Arafāt is the chief rite of the *Hajj*. When asked about the importance of this rite, the Prophet Muhammed (peace be upon him) replied: "The *Hajj* is 'Arafāt." This explains why all the different theological schools agree on this point: that without the rite of standing on 'Arafāt, the pilgrimage is null and void.

The day of 'Arafāt has been compared to the Day of the Last Judgment (*Yawm al-Hashr*). Here the concept of all men's equality before God is not a mere cliché. As on the Day of Judgment, the king and the servant are equals on 'Arafāt. Wearing their plain, identical unsewn *Ihrām* clothing which are so like shrouds, pilgrims feel as though they had just emerged from their tombs and were facing God for the Final Reckoning. So many pilgrims come to Mecca now that the traditional stop-over at Minā on the 9th Thu-l-Hijjah at sunrise is often missed out, as the facilities are inadequate for receiving such great numbers of people. Many therefore go straight from Mecca to 'Arafāt on the 8th Thu-l-Hijjah, or even on the 9th. According to the doctors of Islamic law (*Ulema*), this slight modification does not have any effect on the validity of the *Hajj* for it is dictated by necessity.

According to the Malikites, the Shafe'ites and the Hanifites, the *Wuqūf* begins in the course of the afternoon, whereas the Hanbalites accord the whole day to 'Arafāt. All four schools agree, however, that it ends at dawn on the 10th Thu-l-Hijjah which is the day of the sacrifice.

The *Wuqūf* does not entail a compulsory period of standing, as its name would seem to imply. Pilgrims are free to sit down, to walk about and to converse among one another. But God must be uppermost in their minds throughout, for the day of 'Arafāt is, by definition, the day of invocations and of the quest for Absolute Forgiveness.

Some pilgrims read chapters from the Koran or recite prayers (*Ad'iya*). Others climb the Mountain of Mercy (*Jabal ar-Rahmah*), or listen to orators addressing the multitudes. There is no set pattern of behaviour or specific spot to seek out above all others. Each individual performs the *Wuqūf* according to the dictates of his conscience, and goes wherever he wishes within the limits of the territory of 'Arafāt. The important thing is to be present until sunset, after which a signal is given warning the pilgrims that it is time to set off for Muzdalifah (*Ifādah*).

It must be noted that pilgrims recite abbreviated versions of the *El-Zuhr* (noon) and *El-'Asr* (afternoon) prayers at 'Arafāt. For each of these prayers, they only perform two *Raka'at* or genuflections, instead of the usual four. The Maghrib (sunset) prayer must be celebrated at Muzdalifah.

It is advised not to be late except in cases of emergency, but all latecomers should know that they have the whole night, from the 9th to the 10th Thu-l-Hijjah, in which to accomplish the rite of *Wuqūf*. The Prophet (peace be with him) specified in one of the *Hadeeth* (chronicles of the Prophet's words and deeds) that the pilgrimage of those who reach 'Arafāt before dawn (of the 10th Thu-l-Hijjah) is valid. □

Muzdalifah

■ Having left 'Arafāt after sunset, pilgrims arrive at Muzdalifah after night has fallen. The halt in this place is prescribed by the Koran:

"When you depart from 'Arafāt, invoke God close to the *Mash'ar al-Harām* (Sacred Monument). Invoke Him, for He has set you on the right course, though you had gone astray before then."

Surah of the Heifer, II, 198

First of all, pilgrims must recite the *Maghrib* (sunset) prayer which they have not been able to say at 'Arafāt. They are to say it at the same time as the *'Ishā* (nightfall) prayer, abbreviating the two in accordance with the canonical dispensation granted to travellers.

The pilgrims then go and gather the forty-nine or the seventy pebbles (forty-nine if they are spending three days at Minā, seventy if they remain for four days). These pebbles must be about the size of a chick pea, or a trifle larger, and will be used for the stoning of the Pillars at Minā.

In accordance with the *Sunnah*, some pilgrims spend the night on the spot. They will leave Muzdalifah for Minā only the next morning, just before sunrise, after reciting the dawn prayer, standing before the Sacred Monument.

But the majority of pilgrims will have gone back to Minā on the same night, for as with the *Tarwiyah* (the stay at Minā on the previous day), it is not easy to stay over at Muzdalifah in this day and age, given the great number of pilgrims and the total lack of facilities. Those who stay for the night will not find a roof to put over their heads. Some *Ulema* advise those pilgrims who can to remain on this site until after midnight. □

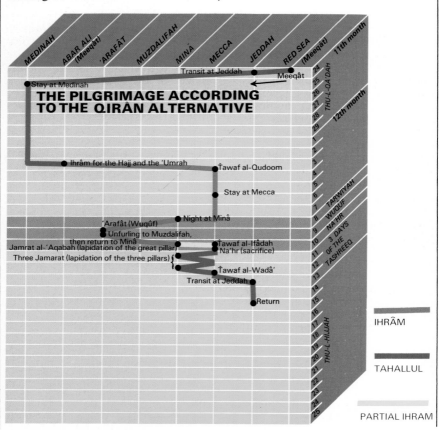

56

Minā

■ After 'Arafāt, pilgrims return to Mecca via Muzdalifah and Minā. As we pointed out earlier, the stay at Muzdalifah is a brief one. The stay at Minā, on the other hand, is a longer one: *a minimum of three days and three nights.*

Pilgrims must spend the day of the 10th Thu-l-Hijjah there, known as the *Yawm an-Na'hr* (or Day of Sacrifice) and the following two or three days, known as *Ayyam at-Tashreeq.*

On the 10th Thu-l-Hijjah, they must stone the Great Pillar or *Jamrat al-'Aqabah* and sacrifice an animal.

They must shave or cut off a lock of hair to put a partial end to the sacred state, and then go on to Mecca to perform the circling known as the *Ťawaf al-Ifādah* (see chapter on the *Ťawaf*).

At the end of this rite, by which pilgrims totally put an end to the sacred state of *Ihrām*, they return to Minā to spend a minimum of two days and a maximum of three there.

The stoning of the pillars symbolizing Satan

The small stones gathered at Muzdalifah for the lapidation of the pillars at Minā are known as *Jamarat* or *Jimār* (sing. *Jamrah*). These pillars are also called *Jamarat* or *Jimār.* They are located at the centre of Minā, over a distance of 272 metres. The smallest of them lies at the far end of the village, in the direction of Muzdalifah. It is called *al-Jamra-ŝ-Soghra,* or again as *al-Jamra-l-Ūla* (the First Pillar).

The second, named *al-Jamra-l-Woŝťā* (the Medium or Middle Pillar), is located 156 metres further on (in the direction of Mecca).

The third pillar, which is called *al-Jamra-l-Kobra* or *Jamrat al-'Aqabah,* is 116 metres beyond the second one, again in the direction of Mecca.

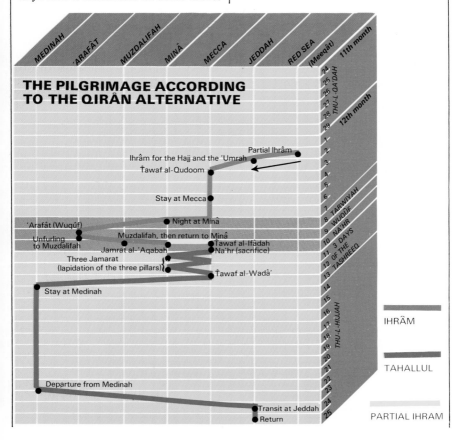

THE PILGRIMAGE ACCORDING TO THE QIRÂN ALTERNATIVE

57

On the 10th Thu-l-Hijjah, pilgrims stone only the last pillar *Jamrat al-'Aqabah.* They must hurl each of the seven pebbles one by one, saying:

"ALLĀHU AKBAR
LA ILĀHA ILLĀ LLĀH".
"God is Greatest,
there is no other god but God".

In accordance with tradition, they will abstain from speaking any other words or making any other invocation.

On the following day (the llth Thu-l-Hijjah) or lst day of the *Tashreeq,* they will go and hurl seven pebbles at the first pillar, then another seven at the middle one, and finally another seven at the Great Pillar.

On the 12th Thu-l-Hijjah (2nd day of the *Tashreeq*) they will once more throw seven pebbles at each of the pillars, starting with the smallest and ending up with that of al-'Aqabah. This rite must be renewed on the 13th Thu-l-Hijjah by those who have stayed on at Minā.

The stoning of the pillars commemorates the Prophet Abraham's gesture when he hurled stones at Satan on three occasions at this spot; it symbolizes the pilgrim's commitment to the principle of resisting future temptations. It is regarded as a duty by all four major theological schools of Islam.

Should a pilgrim fail for any reason to perform all or a part of this rite, he must atone for it by sacrificing an animal or by fasting.

The *Talbiyah,* or response to the divine call (see chapter on *Ihrām),* which the pilgrim never ceases to repeat at all times from the moment he enters the sacred state, is not uttered again once the last pillar has been stoned on the day of the Sacrifice.

The sacrifice
of a head
# of livestock

The memory of Abraham's sacrifice is perpetrated to this day by hundreds of million of Muslims from the four corners of the world who, each year, celebrate the 10th Thu-l-Hijjah, Feast of the Sacrifice or *Eid al-Aḍ'hā,* also known as the *Eid al-Kebeer* or *Bairam.* On the morning after the celebration of the prayer of *Eid,* each family sacrifices one or several heads of livestock (usually sheep, but also oxen or camels) to commemorate the gesture of the Prophet Abraham (peace be upon him).

The luckiest Muslims find themselves actually at Minā, doing a pilgrimage, on this day. Many of them will endeavour to emulate the Prophet Muhammed (peace be upon him) who sacrificed one hundred head of camel on the occasion of his Farewell Pilgrimage. These pilgrims will not hesitate to sacrifice more than one animal if their means allow them to do so.

This rite is not an obligation unless the pilgrim has made a vow or if he must atone for an omission (a rite which he has failed to accomplish, or a failure to observe a rule). It is nonetheless recommended to make a sacrifice, in accordance with the Tradition of the Prophet and with the Divine Proclamation:

"Let them sacrifice on set days and invoke upon their herds the name of God (by immolating them). Eat and feed the unfortunate, the needy."

Koran, the Pilgrimage, XXII - 28

The giving of the flesh of these animals to the unfortunate and the needy is one of the principal objectives of this sacrifice, as another verse of the Koran (XXII-37) attests:

"It is not the meat (of the sacrificial animals) that reaches God, neither their blood; it is your piety that reaches Him."

It is difficult to carry out this particular injunction today though a certain number of needy persons do go to Minā on the Day of the Sacrifice to fetch provisions of meat. The amount that can be distributed in this fashion is insignificant, however, compared to the quantities that are available.

The waste is enormous, for the heat is such that the Saudi authorities must bury thousands of carcasses on the afternoon of the Day of Sacrifice in order to avoid smell and decay.

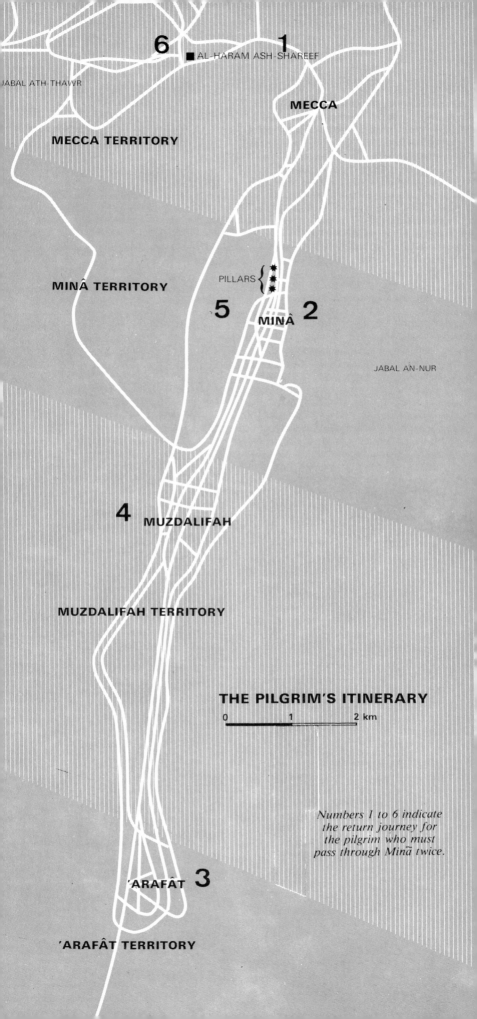

6

1

■ AL-HARAM ASH-SHAREEF

JABAL ATH-THAWR

MECCA

MECCA TERRITORY

MINÂ TERRITORY

PILLARS {

5 2

MINÂ

JABAL AN-NUR

4 MUZDALIFAH

MUZDALIFAH TERRITORY

THE PILGRIM'S ITINERARY

0   1   2 km

*Numbers 1 to 6 indicate
the return journey for
the pilgrim who must
pass through Minā twice.*

'ARAFÂT 3

'ARAFÂT TERRITORY

Ulema have looked into this problem of waste; some of them suggest that the slaughtered animals should be sold to a company that would be equipped to process their flesh, and that the profits thus obtained should go to charity.

Others suggest an even better solution: "That an Islamic organization should take over the conservation and the distribution" of the sacrificial offerings, and that their flesh should be distributed to Muslims who live in countries where food is scarce. One could also realize considerable profits from the sale of the skins if they were tanned, and the money thus obtained would be of great use to a number of Muslim charities in various countries.

Quite a number of pilgrims are under the impression that the deadline for offering a sacrifice is at noon on the 10th Thu-l-Hijjah.

As a result, thousands of pilgrims rush to the Minā slaughterhouses in the first hours of the morning and there is such a scuffle both outside and inside the abattoirs that pilgrims have been known to lose their lives there.

In fact, there is no set time-limit for the sacrificing of an animal. The sacrifice can be performed at any time during the three or four days that the pilgrim spends at Minā; those days are all known as *Ayyam an-Na'hr* (Days of Sacrifice).

Upon completing the *'Umrah,* the pilgrim must shave his head or at least cut off a few strands of hair when he leaves the *Mas'ā* (Procession Gallery: see paragraph concerning the *Sa'y).*

During the *Hajj,* this operation takes place on the 10th Thu-l-Hijjah at Minā, after the stoning of the pillars and the sacrifice (if the pilgrim intends to make a sacrificial offering).

The Malikites, the Hanafites and the Hanbalites regard this rite as a duty. The Shafe'ites consider it a pillar of the *Hajj* whose omission cannot be atoned for by a sacrifice.

All four schools consider that the shaving of the head is preferable to the mere cutting of the hair, but that women need not cut off more than a few symbolic locks of hair. □

Pilgrim camp at Minā.

Jeddah

■ "And call to mind when we assigned the site of the House to Abraham and said: 'Unite not aught with Me in worship and cleanse My House for those who go in procession round it and who stand or bow in worship.'
'And proclaim to the peoples a Pilgrimage. Let them come to thee on foot and on every fleet camel, arriving by every deep defile.' "
Koran, the Pilgrimage, 26-27

In this beginning of the xvth century of the *Hijrah* (Hegira), over two million pilgrims a year heed this call during the prescribed months. In 1930, they numbered only 29,000 from outside the borders of Saudi Arabia. Within half a century, their number has multiplied by thirty, almost 900,000 pilgrims now come from abroad to perform the *Hajj*. To this number must be added almost 1,250,000 pilgrims from Saudi Arabia (350,000 Saudi Arabians and almost 900,000 foreigners residing in that country).

The "fleet camels" of the past have turned into thousands of cars, caravans and buses, dozens of ships and hundreds of airplanes. Almost a third of the pilgrims coming from abroad arrive by land (33 %); nearly 7 % come by sea and 60 % come by air.

Almost all pilgrims going by road head directly for Mecca or Medinah, without going by Jeddah; but most of the pilgrims arriving by sea or air stop at Jeddah.

For the three weeks that precede the decisive days of the pilgrimage, Jeddah airport is thronged both day and night with Boeings, Airbuses, Caravelles, Tristars etc.

According to some, Jeddah is one of the cradles of humanity. This assertion is partially based on the name of the city itself: Jeddah, which means "grandmother" in Arabic, and which would seem to imply that the city harks back to the days of Eve, the mother of all men, who is said to be buried there. Only God knows the whole truth.

With a population of 560,000 inhabitants, Jeddah is the second largest city in Saudi Arabia, as well as the country's diplomatic and economic capital. Though Riyadh is the political capital and houses most of the Governmental departments three-quarters of the year (at Ta'if during the summer months), the Ministry of Foreign Affairs and all the foreign diplomatic missions accredited by the Royal House are located in Jeddah.

But Jeddah is first and foremost a great economic centre. It houses the head offices of all the major commercial companies, both Saudi Arabian and foreign, and it is there that most of the country's business is conducted.

Jeddah is a shopper's paradise. Elegant boutiques sell their wares next to the more traditional souks, offering the latest European merchandise and the newest Japanese gadgets at rock-bottom prices, since there are no taxes in Saudi Arabia.

Jeddah is nothing more than a stopover for most pilgrims, who do not take the time to visit it. They are too much in a hurry to reach the Holy Places and usually go straight on to Mecca or Medinah from the airport or the harbour, both of which are located not far from the city centre.

Formalities

As soon as they enter Saudi Arabian territory, pilgrims must accomplish the following formalities:
Police formalities. These formalities are extremely simple and short for pilgrims who have had a pilgrimage visa delivered to them free of charge by Saudi Arabian consulates abroad. Those who have been unable to obtain such a visa because there was no Saudi Arabian

consulate in their country of origin can obtain the visa upon arrival.

Choosing a Mutawwif. Pilgrims are then sent on to the *Hay'at As'sual Wa-Attawzee'*, an information office where they will be asked the name of their *Mutawwif*.

The *Mutawwif*, plural *Mutawwifeen* (litterally: he who makes others circle round the Ka'bah) is in fact also the person who takes over responsibility for the pilgrim upon his arrival at Jeddah, who finds lodgings for him at Mecca and at the Holy Places in the vicinity of Mecca, who makes his travelling arrangements in connection with all the rites of pilgrimage. The *Mutawwif* takes care of the pilgrim in Mecca itself, as opposed to the *Muzawwir* (literally: he who shows around) who performs the same duties at Medinah. This last journey, which the pilgrim makes before or after the *Hajj* rites, depending on his date of arrival, is not compulsory; but, as we shall see later, the vast majority of pilgrims go there anyway.

Most pilgrims know the name of their *Mutawwif* in advance. Their acquaintances will have recommended so and so, or else they may have a chance to meet him in their home country. Until a few years ago, it was common for the *Mutawwifeen* to travel around various Muslim countries in order to acquire a reputation. They would send a delegate (a *Wakeel*, plural: *Wukala'*) to meet their clients at the various points of entry. But the number of pilgrims has increased to such an extent that the *Mutawwifeen* have had to organize the allotment of pilgrims amongst themselves in a more rational fashion. A *Wukala' Unified Bureau* has been set up to help them in this task.

The 1,200 *Mutawwifeen* of Mecca are divided up into seven groups; each group receives pilgrims from a specific region:
— South-East Asia,
— India, Pakistan, Afghanistan, Bangladesh, Burma, Sri Lanka,
— non-Arab Africa,
— Arab countries,
— Turkey,
— Iran,
— countries of Europe and America.

This last group, which has just been created, has not yet had *Mutawwifeen* appointed to it. Organized as a foundation, it takes care of those persons coming from the countries of Europe and America.

The pilgrim who does not know a *Mutawwif* is assigned one. An important recommendation must be made here: those pilgrims who have come with one or more members of their family and those who wish to remain in a group of persons who have the same nationality as themselves, must specify that such is their intent at the Bureau and ask for the same *Mutawwif* to be assigned to all of them. If they do not take this precaution, they may well find their party dispersed. Even couples have been known to become separated and to have different *Mutawwifeen* attributed to them.

Another important recommendation: before giving up their passports to the Bureau employees in charge of the pilgrims, all pilgrims should remove whatever documents they have been carrying with their passports (tickets, travellers' cheques, etc.). Employees of the Bureau will not return passports to the pilgrims immediately, but will hand them over to the *Wukala' Unified Bureau* for further formalities. Passports therefore will go through a number of hands and there is a chance that any other loose documents will get lost in the process. Indeed, even the passports themselves sometimes get lost. This happens so frequently that some embassies make all the necessary provisions in advance for replacing the missing documents, but of course this cannot be done in the case of lost travellers' cheques, which are sometimes all the money that the pilgrim is carrying with him.

Customs: One the first two formalities have been dealt with, the pilgrim must proceed to luggage identification and inspection by the customs. This formality is also a brief one. Once he has gone through customs, his luggage is taken charge of by special porters connected with the *Wukala' Unified Bureau*, who wear a special badge. These porters will escort the pilgrim to the pilgrim rest-house (*Madeenat al-Hijjāj*) free of charge; they are renumerated by the Bureau itself and do not expect a payment or a tip.

Pilgrims must then attempt to remain in a group with their relatives or their friends and acquaintances in order to accomplish the next formalities, which will require a great deal of time and patience.

Change: Persons arriving from countries where there are strict exchange controls usually only have on them a traveller's cheque established by a bank in their own country. They must proceed to the counter that corresponds to their geographical zone, where the Saudi Arabian representative of their national bank will give them the amount corresponding to their cheque in Saudi rials.

Those pilgrims who have brought cash do not need to go to a bank to convert it into rials. They will find a *Ŝarraf* (change dealer), often out in the street, who will change their currency at a rate often superior to that offered by the banks.

It is a good thing to know in advance that, in Saudi Arabia, all or almost all currencies are convertible into rials, even the most "unconvertible." But the exchange rate is obviously lower in the case of these unconvertible currencies than the official and often artificial exchange rate established by the countries which print them.

The Wukala' Unified Bureau: Once the pilgrim has changed his money (and not before, as he will have to settle certain taxes), he must head for the *Wukala' Unified Bureau* to have his assignment to his *Mutawwif* confirmed, to settle the problem of transport to the Holy Places, to pay the various service taxes and fees relating to the different services provided and to recover his passport.

The assignment to a *Mutawwif* is not a problem if the pilgrim knows the name of his "landlord" and if that person really does correspond to his country of origin. Should there be any misunderstanding, the pilgrim can have his *Mutawwif*

The odd "Machrabiya"
of the ancient houses of Jeddah.

changed, as we have seen earlier on.

The services provided by the *Mutawwif* vary from one to the next, according to the individual's capacity to house, advise and welcome the pilgrims in his charge. His fee will depend on the quality of the services that he provides and also on the demands made upon him by his charges. The averagely well-off pilgrim who is not too demanding in terms of physical comfort can expect to pay roughly 1000 rials during his stay at Mecca, Minā, 'Arafāt and Muzdalifah. The exchange rate of the rial for 1980 is approximately £ 0.13, or U.S. $ 0.30. These expenses are payed over directly to the *Mutawwif* at Mecca and not to the *Wukala' Unified Bureau.*

Various other expenses: Each pilgrim must pay a sum amounting to approximately 294 rials for services provided upon his arrival and at his departure. He must also pay approximately 80 rials for his overnight stay at the Jeddah pilgrim resthouse. These figures are approximative and are liable to change.

Transportation: The *Wukala' Unified Bureau* is responsible for negociations between pilgrims and the various transport companies.

The complete tour (Jeddah, Mecca, Medinah, Jeddah, or, if the pilgrim is going in the opposite direction Jeddah, Medinah, Mecca, Jeddah) costs 295 rials by bus (subject to change). Those who prefer to go by air can do so; the cost of the return flight Jeddah-Medinah-Jeddah is 250 rials. The cost of transport to and from Mecca from Jeddah (30 rials) is, of course, not included in this sum.

Tanazul: Pilgrims wishing to avoid the long delays attendant on getting a seat in a public conveyance can make use of one of the many taxis available. They are advised to go as a group of four or five, according to the number of passenger seats available in the taxi, and would do well to discuss the price of the fare with the driver beforehand. A seat for Medinah in a collective taxi will cost them approximately 200 rials; and one for Mecca roughly 30 rials. But they will first have to pay a tax at the *Wukala' Unified Bureau* which goes to the public transport companies and which represents about 50 % of the cost of the bus ticket. The Bureau will then stamp their passport for, without this stamp, the pilgrims would not be allowed to travel by private means. The use of a taxi is therefore not recommended, insofar as it means considerable extra expense to little advantage.

Transportation at Mecca: Pilgrims must pay approximately 100 rials for bus transport between Mecca, Minā, 'Arafāt, Muzdalifah and Mecca. This sum must be payed over to the *Mutawwif* at Mecca and not to the *Wukala' Unified Bureau* at the point of entry into the country.

Once these formalities have been accomplished and the pilgrim has paid the various taxes, he will be given back his passport. All that remains for him to do is to find out the time when his bus leaves Jeddah, or when his plane takes off if he is flying to Medinah.

Official delegations

Each Muslim country sends an official delegation to accompany its pilgrims.

This delegation often includes theologians, whose task it is to advise the pilgrims in the accomplishment of their religious duties. It comprises health workers who can dispense first aid in case of sickness and qualified personnel that can provide administrative assistance.

The persons who make up these delegations can be invaluable not only to pilgrims but also to the Saudi Arabian authorities, whose task they make much easier, in terms of helping pilgrims from their countries of origin to accomplish police formalities, of advising those who do not know a *Mutawwif* in selecting one, in establishing a list of the people in the delegation's charge for the use of the *Wukala' Unified Bureau*, in settling the various taxes on behalf of the pilgrims, in finding out details concerning the various means of transport put at the pilgrims' disposal and in showing the pilgrims which bank counters they must go to.

Those pilgrims who are not assisted by an official delegation are advised to organize themselves into a group and to appoint delegates among their number who have already been on the pilgrimage and who therefore know what formalities must be accomplished. This will give the others the opportunity to get on with other tasks or just to rest.

Shopping

Before leaving Jeddah, the pilgrim can buy any supplies or equipment that he is likely to need on the pilgrimage. If he has elected to travel lightly and has brought with him only the strict minimum, he need not regret his decision for he will find everything he needs for the *Hajj* on the spot and at extremely reasonable prices. He will appreciate the fact of having travelled lightly on his journey over to Mecca all the more for having to buy a great number of presents for his friends and relatives at home and therefore being heavily loaded on the journey back.

There is no set list of what to purchase for the pilgrimage, and each person must get what he feels he requires. Besides, the pilgrim will be able to purchase anything he needs at Mecca or Medinah if he has not done so at Jeddah. Everywhere the *Hajj* pilgrim goes, he will find merchants peddling their ware.

A certain number of items, however, are to be recommended to the majority of pilgrims:

— *A prayer mat.* Given the great number of persons who congregate at the mosques during the hours of prayer, a large number of faithful will not be able to enter and will therefore have to pray outside, in nearby streets or squares. They will find it extremely useful to always carry a small carpet with them for the purpose of praying.

— *A parasol.* Given the extremes of heat and the fact that pilgrims must remain bareheaded throughout the state of *Ihram*, a parasol is a most useful acquisition. Many pilgrims use an umbrella for this purpose, not realizing that the dark colour of such instruments (which are often black) offers no protection against the sun. It is therefore far better to use a proper, light-coloured or preferably white parasol.

— *Warm clothing.* These will be needed at Medinah, where there is a considerable drop in the temperature at night.

— *An inflatable rubber mattress* or else a foam rubber pad to sleep on for persons in poor health or unaccustomed to hardship. Pilgrims will have to sleep in tents during their stay at Mina and the *Mutawwifeen* often do not provide sufficient bedding.

— *Tablets for purifying the water.* Some of the places where the pilgrim will sojourn have an inadequate water supply. What water there is has been stored in unhygienic containers. Cheap chloramine tablets can be purchased at any chemist, and will enable the pilgrim to sterilize any water he suspects is contaminated, for drinking purposes or for washing food and eating utensils.

The departure from Jeddah to Mecca or Medinah

Once pilgrims have accomplished the necessary formalities at Jeddah, they are free to proceed either to Mecca or to Medinah. The decision to go first to one or to the other town will depend upon their date of arrival in Saudi Arabia. It must be recalled that the latest date a pilgrim can arrive in Mecca for the *Hajj* is the 4th or the 5th Thu-l-Hijjah. Traditionally, pilgrims spend a minimum of eight days at Medinah, so as to be able to recite forty prayers there, at a rate of five a day. Pilgrims who arrive in Saudi Arabia before the end of the month of Thu-l-Qa'dah can visit Medinah before the *Hajj*. Those who arrive in Saudi Arabia after the 29th Thu-l-Qa'dah will not have enough time to go to Medinah first. The best thing for them is to go straight to Mecca for the pilgrimage, and to go and spend some time in Medinah after the *Hajj* (see calendars and itineraries on page 90). ☐

The Maghreb (sunset) prayer.
In the foreground, to the left,
the ancient Zamzam well
which has been modernized :
the water now comes out of taps.

Mecca
Makkah

■ "Truly the first temple establish-ed for the people was that of Bakkah (ancient name for *Makkah* or *Baccah*), a holy place that gives guidance to all beings.

"The signs are clear. It was there that Abraham came to a halt and whosoever enters this place is in security. It is the duty of all men towards God to go to the House as pilgrims, if they are able to make their way there. As for the unbeliever, God is All-Sufficient nor needs any being."

Koran III, 96-97, the House of 'Imrān.

There is no other place in the whole world which has been so honoured and respected as Mecca. Five times a day, hundreds of millions of Muslims turn to face the very heart of this city, which is the Ka'bah, the "blessed sanctuary which gives guidance to all beings". All those who turn to face Mecca in this fashion hope that one day God will grant their prayers and that they will have the immense privilege of going to the holy city to accomplish the fifth pillar of Islam, in other words the *Hajj*.

Mecca is the spiritual capital of the Muslim world, a land made blessed and noble by God. It is the cradle of monotheism (faith in the One and Only God), where according to Divine Revelation "the first temple established for the people", the Ka'bah, was built. It was also here that the Prophet Muhammed (peace be upon him) was born and received the first verses of a Revelation that was to change the face of the world.

Mecca is located on the 21° 30' latitude north and 40° 20' longitude east. It lies 73 kilometres south-west of Jeddah and is surrounded by two mountain chains that are gradually drawing together to the east, the west and the south. The city itself is constructed on a number of hillocks and alluvial valleys. Its central point is the *Harām ash-Shareef* (the Forbidden Sanctuary) which shelters the Ka'bah. The *Harām* lies in one of the low parts of the city, at an altitude of 277 metres above sea level.

Mecca has several different names. Apart from its present denomination, it is often referred to in the Koran as "Umm al-Qūra" (the Mother of Cities), "Al-Balad al-Ameen" (the City of Peace, or Safety), "Al-Bayt al-Ateeq" (the Ancient House), "Al-Bayt al-Harām" (the Forbidden Temple). It is also known by the name of "Umm al-Rahmah" (the Source of Mercy), "Al-Raas" (the Head: ie the origin), "Al-Haram" (the Forbidden, the Sacred), "Al-Akdes" (the Holy of Holies) and "Al-Mukaddassah" (the Sacro-Sanct). Its history began at the very dawn of humanity and has been traced back to Adam, father of mankind and the world's first Prophet, who according to tradition was the original builder of the Ka'bah, or ancient temple (Al-Bayt al-Ateeq). The original temple is said to have been destroyed (perhaps in the Deluge), and was later rebuilt by the Father of Prophets, Abraham (peace be upon him) and his son Ismāel (Ishmael). There is considerable controversy amongst Islamic scholars, chroniclers of the *Hadeeth* (sayings of the Prophet) and historians concerning the identity of the first builder of the "ancient temple" and how many times it was rebuilt. All agree, however, that it is a very ancient site indeed and that the Ka'bah is the very first place where the One and Only God was worshipped.

"Archeologists claim that the Arabian Peninsula once enjoyed a rainy and temperate climate, a fertile soil . It was the cradle of a number of civilizations." At a later date, the desert encroached upon the area as it did upon many other parts of the globe which were once fertile. Mecca lies in the middle of the Western part of the Arabian Peninsula, and this situation soon earned it an important commercial position as a meeting-place for caravans.

The road between Jeddah and Mecca is not a long one: hardly 75 kilometres, under an hour by car if there is not too much traffic. Yet those kilometres seem endless to the pilgrims who have travelled thousands of miles to reach the Holy Land. Before they can enter Mecca, they must first make a brief stop outside the city to have their identity checked; for it must be remembered that only Muslims can go beyond this point. Both Mecca and Medinah are *Harām*, in other words sacred territory forbidden to all non-Muslims.

As soon as they catch sight of the first houses of Mecca, the pilgrims stop constantly uttering the *Talbiyah*, in answer to the Divine Summon, and start reciting the *Du'a* or invocation known as:
"BISMI L-LĀHI AR-RAHMĀNI AR-RAHEEM
ALLĀHUMMA J'ALLEE BIHA QARĀRĀ WA-RZOUQNEE FIHA RIZQANE HALĀLĀ."
"In the name of God the all-merciful, the all-compassionate, o Lord!
Grant that I may sojourn here and live by lawful provision."

The above shows how deeply concerned the pilgrim is not to compromise his pious action by paying for it out of dubiously acquired funds. He has already taken care to settle all his debts before leaving his home country. After all, he is rehearsing his ultimate appearance before God on the Day of Judgement, and besides, who can tell where death may strike one?

Afterwards, when the pilgrim enters the city, he salutes Mecca in the following words:
"O God, this Sanctuary is Thy Sacred Place!
And this city is Thy City!
And this slave is Thy Slave!
I come with many sins,
From a far land,
And I petition with the petition,
Of those who are compelled,
And fearful of Thy punishment.
And I beseech Thee to forgive me,
And accept me with Thy complete forgiveness,
And admit me into Thy spacious Heaven of Beatitude."

The Mutawwif

Naturally, the pilgrim is keen to go straight to the *Harām ash-Shareef* (the Great Mosque) and to the Holy *Ka'bah*; but before he can go to the spot he has yearned to see for so long, he must find the *Mutawwif* he has selected, or who has been assigned to him, to deposit his luggage.

The *Mutawwif* will understand that he is in a hurry and will discuss practical matters with him later. He will show the pilgrim where he is to sleep and will take his passport, which he retains until the end of the pilgrimage to avoid any risk of loss.

The pilgrim should, from the very first moment of arrival, write down the name of his *Mutawwif* or get some one else to write it down for him, preferably in Arabic. This information should be set down on a piece of paper which the pilgrim is well-advised to keep on him at all times. At places like Minā and 'Arafāt, where pilgrims sleep in tents that are all identical, it is extremely common to get lost. Many a pilgrim does not recall the name of his *Mutawwif* or, if he is non Arabic-speaking, pronounces it incorrectly.

If the pilgrim shows his piece of paper to the authorities, he will have little trouble finding his way back to his group. In case of accident, the paper will also be of use in identifying the pilgrim.

The settling up of lodgings and other expenses usually takes place after the accomplishment of the first rites (the *Tawaf* of arrival and the the *Sa'y*).

One must allow a minimum of 1,000 rials for lodgings alone (not all *Mutawwifeen* provide food) and about 100 rials for transport from Mecca to Minā, 'Arafāt, Muzdalifah, Minā and back again to Mecca, which is the circuit that all *Hajj* pilgrims must make if they want to perform the necessary rites of pilgrimage. Many pilgrims will find housing conditions extremely rudimentary (a mattress on the floor in a dormitory at Mecca and a tent at Minā); but it must be remembered that Mecca is a city of no more than 400,000 inhabitants in normal times, whereas it has to shelter over two million pilgrims during the pilgrimage season, in other words five times its usual population. No wonder then that sleeping quarters are somewhat cramped!

Those who can afford better housing conditions can reserve hotel rooms a long time in advance and at very high prices. Those who have left it too late will have to make do with a simple mattress in a corridor, whatever the price is they can afford to pay.

The pilgrim must perform his ablutions before going to the *Harām ash-Shareef* (or *Harām* for short), with a view to accomplishing the *Tawaf* of the Ka'bah and of reciting prayers that demand a state of complete purity (*Taharah*.)

The *Harām ash-Shareef* is a vast building with seven minarets that rise 85 metres high. Now that it has been enlarged by the Saudi Arabian authorities, it can receive over 500,000 faithful.

The Sacred Mosque houses the holiest relics of Islam, the most important of which are:
• the Holy Ka'bah which encases the Black Stone,
• the *Maqām Ibraheem* (station of Abraham),
• the Zamzam well,
• the procession gallery or path between Aŝ-Ŝafā and Al-Marwah.

The pilgrim's first entry into the *Haram* should, in theory, be by the Gate of Salvation (*Bab as-Salam*). Entering through this gate, he should recite the following short prayer:
"O God, Thou art Salvation and from Thee comes Salvation.
Grant us Salvation and that we may enter the portals of Thy Paradise, wherein Salvation lies."

If it is not possible to enter by the *Bab as-Salam* because there are too many people, the pilgrim can enter the Great Mosque by any of the other entrances.

The Ka'bah

Once the pilgrim has crossed the threshold of the Forbidden Sanctuary he will catch sight of the Ka'bah in the centre of the inner courtyard of the *Harām*, an unforgettable vision.

The Prophet Muhammed himself (peace be upon him) was extremely moved when he arrived before the Ka'bah on his Farewell Pilgrimage. Raising his hands to the heavens, he declared:

The Maqām Ibraheem
(place where Abraham was in the habit of standing).
It is opposite the Multazam,
the only door of the Ka'bah.

"O God, increase the dignity of this Thy House,
And its honour and its renown,
And its majesty, and its eminence,
On the part of those who accomplish the *Hajj* and the *'Umrah.*"

Few people have ever been able to adequately describe the emotion they felt upon first seeing the Ka'bah. Etienne Dinet, a French scholar and painter who became converted to Islam and later changed his name to Nacir Ad-Dine, wrote that when he started circling the Ka'bah and reciting the ritual invocations, he felt such an "ecstatic intoxication" come over him that he lost all notion of time and of worldly things, and was even unable to keep a count of his circumambulations. He added that his emotion was even stronger upon seeing the temple for the fourth time; never, he says, had he known "such hours of sublime ecstasy."

E. Guellouz, a Tunisian pilgrim, burst into tears when he saw the Ka'bah, a simple cube covered by a plain drapery, which seemed "suspended in space rather than resting on the ground" and to which "the hallucinating circling of the pilgrims seemed to provide a base, as though they were bearing it up in triumph". He no longer recognized the "unbeliever or the indifferent, or indeed the believer in theory" that he had been a few moments earlier, "nor the believer intent upon understanding everything, analyzing and explaining to intellectuals like himself. He no longer recognized the philosopher-believer that he had been".

The Ka'bah, or *Bayt al-Harām* (Sacred House of God), is a cube measuring about thirteen metres in length, twelve metres across and fifteen metres in height. It is shrouded almost down to its base in a rich black drapery, the *Kiswah*, on which are embroidered in gold thread quotations from the Holy Koran.

The Ka'bah possesses a single door, about two metres from the ground, probably as a precaution against floods.

The Black Stone is mounted in silver and set more than one metre from the ground. Pilgrims must start their circumambulation in front of this stone, which they kiss upon each circling as did the Prophet (peace be upon him), or which they hail from a distance if the crush of pilgrims is too great for them to get any closer. This is often the case during the *Hajj*, and people have been known to lose their lives in the stampede that ensued because certain pilgrims were determined to kiss or to touch the Black Stone whatever the cost.

Neither the Black Stone nor the Ka'bah itself are objects of adoration. The Muslim pilgrim is invoking the Master of the Ka'bah in his prayers and his *Ad'iya*. It is God he has come out to seek in this sacred place. The homage he pays to the Black Stone is but the expression of his submission and his devotion to the Master of the whole Universe.

The second Caliph and disciple of the Prophet (peace be upon him), 'Umar Ibn al-Khattab, unequivocally proclaimed this truth loud and clear. He addressed himself to the Black Stone in the following terms: "I know that you are but a stone which can do neither good nor evil. If I had not seen the Prophet bestowing a kiss on you, I would not have kissed you."

The kissing or touching of the Black Stone are non-compulsory Traditions. Under Islam, the believer is exempted even from that which is a duty, if he is not in a position for physical, moral or material reasons to accomplish it. Thus he is dispensed from the *Hajj*, which is one of the pillars of his faith, if he does not have the means to perform it. How much more so then is he exempted from performing a Tradition which is not even compulsory! As the verse from the Koran makes it quite clear: "God does not burden any man beyond his capacities."

The *Maqām Ibraheem,* or place, or oratory, of Abraham, is a sanctuary located a few feet from the *Ka'bah.* It is the place where the Prophet Abraham (peace be upon him) stood and prayed, containing the stone that his son Ismäel brought here while they were building the Ka'bah. This stone still carries the imprint of the Prophet's footprint; he stood upon it as he erected the walls of the *Ka'bah* ever higher.

At some time during the first centuries of the *Hijrah*, this stone was set into a stone base, to which it was fastened by strips of lead. These were replaced by strips of silver during the rule of Caliph al-Muntassir Bi-l-Lāh in the IIIrd century of the *Hijrah* (IXth Century A.D.). An ornamental dome was built to shelter it later on.

It remained like that until 1966, when the increase of pilgrims and the proximity of the *Maṭaf* to the place of circumambulation made it necessary to replace the cumbersome structure with a newer one.

The Stone was therefore encased in a glass cloche, 80 centimetres in diameter and one metre high, and the whole thing was protected by a metal grill. It was also raised on a marble base 75 centimetres high.

When they have completed their circumambulation, the faithful must go to the *Maqām* and pray two *Raka'ah* (genuflections), known as the *Raka'atay aṭ-Ṭâwaf*.

The Zamzam well

There is one Tradition of the Prophet which each pilgrim performs after the circumambulation around the *Ka'bah*: that of drinking the waters of the Zamzam well, which is only a few yards away from the circling ground of the *Ṭawaf*. All Muslims regard this water as blessed and possessing miraculous qualities.

Pilgrims invariably take away some of the water from this well, in gourds, water-bottles or small sealed tins known as *Zamzamiyāt*. They take this water home with them, for no gift will be more highly valued. Some of them keep the precious liquid for the rest of their lives, and request that at their death their corpse shall be sprinkled with it.

Others purchase a piece of white cloth in Mecca itself, which they dip into the waters of the Zamzam well and keep until their death. The cloth will then be used as a shroud, in which they will be buried.

The history of the Zamzam well is narrowly linked to that of the going between Aŝ-Ŝafā and Al-Marwah.

The hillocks of Aŝ-Ŝafā and Al-Marwah

"Aŝ-Ŝafā and Al-Marwah are rites prescribed by God. He who accomplishes the *Hajj* of the House or the *'Umrah* acts well in going between them. Those who do it with all their hearts do it for their own good, for God is Grateful and Omniscient."

Koran, the Heifer

Aŝ-Ŝafā (which is derived from the word "rock") and Al-Marwah (etym. : gravel) are two hillocks located not far from the *Ka'bah* on a north-south axis. For the *Hajj*, as for the *'Umrah,* pilgrims are expected to walk or run seven times the distance which separates the two hillocks (rite of *Sa'y* or procession).

The *Mas'ā,* or Sacred Way, which is about 395 metres long, once lay outside the precincts of the *Holy Mosque*. In 1957 however, the Saudi Arabian authorities enlarged the *Harām* so that the *Mas'ā* now lies within its boundaries.

The *Mas'ā* is paved in marble and is divided into two tracks: one for each direction. Between the tracks are small pathways, sheltered by low walls, for persons too old and feeble to perform the rite of *Sa'y* except in wheelchairs pushed by special "porters".

According to tradition, the very first *Sa'y* dates back to Abraham (peace be upon him), when Mecca was nothing but a desert valley. All that remained of the original Ka'bah then was a sort of mound which marked out the site, deeply furrowed all around by endemic floods.

The Prophet Abraham (peace be upon him) had two wives : Sarah, who was barren, and Hājir (known as Agar in the Bible), whom he had married for the purpose of begetting a son, with his wife's consent.

It is said that the two wives came into conflict from the time that Hājir gave birth to (Ismāel). Out of jealousy, Sarah never missed an opportunity to make Hajir's life wretched, and was not satisfied until she had devised a way to get rid of the woman who had given Abraham a son. In order to put an end to a situation that had become unbearable, Abraham finally agreed to send away his second wife and his child. Allowing himself to be guided in his decision by God, he led them to the valley of Bakkah (the ancient name for Mecca and a crossroad for caravans), where he left them for a time with only a sac of dates and a goat-skin full of water.

As he was about to depart, Hajir asked the Prophet :

"Who then will you forsake us to in this waterless desert ? Who has commanded you to act in this fashion?"

"God," replied Abraham.

"If God has ordered it, He shall not fail to come to our aid."

As Abraham walked off, he implored God in the following words:

"Our Lord! I have settled a part of my offspring in a valley unproductive of fruit near Thy Sacred House*, Our Lord, that they may keep up prayer: so make the hearts of some people yearn towards them and provide them with fruit, that they may be grateful unto Thee."

Coran, Ibrâhîm, XIV-37

Hajir remained alone with her infant son, who soon began to suffer from thirst once their meager water rations were drunk. She set off looking for help, without much hope of finding any, climbing on the hillock of Aŝ-Ŝafa to try and see if any caravan happened to be passing. From there, she ran to Al-Marwah, also in the hope of getting some help; she then turned back and went to Aŝ-Ŝafa once more. Altogether, she went seven times between the two hillocks, and it is this walk which is commemorated by Muslim pilgrims in the *Sa'y*. On her last journey, while she was still on Al-Marwah, she saw an angel standing

*) At the time, nothing remained of this temple, built by Adam and Eve and their first children, and restored throughout the ages by the prophets who succeeded Adam until Noah cincluding Enoch: Hermes in Egyptian and Idrees in Arabic -*Koran* XIX-Mary-56; XXI-the Prophets-85). It was rebuilt by Abraham and Ismāel.

The Jabal-r-Rahmah (Mercy Hill)
which overlooks
the vast plain of ‘Arafāt.

by her son, who was writhing with thirst. The angel, obeying divine orders, caused a spring to spout from the earth and said to Hajir:

"Fear not, for God's House is near, which the boy and his father will build. God does not forsake his creatures."

Hajir rushed to the spring and made a little wall of earth around it to dam the water, saying *"Zamzam"*, which means the sound made by rushing water in Babylonian. She drank from it and suckled her son.

The water, which poured out profusely, attracted animals. A nomadic tribe which was wandering in the neighbourhood saw birds circling over the valley and thus guessed that water was nearby. They went to the place and found Hajir and her son by the Zamzam.

These nomads, who were called the Jurhumites, asked Hajir's permission to settle near the Zamzam. Ismāel grew up among them, learnt their Arabic dialect and, at a later date, married a member of the Jurhumite tribe. It was during his adolescent years that Ismāel helped his father to build the Ka'bah.

Many years later, the Jurhumites and the descendants of Ismāel filled in the Zamzam.

The Zamzam was rediscovered a long time afterwards by 'Abd al-Muttalib, the Prophet's grandfather, who saw its location in a vision. He dug down deeply, reinforced the sides of the well with masonry, and the Zamzam yields up its waters to this day.

Optional visits of historical sites of Mecca

If the pilgrim has sufficient time he can take advantage of his stay at Mecca to visit places of key historic interest for Islam.

Amid the chain of mountains to the north-east of the city there is a cone-shaped hill 634 metres high which is called *Jabal an-Nur* (the Hill of Light). There is a grotto in the side of this hill which is known as *Ghâr Hirâ'*. Long before the Revelation, the Prophet (peace be upon him) was in the habit of spending whole days and nights there in order to meditate. It was there that one night, during the last few days of Ramadān, a night blessed amongst all others (*Laylat al Qadr* or Night of Destiny), the archangel Gabriel (or Jibreel) came upon Muhammed and ordered: « Read. « I cannot read », replied Muhammed.

The archangel insisted:

« In the name of Thy Lord, who created thee, read ! Who created man out of a clot of blood. Read by the infinite grace of thy Lord, Who taught man to use a pen, and who taught man that which he knew not. »   *Koran* XCVI, 1-5

These were the first verses of the first *surah* (collection of chapters of Revelation). The archangel then disappeared. Overwhelmed, Muhammed (peace be upon him) felt suddenly illuminated.

Believing himself to have been the victim of a hallucination, he ran to his wife, Khdîdjah, for refuge, crying out: « Cover me ! »

The archangel came to seek him out and ordered him thus:

« O thou who hides beneath a cloak ! Rise and bear witness ! Magnify thy Lord. »

It was in a grotto in this hill south-west of Mecca that the Prophet (peace be upon him) and his companion Abu Bakr sought refuge when they left Mecca for Medinah. They remained in hiding for three days. The Qureishites, who had promised a reward of one hundred camels to whoever should find the Prophet, organized a search-party. They passed in front of the grotto many times but, seeing that the entrance was covered with spiders' webs, they did not bother to search the grotto, convined that no-one had been there recently.

Upon hearing the footsteps of their enemies, Abu Bakr said to the Prophet: « If they find us, it will be the end of the religion of God ». « O Abu Bakr, replied the Prophet, what would you think of two people, the third of them being God ? »

The Koran tells this story, adding that the Prophet also said:

« Do not be afraid, for God is with us. » *Koran,* IX the Limbos - 40 ☐

'Arafāt

■ 'Arafāt is the name given to the valley that lies 21 kilometres east of Mecca. The cone-shaped granite hill located in the north-eastern corner of this valley is known as *Jabal 'Arafāt* or, even more commonly, *Jabal-r-Rahmah,* or hill of Mercy.

The valley of 'Arafāt is about ten kilometres long and six kilometres wide. It lies outside the *Harām* or sacred territory of Mecca. It can be reached coming from Mina and Muzdalifah, through a gorge debouching on a hollow known as *Urana.* On the far side of this hollow, or *Wadee,* there is a mosque called *Namirah,* in the centre of which begins the territory of *'Arafāt* where all pilgrims must perform the rite of standing on the 9th Thu-l-Hijjah.

The origin of the name *'Arafāt* is unknown. According to one tradition, the name is derived from *Ta'Arafa* (they recognized one another), for it is said that Adam and Eve met up in this place and recognized one another; after their expulsion from Paradise, they had been parted and had wandered across the earth for many a year looking for each other.

The day of *'Arafāt* is looked upon as the very foundation of the *Hajj.* The Prophet Muhammed (peace be upon him) said on this subject : "No day is more highly favoured by God than the day of 'Arafāt. On that day, the blessed and exalted God descends to that part of the Heavens closest to the Earth to point out the people of the Earth to those of Heaven, and to say, "Behold my servants! They have come to me in a bad condition, covered with dust and burnt by the sun. They come from the far corners of the Earth to ask for my mercy."

Before Islam, the Arabs had adulterated the message of Abraham (peace be upon him) and had introduced heretical practices such as the idolatrous notion that idols could intercede on their behalf before God. They had also introduced a class system in the accomplishment of the rites of the pilgrimage. Thus the Qureishites did not go to 'Arafāt for the *Wuqūf,* or rite of standing. Their procession and those of their allies would stop at Muzdalifah. Whereas the rest of the Arab pilgrims would perform the *Wuqūf* and the unfurling from 'Arafāt, the others considered that, as they were the masters of the Holy Places, they had no cause to leave the sacred territory of which Muzdalifah but not 'Arafāt is a part.

Muzdalifah

■ After the *Wuqūf* (standing) at 'Arafāt, pilgrims set off for *Muzdalifah,* a valley located approximately half-way between 'Arafāt and Mina. In theory, they should spend the night of the 9th to the 10th Thu-l-Hijjah and stand before the *Mash'ar al-Harām,* or Sacred Monument, before sunrise.

However, there are so many pilgrims today during the *Hajj* that the stopover at *Muzdalifah* has been shortened to a brief halt, during which pilgrims celebrate the prayers of *al-Maghrib* (sunset) and of *al-'Isha* (middle of the night), and gather the forty-nine or seventy pebbles with which they will stone the pillars of *Minā* during the following days.

Before Islam, *Muzdalifah* was the place where the Qureishites and their allies gathered, their *Mawqif.* The spot which was regarded as particularly sacred was the hill of *Quzah,* which later came to be known as *al Mash'ar al-Harām.* The rest of the Arabian tribes would stay at 'Arafāt.

Islam, which is an egalitarian religion, stressed that pilgrims were all to wear the same white robes, without any seam or decoration, so as to abolish all distinction. It could therefore not tolerate such a practice.

Though the Prophet himself was of Qureishite origins, he nonetheless insisted upon performing the rite of standing on 'Arafāt, amidst the other people, for in his eyes they were all part of the same community.   □

Minā

■ *Minā* is a spot located in a valley of the same name set amid mountains, east of Mecca.

Pilgrims go through Minā twice in the course of the *Hajj*, at least in theory: the first time from the 8th to the 9th Thu-l-Hijjah (in the morning) before going on to 'Arafāt, the second time from the 10th to the 12th or even the 13th Thu-l-Hijjah on their way back to Mecca.

The first of these two halts at Minā is called the *Yawm Attarwiyah*. Many pilgrims leave it out of their itinerary, proceeding straight on to 'Arafāt. This is not true of the second halt, called the *Ayyam at-Tashreeq*, which is the ultimate stage of the *Hajj* pilgrimage. It is during these final days that pilgrims leave the sacred state of *Ihrām*, after having accomplished a certain number of rites which are listed above.

Minā itself is thinly populated except on the three days of the *Tashreeq*, when over two million pilgrims converge here. The main road, on an east-west axis, is called *Shari 'al-Jamarat*, or Street of the Pillars. The first of the pillars lies on the western tip of this street; it is called the *Jamrat al-'Aqabah*, or *Jamra-l-Kobra*. A little further on, towards the east, one comes upon the second pillar, which is called *al-Jamra-l-Wosta* or middle pillar. Then, proceeding still further east, one reaches the third pillar, called *al-Jamra-s-Şoghra*. It was here that Satan appeared three times before the Prophet Abraham (peace be upon him) to tempt him away from his mission. Abraham showed his contempt by hurling seven stones at him on each of the three occasions. This gesture is repeated by all the pilgrims who, during the three days they spend at *Minā*, throw seven stones at each of the pillars, which symbolize the Tempter, to show their determination to resist.

During these days at *Minā*, pilgrims must go to Mecca briefly in order to accomplish the rite of circumambulation called the *Tawaf al-Ifadah*, which is compulsory.

The pilgrim can take advantage of his stay at Mecca to visit those places which have played a crucial part in the history of Islam. □

Medinah
Al-Madinah al-Munawwarah

■ The visit to Medinah does not in fact make up a part of the *Hajj* ritual, and is therefore not compulsory; but no pilgrim would dream of missing it out. Those who arrive in time, before the decisive days of the *Hajj,* tend to go there before going to Mecca. Those who arrive later go to Medinah after the pilgrimage.

Medinah is the second holiest city of Islam, beloved by all Muslims. It was in this city that the Prophet (peace be upon him) found refuge when he was chased out of Mecca by the Qureishites, who wanted to get rid of him.

It was from its base in Medinah that Islam expanded, starting off by ridding Mecca of its polytheistic religion to spread later to other parts of the world.

It was also at Medinah that the Prophet Muhammed (peace be upon him) was buried upon his death, along with a sizable number of his followers.

The Mosque which the Prophet built with his own hands and later enlarged is also located at Medinah. One prayer in this particular mosque is worth a thousand prayers anywhere else, with the exception of the Great Mosque at Mecca (where a single prayer is worth a hundred thousand recited elsewhere), and of the *Masjid al-Aqsā* at Jerusalem.

The Prophet said on this subject: "One sets off on a long journey to visit three mosques only: *al-Masjid al-Harām* (the Holy Mosque at Mecca), my mosque (at Medinah) and *al-Masjid al-Aqsā* (at Jerusalem)."

How, therefore, can any pilgrim be content to go on the pilgrimage to Mecca and to miss out the *Ziyyarah* (visit) to Medinah?

Medinah is located 425 kilometres from Jeddah and 447 kilometres from the holiest city of Islam, Mecca. It is surrounded by fertile oases such as those of *Bathan, al-Agik Kanah*, etc. Its territory is *Harām* (sacred) and therefore forbidden to all non-Muslims.

Medinah, like Mecca, has many different names, about 90 in all.

Before the *Hijrah,* it was called *Yathrib.* The Prophet (peace be upon him) deliberately changed this name because of its meaning. Yathrib is derived from an ancient

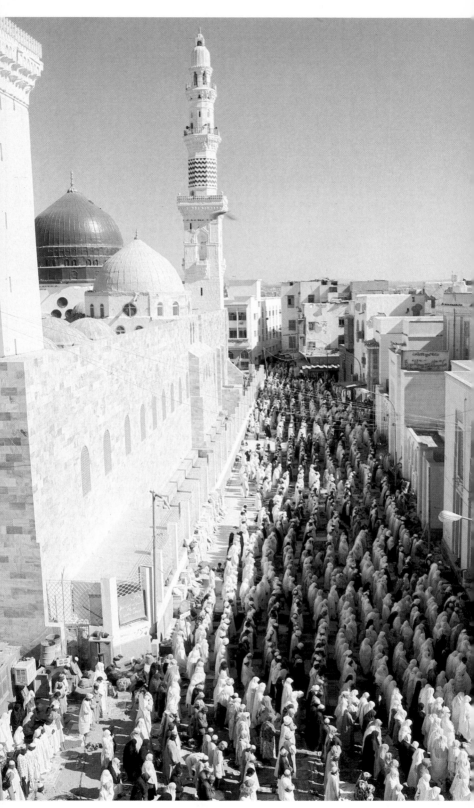

*Pilgrims praying
at the Great Mosque of Mecca.*

verb-form whose root, *Tharāb*, means: corruption, depravity. Muhammed therefore called it *Aṭ-Ṭayyibah* (Pleasant) and *al-Madinah al-Munawwarah* (the Enlightened or Illustrious City). The other names of Medinah are *Madīnatu-n-Nabī* (the City of the Prophet), *Dar as-Salam* (the House of Peace), *Qaryet al-Ansār* (the City of the Allies of the Prophet), *al-Mubārakah* (the Blessed), *al-Mukhtarah Dar al-Abrār* (the City of the Pious and the Just), *Kubbat al-Islām,* etc.

Yathrib was a very ancient city indeed, and was famous from the earliest times as a major halting-place on the caravan route between Yemen and Syria.

A tradition which has no established basis has Yathrib dating back to Noah's immediate descendants on the side of his son, Sem. On the other hand, Minean records prove that the city existed at the time of the Ma'eeneet Empire which had spread across parts of Arabia towards the xvth century B.C.. According to geologists, the hills surrounding Yathrib suffered from an important volcanic explosion in 1266 B.C. which altered the course of local rivers in the direction of the actual location of the city. This upheaval made the area one of the best-irrigated in Northern Arabia. One only has to dig a few yards down to come upon large underground sheets of water. The earthquake also made the ground particularly fertile; the date-trees of Medinah are famous, and have been so from earliest times. At least 172 different varieties of dates are still grown in the area.

The celebrated Graeco-Egyptian astronomer-geographer Ptolemy, who lived in the IInd Century A.D., mentions Yathrib, known as Jathrippa, in one of his works.

The city's real hour of glory was to strike in the year 622 A.D., for it was here that the Prophet and his companions decided to take refuge from the persecutions of the Qureishites of Mecca. Some of the inhabitants of Yathrib had become converted to Islam and had sworn allegiance to the new faith in two historic oaths known as the first al-'Aqabah oath (620) and the second 'Aqabah oath (622). After this came the *Hijrah* (Hegira), or immigration.

The most significant date in the city's history occurred on the 24th of September, 622, when the Prophet and his companion, Abu Bakr, entered the Yathrib oasis. It was also a turning-point for Islam, and heralds the beginning of the *Hijrah,* which is the Muslim era.

The first Muslim State was founded at Medinah. After many difficulties and conflicts with the Qureishite middle-class, which felt threatened by the new religion and therefore persecuted it remorselessly, the Prophet and his followers were finally able to enter Mecca without bloodshed on the 20th of the month of Ramadan, in the 8th year of the *Hijrah,* in other words on the llth of January, 630. The Prophet decided to stay on at Medinah and to make it the capital of the *'Ummah* (the Islamic nation, or community).

Mecca remained the spiritual community of the Muslims and the direction (*Qiblah*) towards which they turned to pray.

After his Farewell Pilgrimage to Mecca in the year 10 of the *Hijrah,* which has remained the model for pilgrimage of every subsequent generation of Muslims, the Prophet died on the 8 of June, 632. In accordance with his wishes, his funeral was held in his own home, for he had proclaimed: "Prophets are buried at the spot where they expire."

Medinah remained the capital of the Muslim world under the first three orthodox Caliphs (*Rashidīn*) who came after the Prophet, but for political reasons the fourth Caliph, 'Ali (cousin and son-in-law of the Prophet) chose to go to Cūfa, in Iraq.

All his life, God's Messenger was concerned to know if he was worthy of his mission. In his sermon on Mount 'Arafāt, which he made during the Farewell Pilgrimage, he cried out: "O God, have I truly proclaimed Thy commands?" "Yes, O Prophet of God," cried the gathering. The Prophet then raised his eyes to Heaven "O God", he said, "Be my witness this day."

Generations of Muslim faithful have since flocked to the Prophet's tomb and to implore God to bless and to reward him according to his merits. They have borne witness to the fact that Muhammed truly proclaimed God's command for fourteen centuries.

The Mosque of the Prophet

The first time a pilgrim enters the Mosque of the Prophet (al-Hāram an-Nabawee) he must do so through the *Bab as-Salam* (gate of Salvation), then proceed under a peristyle to the chamber where the Prophet's tomb lies, reciting:

"BISMI L-LĀHI AR-RAHMĀNI AR-RAHEEM"
"In the name of God the all-Merciful, the all-Compassionate."

Guides called *Muzawwireen,* who must not be confused with those "landlords" that are called by the same name, come forward to offer their services to visitors, whom they guide through the Mosque, helping them to recite the invocations appropriate to each spot. The pilgrim can hire their services during his visit, or else he can do without them and recite either the *Ad'iya* which are dictated by others, those which are contained in a book or else those which are dictated by his own individual inspiration.

When the pilgrim reaches *ar-Rawdyya an-Nabawiyya* (the Garden of the Prophet), he must recite a prayer of two *Raha'ah* (genuflections) of salutation of the Mosque. The *Rawdyya an-Nabawiyya,* which is also called *ar-Rawdyya al-Mutahhara,* is the space which lies between the Prophet's tomb and his chair (*Minbar*). God's Messenger himself used to say of this spot: "Between my house (now his last resting-place) and my *Minbar* lies a garden of Paradise."

For the faithful to recite a prayer here is tantamount to praying in a corner of Paradise. No wonder then that this small space is in such demand by pilgrims, all of whom want to pray there. But, once again, it must be emphasized that it is not an obligation. "God does not burden any man beyond his capacities." If there are too many people crowding round this spot, the visitor can pray in any other part of the Mosque equally well.

The pilgrim then goes over to the actual tomb of the Prophet, repeating :
"God and his angels shower blessings upon the Prophet. O ye who believe, bless him and salute him."
Koran, al-Ahzab, XXXIII - 56
The pilgrim can transmit to the Prophet the greetings of all those who have asked him to do so. He then goes over to the tomb of the first Caliph, Abu Bakr Aŝ-Ŝiddiq, which is located a few feet away from that of the Prophet. After greeting the companion of the Messenger of God, the pilgrim goes over to the tomb of the second Caliph, 'Umar Ibn al-Khattab, just next to that of Abu Bakr, which he also salutes. Before each of these tombs, the pilgrim must make salutation and recall the merits of he who lies beneath.

Thus ends the visit to the Mosque of the Prophet. Traditionally, pilgrims stay at Medinah for eight days, which is the time required for the utterance of forty ritual prayers at the proper times in the Mosque of the Prophet.

The Cemetery of Al-Baqee' and the mosques of Qubā and the Two Qiblah

The third Caliph, 'Uthman Ibn 'Affān, the wives of the Prophet, the mothers of many believers, including 'Ayesha the daughter of Abu Bakr Aŝ-Ŝiddiq and Hafsa, the daughter of 'Umar Ibn al-Khattab, the uncle of the Prophet, Al-Abbas, his grandson, Al-Hassan Ibn 'Ali, the Imam Malik Ibn Anas, founder of the Malikite School, and a host of Ŝahābah (companions of the Prophet) are all buried inside this cemetery.

The visitor is always struck by the extreme simplicity of the Cemetery of Al-Baqee'. The tombs of so many heroes of Islam are marked only by small stones. In order to cut short any cult of the saints, which tended to degenerate into idolatry, the

*Pilgrims at the Mosque
of the Prophet
at Medinah.*

Wahhabites destroyed all the cupolas and mausoleums that once ornamented these tombs, under the reign of the founder of modern-day Saudi Arabia, King 'Abd-al-'Aziz al-Sa'ūd.

The Mosque of Qubā, or Qibā, better known as *Masjid at-Taqwā* (the Mosque of Piety), was rebuilt on the site of a mosque put up by the Prophet in person. It was at this spot that the Prophet entered Medinah during the *Hijrah* (immigration), and it was also in this mosque that he received the following divine revelation:

"There is a mosque whose base was founded from the very first day upon piety; it is worthier for those who can to rise (in other words pray) within its boundaries. Within it are men who yearn to be purified, and God loves those who purify themselves".

Koran, IX, At-Tawba, 108.

Prayer in the mosque is looked upon as a Tradition. The Prophet (peace be upon him) was in the habit of going there from time to time, of a Saturday, in order to pray. It is thus desirable to go there on a Saturday.

As its name implies, this mosque has two *Mihrab* which both indicate a different *Qiblah*. Only vestiges of the first remain, and this one indicated the direction of Jerusalem. It was abandoned and a second *Mihrab* took its place when the Prophet decreed that prayers should be addressed to Mecca instead.

Masjid al-Jumu 'ah (the Friday Mosque)

It was here that the Prophet (peace be upon him) celebrated the first Friday prayer at Medinah. A Mosque was built in his lifetime on the very spot where that first Friday ceremony was held.

There are seven small, open-air mosques west of Mount Selaa. Their foundations are sometimes no more than low walls, and all that remains of the site.

Amid these seven mosques are the *Masjid al-Fat'h* (the Victory). There are two theories concerning the origins of this name.

According to one, this was where the Prophet (peace be upon him) prayed for the victory of Islam over the coalition of al-Ahzab. According to the other theory, it was also here that Muhammed received the revelation of the Surah of Al-Fat'h, XLVIII: Victory.

What was meant by the approximative term "coalition"? *Ahzāb* was the word used in the Koran to designate the coalition instigated by the Medinah Jews in the year 5 of the *Hijrah* against the Prophet. This coalition included the Qureishites and their mercenaries, the Bedouins, who had rallied to the cause either out of self-interest or because they had been influenced by insidious Jewish propaganda. It also included powerful warrior tribes such as the Kinanah, the Ghatafān, the Fazārah, the Murra, the Sulaym, the Asad, etc. The members of the coalition had accomplices within Medina itself: the *Munafiqun* (hypocrites) of 'Abd Allah Ibn Ubayy, and the important Jewish clan of Banū Quraydha.

This army of an estimated 10,000 men attacked the Muslims under commander Abu Sufian, during a particularly harsh winter. The Prophet (peace be upon him) disposed of an army of only 3,000 men, but his soldiers were hardy, well-disciplined and under good leadership.

Mount Uhud, which was described by the Prophet as one of the mounts of Paradise, is located about five kilometres north of Medinah.

It was at the foot of this hill that the famous battle which bears the same name was fought. The Qureishites had assembled an army of 3,000 men, including 200 horsemen, to avenge their defeat at Badr in the year 2 of the *Hijrah*.

The Muslim army, led by the Prophet himself (peace be upon him), numbered only 700 soldiers, including a few horsemen under the orders of Zubair Ibn al-Awwām. It stood with its back to Mount Uhud.

Its right flank was covered by about fifty archers, commanded by 'Abd Allah Ibn Jubayr, who stood facing the Qureishite cavalry.

The Muslim side scored an early victory. Its archers stopped the first charge of the Qureishite cavalry, and soon both sides were locked in combat. The Prophet's uncle, Hamzah, and his cousin and son-in-law, 'Ali Ibn Abu Ṭālib, Sa'd Ibn Abi-Waqqas and Abu Dujana all fought with outstanding bravery; their exploits on this day have become legendary. The Qureishites fell back and their women, who beat the drums at the rear in accordance with Arab tradition, started fleeing from the battle-field.

Believing the battle to be won, the Muslim archers left their post (Mount *Arrumah,* which can be visited to this day) and rushed forward to look for booty, notwithstanding the Prophet's orders and the interdiction of their leader.

The commander of the Qureishite cavalry, Khālid Ibn al-Waleed, who would later put all his courage and all his military ability at the service of Islam, grasped that the enemy had made an error of judgement. He therefore swept into the breach and charged the Muslim army from the rear. The Muslims suffered total defeat that day. Hamzah, the Prophet's uncle, and approximately seventy other Muslim warriors were killed in the battle.

Two women, one on each side, are remembered to this day for the part they played during and after the battle. One of them, a Qureishite, is remembered for the savagery of her behaviour; the other, a Muslim, for her bravery.

The Qureishite woman, Hind, daughter of Utba and wife of Abu Sufian, searched the battle-field once the fighting was over, looking for the corpse of Hamzah. Once she had found it, she slashed it open and ripped out the liver, which she bit with rage several times to assuage her vengefulness before hurling it away in disgust.

The Muslim woman is almost unknown. Her name was Umm Imāra Nusayba, daughter of Ka'b. She had gone over to the Prophet's camp to give his warriors something to drink. When the tides of war turned against the Muslims and she saw that the Prophet was encircled, she seized hold of a sword and rushed to his aid. Though she was wounded, she held the assailants at bay until the arrival of 'Ali, son of Abu Ṭalib, one of the greatest warriors in history.

Her example can be pointed out to those adversaries of Islam who claim quite wrongly and in order to discredit the Muslim religion that it is misogynist in its outlook.

The Prophet's uncle and the other companions who had been slain in battle at Uhud that day were buried on the battlefield itself. Verses in the Koran say of all those who die for the cause of Islam and of God:

"And repute not those slain on God's path to be dead. Nay, alive with their Lord, are they richly rewarded.

"Rejoicing in what God of His bounty hath vouchsafed them, filled with joy for those who follow after them, but have not yet overtaken them, that on them nor fear shall come, nor grief.

"Filled with joy at the favours of God, and at His bounty: and that God suffereth not the reward of the faithful to perish.

"As to those who after the reverse which befell them, respond to God and the Apostle — such of them as do good works and fear God, shall have a great reward."
Koran, the Family of 'Imrān, 169-172 □

MEDINAH

Transportation : One can go from Jeddah to Medinah either by road or by air. From Mecca, one can only go by road to Medinah.

Lodgings: During the pilgrimage season, lodging is provided by the *Muzawwireen.* The pilgrim is under no obligation to give the name of his *Muzawwir* to the authorities upon arrival in Saudi Arabia, as he must do the name of his *Mutawwif.*

Visiting Medinah and its surroundings: most people are able to walk to the Mosque of the Prophet, as well as to the Cemetery of Al-Baqee', which is a few hundred yards from the Harām an-Nabawee. There are no organized visits of the mosques of Qubā, Al-Qiblatayn, etc.., or of Mount Uhud. One can go to these places by taxi. One's *Muzawwir* can provide useful information on this subject.

preparation for the pilgrimage

■ *The Muslim calendar and the pilgrimage from 1980 to 1989:* The Hegiran year comprises twelve lunar months of 29 or 30 days. It therefore makes up a year of 354 or 355 days, instead of the 365 days of the solar or Gregorian year.

The Hegiran months are thus mobile, as opposed to the static months of the Gregorian calendar. Muslim feast days therefore fall in all four seasons over a period of 34 solar years. The Muslim months are as follow:
1 - Muharrām,
2 - Ŝafar,
3 - Rabi'al-Awwal,
4 - Rabi'ath-Thani,
5 - Jumada-l-Ūlā,
6 - Jumada-th-Thani,
7 - Rajab,
8 - Sha'ban,
9 - Ramadan
10 - Shawwal,
11 - Thu-l-Qa'dah,
12 - Thu-l-Hijjah.

The duration of the Hegiran month (29 or 30 days) is, in theory, determined by the new moon. Attempts to fix the exact number of days in the month in advance are usually unsuccessful.

What are the dates of the Pilgrimage?

To give the pilgrim some idea of the correspondence between the dates of the *Hajj* and those set according to the Gregorian calendar, the chart printed below provides some indication, give or take a day or two, of the dates of certain Muslim feast days for the decade of 1980. These feast days are the *Ra's al-Am* (New Year's day), the 1st of *Ramadan, Eid al-Fiŧr* (Feast of the ending of the fast) and *Eid al-Aḋ'hā* (Feast of the Immolation).

This last feast day is the one which the pilgrim should use as his guideline. Knowing that it is celebrated on the 10th Thu-l-Hijjah,

THE MUSLIM CALENDAR
(correspondences with the Gregorian calendar)

Hegiran Year	New Year's day (Ra's al-Am)	1st of Ramadan	1st of Shawwal (Eid al-Fiŧr)
1400	20/11/1979	13/07/80	12/08/80
1401	09/11/80	2/07/81	01/08/81
1402	29/10/81	21/06/82	20/07/82
1403	18/10/82	10/06/83	09/07/83
1404	07/10/83	30/05/84	29/06/84
1405	26/09/84	19/05/85	18/06/85
1406	15/09/85	08/05/86	07/06/86
1407	04/09/86	27/04/87	26/05/87
1408	24/08/87	16/04/88	15/05/88
1409	13/08/88	05/04/89	04/05/89

Previous pages:
The tents of the pilgrims
in the great plain of 'Arafāt.

the day after the decisive day of the *Wuqūf* at 'Arafāt, the pilgrim can work out the exact date at which he must find himself in the Holy Places.

To make it easier to work out the dates, the dates corresponding to the 1st and the 9th Thu-l-Hijjah during the Hegiran years from 1400 to 1409 are also provided in the chart.

Travel documents required for the Hajj

Preparing for the *Hajj* is a long and arduous undertaking. The pilgrim must set about it long in advance if he wishes to accomplish the necessary formalities in good time. He will have to acquit himself of a number of administrative, health and other formalities in his country of origin, and is wise to start preparations in the month of Ramadan. Some pilgrims start well before then, at least 3 or 4 months before the pilgrimage.

These formalities vary from one country to another. In most Muslim countries, the authorities issue a list of the dates by which the necessary formalities must be accomplished, as well as a list of the documents that must be provided and the conditions that must be fulfilled.

The pilgrim must usually start off by addressing himself to the administrative authority in charge of issuing passports: Home Office, Prefecture, Wilaya or Consulate of his country if he is a resident abroad, etc.

Certain countries issue special passports, whose validity are limited to the duration of the pilgrimage. Ordinary passports are accepted if the individual's membership in the Muslim community is beyond doubt.

Given the fact that the pilgrimage is very tiring, the authorities of certain countries require that each pilgrim provides a medical certificate

FROM 1980 TO 1989

	1st Thu-l-Hijjah	9th Thu-l-Hijjah (Wuqūf)	10th Thu-l-Hijjah (Yawm an-Na'hr)
1400	10/10/80	18/10/80	19/10/80
1401	29/09/81	07/10/81	08/10/81
1402	19/09/82	27/09/82	28/09/82
1403	08/09/83	16/09/83	17/09/83
1404	28/08/84	05/09/84	06/09/84
1405	17/08/85	25/08/85	26/08/85
1406	06/08/86	14/08/86	15/08/86
1407	26/07/87	03/08/87	04/08/87
1408	15/07/88	23/07/88	24/07/88
1409	04/07/89	12/07/89	13/07/89

before departure. The authorities are extremely lenient on this score, however, and it is very rare for a would-be pilgrim to be forbidden access to the Holy Places for reasons of health.

Vaccinations. The pilgrim must be in possession of an international cholera and smallpox vaccination certificate. The Saudi Arabian authorities require this certificate before delivery of a visa to their country. The smallpox vaccination certificate is valid for three years, the cholera certificate for six months. Persons coming from countries or areas where there are cases of yellow fever, as reported by the World Health Organization, must also be vaccinated against this disease.

During the period of the pilgrimage, all persons not in possession of the required vaccination certificates are either vaccinated upon their arrival at Jeddah or placed in quarantine immediately.

Transport

In certain countries, the would-be pilgrim is not given a pilgrimage passport unless he is in possession of a return ticket. He must also possess a return ticket if he wishes to export currency from countries where there are strict exchange regulations. The Saudi Arabian authorities demand to see the pilgrim's return ticket before issuing a visa.

Group travel. In Muslim countries, both the authorities and private companies organize collective tours of the Holy Places, setting out either by land, sea or air according to the geographical location of the country. There are special low cost for this type of journey and the organizers often also look after the departure and arrival formalities. This is far and away the best method of travelling to Mecca.

Individual travel. This method can be more convenient but requires some preparation and a certain amount of travelling experience, for it is impossible to improvise on a pilgrimage. It is, at any rate, often the only way a pilgrim can travel, particularly if he is coming from a country that is not predominantly Muslim.

Travelling by road. It is possible for pilgrims coming from countries bordering Saudi Arabia, or not too far distant, to travel there by road, either privately or in groups. This is often done by pilgrims coming from the Yemen, Qatar, Kuwait, Iraq, Iran, Jordan, Syria, Lebanon, Turkey and occasionally Europe. Pilgrims from North Africa used to go by road to Suez, from which they sailed either to Jeddah or to Yambu, but this is no longer possible now that the frontier between Libya and Egypt is closed. Those pilgrims who intend to go to the Holy Places by road, coming from countries that do not border Saudi Arabia, are well advised to make enquiries concerning all the necessary formalities to be accomplished for travelling within those countries that they will have to cross to get to Saudi Arabia.

Travelling by sea. This used to be an inexpensive and convenient method of travel, but is no longer employed now except by pilgrims coming from a few Asian and East African countries. Today, pilgrims coming by ship from abroad to accomplish the *Hajj* make up no more than about 7 % of the total.

Travelling by air. Nearly two thirds of all foreign pilgrims travel by air today to go to the Holy Places. There are several possibilities:

— *by charter.* Many airlines and travel agencies provide charter trips, which is by far the cheapest method of air travel. The one disadvantage about this method is that the departure and the return dates are fixed well in advance and cannot be altered.

— *by regular flights.* Quite a few airlines have regular flights to Saudi Arabia (see list). Pilgrims can pay much less for their ticket if they take advantage of the economy class excursion rate, which is usually valid for a period of 30 days. However, pilgrims are advised to notify the airline at the check-in desk that they are *Hajj* pilgrims if they are flying on a regular flight,

*Pilgrims arriving at
Jeddah harbour.*

for non-pilgrims are sent to a different terminal upon arrival at Jeddah. A special label attached to the luggage of *Hajj* pilgrims will ensure that their suitcases reach the right destination.

Visa and change

The Saudi Arabian authorities deliver a special visa for the *Hajj* or the *'Umrah* solely to persons of the Muslim faith. The only persons who do not require such a visa are those of Saudi Arabian nationality and those from Kuwait, Qatar and the United Arab Emirates.

This visa is delivered free of charge by Saudi Arabian Embassies and Consulates abroad (see list). It can be obtained at Jeddah by pilgrims coming from countries which do not have diplomatic relations with Saudi Arabia.

Documents which must be furnished in order to obtain a visa for the pilgrimage (this list is not exhaustive):
1. Passport.
2. Return ticket to and from country of departure.
3. Vaccination certificate.

In Muslim countries where there are exchange controls, a currency allocation is granted to pilgrims which is usually higher than that granted to ordinary tourists. The sum which the future *Hajj* pilgrim can take out is generally allotted in the form of a cheque that can be cashed at a Saudi bank.

Pilgrims who are able to export currency are advised to carry cash rather than cheques, since banknotes can be changed in Saudi Arabia at a slightly better rate than travellers' cheques. This is especially true if pilgrims go to private exchange dealers, who can be found everywhere.

Credit cards, especially American Express and Diners' Club, are accepted without difficulty by most banks and at a large number of hotels and shops.

Entrance formalities upon arrival in Saudi Arabia

The Delegation in charge of the questionnaire and the allocation of pilgrims. After a police control, which is generally rapid, pilgrims must hand over their passport to the employees of the Delegation which is in charge of the questionnaire and the allocation of pilgrims (*Hay'at assu āl-wal-jawāb*). Pilgrims will be given back their passports much later at the *Wukala' Unified Bureau* (authorized agents) when all formalities have been accomplished.

Customs. This formality is usually extremely brief, given the flexibility of Saudi Arabian legislation with regards to customs controls. Weapons, alcoholic beverages, drugs, pork meat products and books, pictures or magazines regarded as contrary to Islamic morality are not allowed into the country, however. Camera owners should know that they may have to pay a deposit on their camera, which will be refunded when they leave the country if they do so within 90 days.

The *Wukala' Unified Bureau.* Pilgrims must accomplish the greatest number of formalities at this bureau before they can recover their passports.

They must pay a sum of money (approximately 294 Saudi rials) which will cover various charges and services rendered during their stay. Pilgrims arriving by air or by sea must also pay a sum which will cover their expenses at the pilgrim resthouses during transit; this will cost them approximately 80 rials*.

Pilgrims will then have to pay for the cost of transportation to Medinah or Mecca. They must demand a receipt for all the sums they pay out or, failing this, at least ask that the payment of these taxes be recorded in their passport. Otherwise, they run the risk of having to pay these sums all over again at a control checkpoint. ☐

---

* The pilgrim must draw out a cheque issued by a Saudi Arabian bank which will cover these expenses. To find out the exact amount of these various taxes, he must enquire at the Saudi Arabian Consulate. He can also pay these taxes in cash.

the pilgrimage on a day to day basis

■ *Road transport.* State-owned and privately-owned buses, as well as taxis, make the journey between Mecca, Jeddah and Medinah. Reservations can only be made at the *Wukala'Unified Bureau.* Should the pilgrim wish to travel by his own means, he must first pay a tax called the *Tanazul* which amounts to 50 % of the price of transportation. Transport between the Holy Places of Mecca (Mecca - Minā - 'Arafāt -Muzdalifah - Minā -Mecca) is taken care of by the *Mutawwif.*

Air transport. Exists solely between Jeddah and Medinah. A practical and restful way of making the trip. The flight lasts only 30 minutes, whereas to go by road takes 7 or 8 hours. A return ticket costs 250 rials. Reservations can be made either through the *Wukala'Unified Bureau* or else directly through the Saudi airlines.

Lodgings

Pilgrims are lodged by the *Mutawwifeen* at Mecca and at the Holy Places. They sleep in houses at Mecca, and under tents at 'Arafāt and Minā (one day, from morning to night at'Arafāt, three or four days at Minā). Total cost: about 1000 rials. Besides this, they must also pay for the cost of transport between Mecca, Minā, 'Arafāt, Minā and Mecca. Cost: approximately 100 rials.

Pilgrims must hand over their passports to the *Mutawwif* upon arrival. The *Mutawwif* is entitled to hold onto the pilgrims' passports until their departure from Mecca. Pilgrims should demand that their *Mutawwif* give them a card bearing his name, address and telephone number, as well as their own particulars.

Pilgrims should also demand a receipt for the sums of money they have handed over to their *Mutawwif.* This receipt could be required of them upon leaving Saudi Arabia.

Lodgings are provided in similar circumstances by *Muzawwireen* at Medinah. The cost of a stay there (usually eight days) is not as high: approximately 500 rials.

Hotels and restaurants

Hotels. There are many hotels at Jeddah, Mecca and Medinah, most of them modern and some of them of international standards. It is practically impossible to book a room in one of them during the pilgrimage season, however, and making a reservation at this time is out of the question. One would have to go about reserving several months in advance while on the spot. Pilgrims who are carrying out an *'Umrah* pilgrimage considerably ahead of the *Hajj* may, however, be able to take advantage of this opportunity to book a room for the *Hajj* season at one of the local hotels.

There are international-class restaurants at the hotels of Jeddah, Mecca and Medinah, but there again it is often difficult to book a table. It is far easier to get a seat at one of the many small places that provide meals at all the pilgrims' stopping-places, or else to buy roast chickens in the market, meat sandwiches (*Shawarma*) and every variety of fruit. These items can then be eaten at home. It is the only solution to the feeding problem during the days spent "camping" at Minā.

Drinking supplies

There is a sufficient supply of drinking water in the cities, generally speaking. At Mecca, pilgrims prefer to drink the waters of the Zamzam well, which they can go and fetch themselves at the Holy Mosque. But the water supply in neighbouring localities ('Arafāt and especially Minā) leaves much to be desired. It is highly recommended to disinfect all drinking-water and the water used for washing food and eating utensils. Lebanese bottled mineral water is available almost everywhere, as are international non-alcoholic beverages such as Pepsi-Cola,

Precious craftsmanship :
gold and silver thread embroidery
of the verses of the Koran
on the Ka'bah covering.

Seven-Up, etc. The price of tinned fruit juice is extremely reasonable.

Tea is the hot drink most widely available, though coffee too is drunk in considerable quantities.

Presents and souvenirs

The relatives and friends of the *Hajj* pilgrim await his return eagerly. They will be thrilled to receive a present from the Holy Places — indeed, some of them will have demanded one in advance. This will hold true even if the gift has been manufactured in another part of the world. The pilgrim will be lost for choice as far as purchases are concerned.

Gift suggestions

Rosaries of varying quality, usually sold by the dozen, make suitable gifts for everyone and are therefore an extremely convenient object to purchase.

Zamzamiyāt are small, sealed metallic flasks containing water from the Zamzam. They too are in very great demand as souvenirs.

Korans of assorted sizes and bindings also make highly popular gifts.

Scarves with a picture of one of the Holy Places on them are popular too, even when they carry a discreet label in one corner printed: "Made in China" (Taiwan), or "Made in Hong-Kong".

Radios, tape-recorders and other transistor equipment attract many a buyer because of their low prices. They are frequently purchased by *Hajj* pilgrims.

Jewellers' windows also draw many pilgrims' eyes because of the amazingly reasonable price of *jewellery* in Saudi Arabia. Necklaces, bracelets, rings, etc, are usually sold for no more than the actual cost of the precious metal from which they are made (usually gold).

Health

Saudi Arabia has one of the best medical-care systems in the world, and also one of the most modern. Medical care and prescriptions are free to all, including foreign pilgrims. Furthermore, pilgrims have the possibility if they so wish to address themselves directly to the medical staff which accompanies the delegations of each country. These missions have representatives in Jeddah, Mecca and Medinah. They accompany pilgrims throughout the pilgrimage, and are with them also at 'Arafāt and Minā. □

hotels

PLACES ESTABLISHMENTS	Telephone number
JEDDAH	
Al-Attas Oasis, Shara Emir Fahd (Close to the Saudia Building)	20211
Alamin, King 'Abdul 'Aziz Street, Bab Sharif	33191
Andalus (Al), Shara 'al-Jadid	32300
'Arafat, Shara 'al-Jadid, (Basameh Building)	32248
Asia, King 'Abdul 'Aziz Street, Bab Mecca	26218
Atlas, Shara Khalid Ibn al-Walid	38520
Bahauddin, Shara 'al-Jadid	31506
Bahauddin (new), Shara 'al-Jadid	23851
Haramain (al), King 'Abdul 'Aziz Street, Bab Sharif	26655
Haramain (al), Shara Emir Fahd	20211
International, Shara 'al-Jadid, al-Bai'a Square	29022
Istanbul, King'Abdul 'Aziz Street, Bab Sharif	26756
Jazira (Al), King 'Abdul 'Aziz Street	22365
Jeddah Airport, Airport	33261
Jeddah Palace, Al-Bai'a Square	32225
Kaki (Al), Airport Road (close to the Passport Bureau)	48071
Kandara Palace, Airport (close to the National Hospital)	23155/25700
Khayyam (Al), Shara 'al-Jadid	33560
Medina (Al), Shara 'al-Jadid	32650
Meridien, Mecca Road (near King Khalid bridge)	45011
Nahdha, Harbour Road (close to the Arab Bank)	23956
Quds (Al), Mecca Gate (close to the Bakhshab Building)	33477
Quraish, Mecca Gate	29627
Red Sea Palace, Top of King 'Abdul 'Aziz Street	28555
Rehab (Al), Shara 'al-Jadid	32216
Riyadh, Airport Road, Sharafiyah	33950
Royal, Shara 'al-Jadid	42048
Sands, Al-Hamra	57996
Shaheen, King'Abdul 'Aziz Street	26582
Sheraton, Airport Road, (Kaki Building)	24018
Taj al-Jadid, Sharafiyah	26815
Waha (Al), Shara Emir Fahd	50960

MECCA	
Abdul 'Aziz Khogir, Al-Suq Assaghir (the small market)	27090
Abdul 'Aziz Khogir, Al-Suq Assaghir (the small market)	36331
Africa, Al-Suq Assaghir (the small market)	27067
Amin (Al), Jiyad	28240
As-Salam, Al-Ghaza	22880
Aŝ-Safā, Aŝ-Ŝafā	24748
Aŝ-Ŝafā (annexe), Aŝ-Ŝafā	33437
Hafiz, Al-Suq Assaghir (the small market)	31931
Haram (Al), Al-Hijla	27720

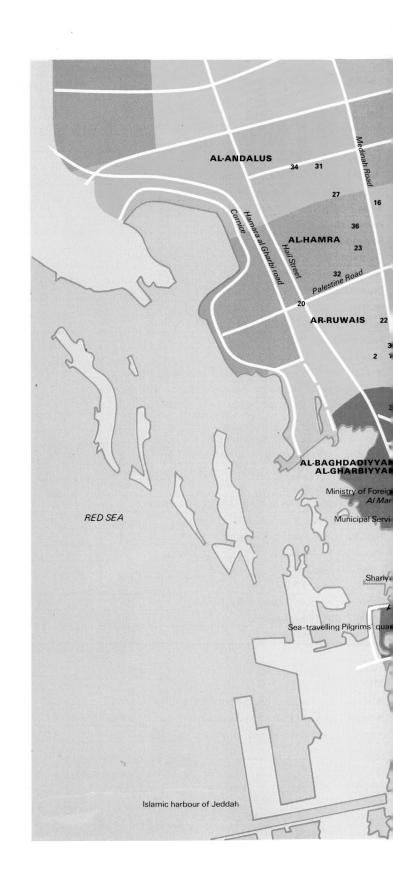

AL-ANDALUS
34 31

Medinah Road

27

16

Cornice

Hamara al Gharbi road

Hail Street

AL-HAMRA
36
23

32

Palestine Road

20

AR-RUWAIS 22

3
2 1

3

AL-BAGHDADIYYA
AL-GHARBIYYA

Ministry of Foreig
Al Mar

Municipal Servi

RED SEA

Shariy

Sea-travelling Pilgrims' qua

Islamic harbour of Jeddah

MAP OF JEDDAH

0   2   3 km

Embassies
1. Algeria
2. Bahrain
3. Cameroon
4. Egypt
5. Ethiopia
6. France
7. Gabon
8. Gambia
9. Ghana
10. Guinea
11. India
12. Iran
13. Irak
14. Jordan
15. Lebanon
16. Libya
17. Mali
18. Mauritania
19. Morocco
20. Niger
21. Nigeria
22. Qatar
23. Senegal
24. Sudan
25. Syria
26. Tunisia
27. Turkey
28. Uganda
29. United Arab Emirates
30. Yemen (North)
31. Yemen (South)
32. Zaire
33. Afghanistan
34. Kenya
35. Kuwait
36. Oman
37. Somalia

'YAH

HRAFAH

AR-RIHAB

AL-KHADHIRA

lestine Road

NAZLAT BANI   MALAK

12

25

AL-MATAR   AL-QADIM

International Airport

ing Pilgrims' quarter

GHDADIYYAH
HARQIYYAH

rport road

AL-KUNDARAH

MARIYYAH

ASH-
SHUHDDA   AL-
KHALIDIYYAH

AS-SULAIMANIYYAH

AL-JAMI'AH

University

AS-SABIL

Al-Janubi al-Matar road

ATH-THAGHR

Mecca road

KHOZAM
PALACE

MASHRAFAH

'AH

Road

AN-NAZLAH
AL-YAMANIYYAH

AL-QURAYYAT

MADAIN FAHD

GHULLIL

N

AL-WAZIRRIYYAH

Stadium

101

hotels *(cont.)*

Faruq Jamil Khogir, Al-Ghaza	28514
Fat'h (Al), Bab Al-Umra	31242
Madina (Al), Al-Suq Assaghir (the small market)	24948
Marzo'qi, Al-Suq Assaghir (the small market)	31394
Mecca, Al-Shubeikah	24987
Mecca Intercontinental, Umm al-Joud	31580
Mufti (Al), Jiyad	24163
Muutaz (Al), Jiyad	24163
Qatan (Al), Al-Ghaza	34462
Quthaddin, Al-Shubeikah	25382
Shubra, Jiyad	28240
Taibah, Jiyad	36868
Umm Al-Qura, Bab al-Malik (King's Gate)	27652
Zamzam, Al-Qararah	29201

MEDINAH

Abuljud, Shara Malik 'Abdul 'Aziz	25925
'Arafāt, Bab al-Majidi	24882
Bahauddin, Bad al-Majidi	21350
Dar al-Ansar, Shara as-Sumbulia	21743
Dar al-Hijah, Shar'a Malik 'Abdul 'Aziz	29110
Firdaws (Al), Bab al-Majidi	21180
Haram (Al), Shara As-Saha al-Jadid	23200
Hijaz (Al), Shara As-Sumbulia	21120
Jazirah (Al), Abu Dharr	21235
Khalid, Shara Malik 'Abdul 'Aziz	27157
Nour (An), Bab as-Salam	23165
Qasr Al-Madina, Bad al-Majidi	21350
Rawdha (Ar), Shara Malik 'Abdul 'Aziz	21016
Rihab (Ar), Shara As-Saha al-Jadid	23200
Sa'ada (Al), Shara Malik 'Abdul 'Aziz	22922
Taisir, Shara as-Sumbulia	21425
Zahra (Az), Shara as-Sumbulia	21231

banks

PLACES ESTABLISHMENTS	Telephone number

JEDDAH

National Commercial Bank, King 'Abdul 'Aziz Street	33580
Riyadh Bank, King 'Abdul 'Aziz Street	23126
Arab Bank, Harbour Road	23133
Al-Bank Al-Saudi, Al-Britanni King 'Abdul 'Aziz Street	42868

banks *(cont.)*

City Bank, Sharafiyah	47350
Al-Jazira Bank, King 'Abdul 'Aziz Street	32888
Cairo Bank, King 'Abdul 'Aziz Street	23266
Meli Bank (Iran), King 'Abdul 'Aziz Street	23808
Bank of the Lebanon and Overseas, King 'Abdul 'Aziz Street (near the Sharbatti Building)	23285

MECCA

National Commercial Bank, Shara Emir 'Abdallah al-Faisal	42639
National Commercial Bank, Al-Muddā 'a, Shara Emir 'Abdallah al-Faisal	41405
National Commercial Bank (Branch), Al 'Otaibiya	34708
National Commercial Bank (Branch), Al-Suq Assaghir (the small market)	36754
National Commercial Bank (Branch), Al-Shubeika	21814
Riyadh Bank, Al-Ghaza	40203
Riyadh Bank, Al-Kararah	32158
Riyadh Bank, Al-Suq Assaghir (the small market)	20996
Arab Bank, Al-Ghaza	43455
Arab Bank, Manzil Azzahra	35263

MEDINAH

National Commercial Bank, Shara al-Manakha	25340
Riyadh Bank, Shara al-Manakha	20550
Al-Jazirah Bank, Shara al-Manakha	20122
Al-Rajihi Bank, Bab al-Majidi	23330
Al-Kaaki Bank, Shara Malik 'Abdul 'Aziz	24780
Al-Sibei Bank, Shara as-Saha Al-Jadid	24550
Ba Ghalf Bank, Shara Malik 'Abdul 'Aziz	23897

embassies

SAUDI ARABIAN EMBASSIES
AND CONSULATES ABROAD

Algeria (Algiers)	**Malaysia** (Kuala Lumpur)
Austria (Vienna)	**Morocco** (Rabat)
Bahrain	**Netherlands** (The Hague)
Belgium (Brussels)	**Nigeria** (Lagos)
Chad (N'Djamena)	**Pakistan** (Karachi)
Egypt (Cairo)	**Senegal** (Dakar)
Ethiopia, (Addis Ababa)	**Singapore**
France (Paris)	**Somalia** (Mogadiscio)
Ghana (Accra)	**Spain** (Madrid)
Greece (Athens)	**Sudan** (Khartoum)
Guinea (Conakry)	**Sweden** (Stockholm)
India (Delhi)	**Switzerland** (Bern)

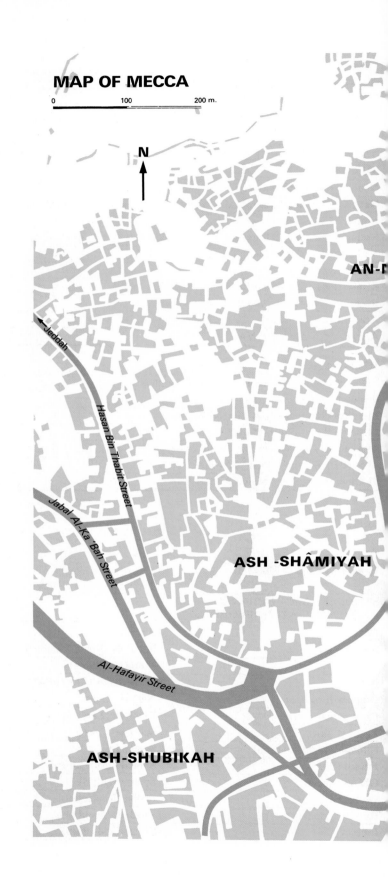

MAP OF MECCA

0   100   200 m.

N

Jeddah

Hasan Bin Thabit Street

Jabal Al-Ka'Bah Street

Al-Hafayir Street

AN-

ASH -SHÂMIYAH

ASH-SHUBIKAH

Minâ POST

Al-Ghazah Street

SUQ AL-LÎL

AL-MARWAH

BÂB AS-SALÂM

JMRAH

KA'BAH

AŜ-ŜAFÂ

BAL AL-MALIK
'ABDUL 'AZÎZ

AL-QUSHASHIYAH

HOSPITAL

embassies *(cont.)*

Indonesia (Djakarta)	**Syria** (Damascus)
Iran (Teheran)	**Thailand** (Bangkok)
Iraq (Baghdad and Basrah)	**Tunisia** (Tunis)
Italy (Rome)	**Turkey** (Ankara)
Japan (Tokyo)	**United Kingdom** (London)
Jordan (Amman)	**United States** (Washington DC and New York City)
Kuwait	
Lebanon (Beirut)	**Venezuela** (Caracas)
Libya (Benghazi and Tripoli)	**West Germany** (Bonn)

FOREIGN EMBASSIES AND CONSULATES

JEDDAH

Algeria Melinah Road, Ahmed Shawqui Street	53202
Bahrain, Al-Ruwais (near the Old Royal Palace Hotel)	51905
Bangladesh, Mecca Road, Kilom. 3	78465
Cameroon, Mecca Road, Kilom. 4 Maidan (place) Al-Fahd	71782
Chad, Medinah Road, Sharafiyah	53662
China (Taiwan), Palestine Road	59162
Egypt, Airport Road, Sharafiyah	21011
Ethiopia, Mohammed Ibn 'Abdul-Wahhab, Baghdadiyah	23013
France, Baghdadiyah	21233
Gabon, Medinah Road (near the Japanese Embassy)	52468
Ghana, Medinah Road (near the As-Salam Mosque)	52779
Greece, Medinah Road	58701
Guinea, Abu Feras Street, Ruwais	53718
India, Medinah Road, near the Al-Ettihad sports club	21602
Indonesia, Villa 'Abdul-Malik Ibn Ibrahim, Baghdadiyah	21681
Iran Medinah Road, Abu al-Tayeb Street (near the Defence Ministry)	53145
Iraq, Medinah Road, Kilom. 5 (near the Lebanese Hospital)	52948
Italy, Sharafiyah	21448
Jordan, Mecca Road (near the Al-Essaie display)	78474
Kenya, Medinah Road, Emir 'Abdallah Ibn 'Abdul 'Aziz Street	56718
Kuwait, 'Ali Ibn Abi Taleb Street (near the American Bank), Sharafiyah	53163
Lebanon, Medinah Road, Kilom. 3	52488
Libya, Medinah Road, Kilom. 5	51273
Malaysia, Medina Road, Kilom. 3 (near the King Saud Mosque)	52371
Mali, Medinah Road	57704
Mauritania, Mecca Road, Baghdadiyah	78171
Morocco, Medinah Road, Al-Hamra Street	52568
Niger, Sharafiyah (near the American Bank)	51551
Nigeria, Madaris Street, Baghdadiyah	32835
Oman, Ruwais	53619
Pakistan, Harbour Road	27333
Philippines, Medinah Road, Kilom. 5	
Qatar, Medinah Road	52538

Senegal, Medinah Road (behind the Telephone Building)	54465
Somalia, Medinah Road, Kilom. 2	51495
Spain, Mecca Road, Kilom. 4 (near the Exhibition Al-'Issai)	73226
Sudan, Harbour Road	20560
Syria, Al-Huda Street, Sharafiyah	51049
Thailand, Madaris Street, Baghdadiyah	31344
Tunisia, Mecca Road, Kilom. 3	73590
Turkey, Medinah Road, Kilom. 7	54873
Uganda, Medinah Road, (behind the Maternity Hospital)	52386
United Arab Emirates, Osman Ibn Affan Street Sharafiyah	53770
United States of America, Palestine Road, Ruwais	52589
North Yemen, Mecca Road, Kilom. 4	74291
South Yemen, Medinah Road	56591
Zaire, Palestine Road (east of the U.S. Embassy)	52973

airlines

SAUDIA
(Saudi airlines)

JEDDAH

Reservations	33333
Reconfirmations	36333
Airport (Information)	22111
Medinah Road office	53725/53765
Mecca Road office	31687/31699
Kandara Hotel (tickets)	23155
Oasis Hotel (tickets)	27836
Freight service	31804

MECCA

Reservations and reconfirmations	33777/33977/33333
Ticket office	23200/23211/23222
Nuzha Office (tickets)	31484/31485

MEDINAH

Sales and reservations	24411 (20 lines)
Freight service	23815

FOREIGN
AIRLINES

JEDDAH

Air Africa, King 'Abdul 'Aziz Street (behind the Bank of Cairo)	22882
Air Algeria, King 'Abdul 'Aziz Street ('Ali Ridha Building)	22233

MAP OF MEDINAH

0   100   200 m

N

HOSPITAL

Airport Road

Bab Ash-Shami

HOSPITAL

Bab Al-Kuma

Shara As-Sahah

Shara Al-Manakhah

AL-MANAKHAH

Shara As-Sayh

POLICE

POST

AL-ANBARIYAH

Shara Al-Anbariyah

Ouba Avenue

Jeddah

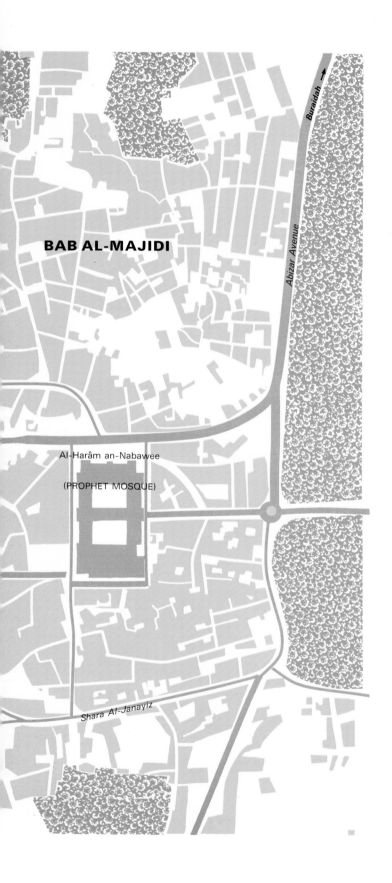

BAB AL-MAJIDI

Abizar Avenue

Buraidah

Al-Harâm an-Nabawee

(PROPHET MOSQUE)

Shara Al-Janayiz

airlines *(cont.)*

Air France, King 'Abdul 'Aziz Street (behind the Bank of Cairo)	22882
Air India, King 'Abdul 'Aziz Street (Al-Faisal Building)	31026
Air Malta, King 'Abdul 'Aziz Street (National Commercial Bank building)	
Alia (Jordan), King 'Abdul 'Aziz Street (Al-Maghrabi Building)	33414
Alitalia, King 'Abdul 'Aziz Street (Mufti Building)	22107
Bangladesh Airlines, Baghdadiyah (Al-Johara Building)	33127
Brazilian Airlines, King 'Abdul 'Aziz Street (National Commercial Bank building)	24432
British Airways, Medinah Road	56424
China Airlines (Formosa), King 'Abdul 'Aziz Street	21172
Cyprus Airways, King 'Abdul 'Aziz Street (Al-Attar Building)	21249
Egypt Air, King 'Abdul 'Aziz Street	21144
Ethiopian Airlines, Baghdadiyah (Al-Johara Building)	33127
Indonesian Airlines, King 'Abdul 'Aziz Street	21172
Iraqi Airways, King 'Abdul 'Aziz Street (Al-'Attar Building)	21249
Japan Airlines, King 'Abdul 'Aziz Street	21172
Kenyan Airlines, King 'Abdul 'Aziz Street (Al-'Attar Building)	21249
KLM, King 'Abdul 'Aziz street ('Ali Ridha Building)	22454
Korean Airlines (South Korea), Baghdadiyah (Al-Johara Building)	26354
Kuwait Airways, King 'Abdul 'Aziz Street (Al-Maghrabi Building)	28349
Libyan Airlines, King 'Abdul 'Aziz Street	21172
Lufthansa (West Germany), King 'Abdul 'Aziz Street	26354
MEA (Lebanon), Jeddah Palace Hotel	21140
Nigerian Airlines, Baghdadiyah (Al-Johara Builing)	33127
PIA (Pakistan), King 'Abdul 'Aziz Street (An-Nichar Building)	44110
Quantas Airlines, King 'Abdul 'Aziz Street (Al-'Attar Building)	21249
Royal Air Morocco, King 'Abdul 'Aziz Street (Queen's Building)	21097
Sabena (Belgium), Baghdadiyah (Al-Johara Building)	33127
SAS, Medinah Road	693732
Somali Airlines, King 'Addul 'Aziz Street	21172
Syrian Airlines, King 'Abdul 'Aziz Street	25612
Tunis Air, King 'Abdul 'Aziz Street (Al-Maghrabi Building)	22169

hospitals

The list given below is not exhaustive. It gives only the names of the principal hospitals of Saudi Arabia. Pilgrims can go to these centres or address themselves to the foreign medical missions that accompany their group. The missions give aid not only to persons of their nationality group, but usually to any pilgrim, regardless of his country of origin. Treatment, consultations and medication are provided free of charge.

PLACES
ESTABLISMENTS

JEDDAH

Central Hospital, Bab Sharif	21133
National Hospital, Airport Road	27715
Lebanese Hospital, Medinah Road	52955
King's Hospital, Harbour Road	22266
Dar Al-Shifa Hospital, Harbour Road	27444
Khalid Idriss Hospital, Airport Road	23555
Maternity Hospital, Medinah Road	53655
Ophtalmology Hospital, Airport Road	24926
Al-Maghrabi Ophtalmology Clinic, Mecca Road, Kilom. 2	23680
Al-Daghistani Hospital, University Road	75255
Bakhsh Hospital, Shara Emir Fahd	58688
Suleyman Faqih Hospital, Al-Hamra, close to the U.S. Embassy	61452

MECCA

Ashisha Hospital, Ashisha	21659
King Faisal Hospital, Ashisha	26411
King 'Abdul 'Aziz Hospital, Az-Zahir	21633
Ajiyad Hospital, Ajiyad district	26111
Maternity Hospital, Jarwal	22050
National Hospital, Al-'Aziziya	37170
Ahmed Zahir Hospital, Al-Nuzha	36569
Emergency Hospital, Minā	64378
Mina Hospital, Minā	66719

MEDINAH

King Faisal Hospital, Bab al-Shami	25226
Maternity Hospital, Bab al-Shami	25406
Pulmonary Ailments Hospital, Al-Hara Asharqiya	21188
Ophtalmology Hospital, Al-Hara Asharqiya	21333
Quarantine, Abar 'Ali	24761
Psychiatric Hospital, Soltana Avenue	27509
Anti-Malaria Centre, Quba	23721

Invocations
(Ad'iya)

AD'IYA OR INVOCATIONS SUGGESTED FOR EACH OF THE HOLY PLACES

(singular Du'ā)

At each of the sacred places and during the performance of each rite except for that of the lapidation of the pillars at Minā, the pilgrim must make an invocation to God known as a Du'a (invocations, which are not to be confused with prayers or Ŝalāt).
In the old days, the chief task of the Mutawwifīn *at Mecca (as their name would imply : those who help to perform the circling) was to make the pilgrims recite the* Du'ā *as they went round the Ka'bah, as* well as aiding them to perform the other rites. At Medinah, this task was carried out by the Muzawwirīn *(literally : those who show visitors around).*
In this day and age, this function has been chiefly taken over by rhetors (or talkers) ; they are also known as Mutawwifīn *and* Muzawwirīn *and can be found at each of the sacred places. Their services can be purchased for a few dozen rials.*
Furthermore, a number of authors have transcribed in their works the Du'ā, or invocations adapted to each rite. These texts possess the great advantage :
« Of revealing the multitude of wishes that can be formulated by a heart brimming with faith, gratitude, veneration and hope » (E. Guellouz, Pilgrimage to Mecca, *Saudi Arabian Ministry of Information, 208 p.).*
The use of printed texts is very common now. This is why we include in this work Du'ā appropriate to every circumstance for the use of those pilgrims who might wish to consult them. The Du'a are printed in Arabic, followed by a phonetic transcription in the Latin alphabet and by a translation into English.
Let us remember, however, that there is no compulsory invocation to be recited at any one Sacred Place, any more than there is such a thing as a clergy in the Islamic religion. Each Muslim can (and must) address God directly, without intermediary. He can invoke God in his own fashion, according to the inspiration of his soul.

Attalbiyah
(Reply to the divine call)

As soon as he enters the sacred state (*Ihrām*) in the appropriate place and at the appropriate time (*Mawāqeet*), and until the partial lifting of the *Ihrām* on the 10th Thu -l-Hijjah, after the stoning of the pillars, the pilgrim must continuously repeat the reply to the divine call (*Talbiyah*) :

**LABBAYKA ALLAHUMMA LABBAYK,
LABBAYKA LA SHAREEKA LAKA LABBAYK,
INNA AL HAMDA WA ANNIMATA,
LAKA WAL MOLK, LA SHAREEKA LAK.**

*Here I am, O Lord, here I am
Here I am. Thou hast no partner. Here I am
Unto Thee is praise due, for Thou art the giver of Grace,
Thou art possessed of Sovereign Power,
Thou hast no partner.*

Upon entering Mecca

Prayers
at the entrance
to Mecca

**BISMI-LLAHI ARRAHMANI ARRAHEEM
ALLAHUMMA EJ'AL LI BIHĀ QARĀRAN,
UARZOQNI FIHA RIZQANE HALALANE.**

*In the name of God, the All-Compassionate, the All-Merciful,
O Allah, make these my place of rest and grant me therein lawful provisions.*

On entering Mecca :

**ALLAHUMMA INNA HADHA AL HARAMA HARAMUK,
WAL BALADA BALADUKA, WAL ABDA ABDUKA,
JE'TUKA MIN BILADIN BA' IDATIN BIDHUNUBIN
KATHIRATIN, WA A'MALIN SAYEATIN, AS-ALUKA
MASALATA AL MUDHTARRINA ILAYKA AL-MUS-
HFIQINA MIN 'ADHABIKA-AN TASTAQBILANI
BIMAHDI AFUIKA WA AN TUDKHILANI FACEEHA
JANNATIKA, JANNATA ANNA'IME.**

*O Allah, this sanctuary is Thy Haram, and this city is Thy city.
The peace here is Thy peace. The servant I am is Thy servant.*

*I have come unto Thee from a distant land, carrying with me to
be pardoned a large number of sins and misdeeds. As an afflict-
ed person seeking Thy assistance, dreading Thy chastisement, I
implore Thee to accept from me my sole and simple desire for
Thy forgiveness and for Thy permission to enter Thy vast Garden, the Garden of delight.*

ALLAHUMMA INNA HADHA HARAMUKA WA
HARAMU RASSULIKA, FAHARRIME LAHMI WA DAMI
WA IDHÂMI 'ALA N'NAR.

ALLAHUMMA AMINNI MIN 'ADHABIKA YAWMA
TAB'ATHU 'IBADAKA, AS' ALUKA BI'ANNAKA ANTA
ALLAHU LA ILAHA IL'LA ANTA, ARRAHMANU ARRA-
HIMI, AN TUSSALIYA WA TUSSAL LIMA 'ALA SYYI-
DINA MUHAMMADIN WA ALA ALIHI TASLIMAN
KATHIRAN ABADA.

*O Allah, this is Thy sanctuary and the sanctuary of Thy Messen-
ger. For this render my flesh, my blood and my bones unlawful
unto the Fire.*

*O Allah, spare me from Thy chastisement on the day when Thou
shalt resurrect Thy servants. I beseech Thee, for Thou art Allah
who alone is worthy of worship and is the Beneficient, the Merciful, to send Thy immense and eternal peace and blessings on
our chief Muhammed and on his posterity and on his companions.*

Invocations
for the
circumambulation
(Ad'iya aṭṭawâf)

Niyah Attawaf
(Declaration of intention of performing the circumambulation of the Ka'bah)

نِيَّةُ الطَّوَافِ

اَللّٰهُمَّ إِنِّى أُرِيدُ طَوَافَ بَيْتِكَ الْحَرَامِ فَيَسِّرْهُ لِى ،
وَتَقَبَّلْهُ مِنِّى ـ سَبْعَةَ أَشْوَاطٍ ـ طَوَافَ الْحَجِّ
(أَوِ الْعُمْرَةِ إِنْ كَانَ مُعْتَمِرًا) لِلّٰهِ تَعَالَى .
ثُمَّ يُقَبِّلُ الْحَجَرَ الأَسْوَدَ، وَيَرْفَعُ يَدَيْهِ وَيَقُولُ:
بِسْمِ اللّٰهِ اللّٰهُ أَكْبَرُ وَلِلّٰهِ الْحَمْدُ.

**ALLAHUMMA INNI URIDU TAWAFA BAYTIKA AL
HARAMI FAYASSERHU LI, WA TAQABALHU MINNI-
SAB'ATA ACHUATIN-TAWAFA AL-HAJJ (OR
AL-'UMRA, Depending on the case) LILLAHI TA 'ALA.**

*O Allah I intend to perform the circumambulation of Thy
Sacred House. Make Thou the same easy for me and accept
from me the seven Rounds to be performed in the name of Allah
the Almighty. To Him belongeth glory and power. In the name
of Allah.*

The pilgrim makes a gesture of greeting towards the Black
Stone, or kisses it if he can, and says :

**BISMILLAHI ; ALLAHU AKBAR, WA LILLAH AL
HAMD.**

*In the name of Allah - Allah is great and unto Allah is praise
due !*

The pilgrim can thereupon begin the circumambulation.

Invocation to be
recited for the Îawaf
(circumambulation)

دُعَاءُ الشَّوْطِ الْأَوَّلِ

سُبْحَانَ اللهِ، وَالْحَمْدُ لِلهِ، وَلَا إِلهَ إِلَّا اللهُ، وَاللهُ أَكْبَرُ، وَلَا حَوْلَ وَلَا قُوَّةَ إِلَّا بِاللهِ الْعَلِيِّ الْعَظِيمِ، وَالصَّلَاةُ وَالسَّلَامُ عَلَى رَسُولِ اللهِ صَلَّى اللهُ عَلَيْهِ وَقُلْ. اللّهُمَّ إِيمَانًا بِكَ، وَتَصْدِيقًا لِكِتَابِكَ، وَوَفَاءً بِعَهْدِكَ، وَاتِّبَاعًا لِسُنَّةِ نَبِيِّكَ وَحَبِيبِكَ مُحَمَّدٍ صَلَّى اللهُ عَلَيْهِ وَسَلَّمَ.

اللّهُمَّ إِنِّي أَسْأَلُكَ الْعَفْوَ وَالْعَافِيَةَ، وَالْمُعَافَاةَ الدَّائِمَةَ فِي الدِّينِ وَالدُّنْيَا وَالْآخِرَةِ، وَالْفَوْزَ بِالْجَنَّةِ، وَالنَّجَاةَ مِنَ النَّارِ.

وَيَقُولُ بَيْنَ الرُّكْنَيْنِ فِي كُلِّ شَوْطٍ:
رَبَّنَا آتِنَا فِي الدُّنْيَا حَسَنَةً، وَفِي الْآخِرَةِ حَسَنَةً، وَقِنَا عَذَابَ النَّارِ، وَأَدْخِلْنَا الْجَنَّةَ مَعَ الْأَبْرَارِ، يَا عَزِيزُ يَا غَفَّارُ، يَا رَبَّ الْعَالَمِينَ

ASHAWT AL-AWWAL (first circling round the Ka'bah)

SOUBHANA ALLAH, WA AL HAMDU LILLAH, WA LA ILAHA ILLA ALLAH WA ALLAHU AKBAR, WA LA HAWLA WA LA QUWATA ILLA BILLAH, AL 'ALIYE AL ADHIM, WA ASSALATU WA ASSALAMOU 'ALA RASSUL LI'LLAHI SALLA ALLAHOU ALAYHI WA SALLAM

ALLAHUMMA IMANAN BIKA, WA TASDIQAN LIKITABIKA, WA WAF'AN BI'AHDIKA WA ITTIBA'AN LISSOUNATI NABIYYIKA WA HABIBIKA MUHAMMADIN, SALLA ALLAHU ALAYHI WA SALLAM.

ALLAHUMMA INNI AS ALUKA AL'AFUA, WA AL'AFIYA, WA AL MU 'AFATA ADDA 'IMATA FI D'DINI, WA ADDUNYA, WA AL AKHIRAH, WA AL FAWZA BIL JANNATI, WA ANNAJATA MINE ANNAR.

Upon arriving at the Yemenite angle which precedes that of the Black Stone, the pilgrim must recite each time :

RABBANA ATINA FID'DUNIA HASSANATAN WA FIL AKHIRATI HASSANATAN WA QINA ADHAB ANNAR, WAD'KHELNA AL JANNATA MA'A AL-ABRARI, YA AZIZU YAGHAFFARU, YARABBA-AL'ALAMIN.

He then greets the Black Stone with both hands and recites at each round :

BISMI ALLAH ALLAHU AKBAR WA LILLAHI AL HAMD.

Glory be to Allah and all praise is due unto Allah. And none is worthy of worship except Allah. And Allah is most great. There is no might, no power but from Allah the most High, the Great. And blessings and peace be on the Messenger of Allah.

O Allah, I am performing this duty with complete faith in Thee and with belief in the truth of Thy Book, and in the fulfilment of my pledge to Thee, and in the wake of the Tradition of Thy Prophet and Thy beloved friend Muhammed, may peace and blessings of Allah be upon him !

O Allah, I implore Thee to grant me forgiveness, safety and general pardon in the matters of faith, of this world and the hereafter, and also grant me success leading to Paradise and deliverance from the Fire.

Between the Yemenite angle and the Black Stone angle, the pilgrim recites :

O our Lord, give us good in this world and also in the next world, and deliver us from the torment of Hell-fire, and cause us to enter the Garden along with the righteous, O Powerful, O Forgiver, O Lord of all the worlds.

The pilgrim declares as he arrives in front of the Black Stone which he hails :

In the Name of God, God is most Great, Praised be God.

Invocation
for the second round
of the Ṭawaf

دُعَاءُ الشَّوْطِ الثَّانِي

اللّٰهُمَّ إِنَّ هَذَا الْبَيْتَ بَيْتُكَ، وَالْحَرَمَ حَرَمُكَ، وَالْأَمْنَ أَمْنُكَ، وَالْعَبْدَ عَبْدُكَ، وَأَنَـا عَبْدُكَ وَابْنُ عَبْدِكَ، وَهَذَا مَقَامُ الْعَائِذِ بِكَ مِنَ النَّارِ،

اللّٰهُمَّ حَبِّبْ إِلَيْنَا الْإِيمَانَ وَزَيِّنْهُ فِي قُلُوبِنَا، وَكَرِّهْ إِلَيْنَا الْكُفْرَ وَالْفُسُوقَ وَالْعِصْيَانَ، وَاجْعَلْنَا مِنَ الرَّاشِدِينَ. اللّٰهُمَّ قِنِي عَذَابَكَ يَوْمَ تَبْعَثُ عِبَادَكَ، اللّٰهُمَّ ارْزُقْنِي الْجَنَّةَ بِغَيْرِ حِسَابٍ.

ALLAḤUMMA INNAḤADHA AL BAYTA BAYTUK, OUA AL HARAMA HARAMUK WA AL AMNA AMNUK, WAL 'ABDA 'ABDUK WA ANA 'ABDUKA IBNU 'ABDIK, WA ḤADHA MAQAMU AL 'A 'IDHI BIKA MINA ANNAR.

ALLAHUMMA HAB 'BIB ILAYNA AL IMANA WA ZAYYENḤOU FI QOULOUBINA, WA KARRIḤ ILAYNA AL KUFRA WA AL FUSSUQA WA AL 'ICYAN WA AJ 'ALA'MINE ARRACHIDINE.

ALLAḤUMMA QINI ADHABAKA YAWAMA TAB' 'ATHU IBADAKA, ALLAḤUMMA ARZUQNI AL JAN-NATA BIGHAYRI HISSAB.

O Allah, verily this House is Thy House and this sanctuary is Thy sanctuary, and the peace here is Thy peace, and these creatures Thy servants. I am Thy servant and the son of Thy servant. This is an asylum for a person seeking Thy refuge from the Fire. For this render our flesh and faces unlawful unto the Fire.

O Allah, make the faith amiable unto us and prepare the same in our hearts. Render infidelity and iniquity and disobedience hateful unto us, and thereby cause us to walk in the right way.

O Allah, grant me deliverance from Thy chastisement on the day Thou shalt resurrect Thy servants. O Allah, grant me in the Garden provisions superabundantly.

Du'a Ashawt ath-Thalith
(Invocation for the third Round)

ALLAHUMMA INNI A OODHU BIKA MINA ACH SHAKKI, WA SHERKI WA ASH 'SHIQAQI WA AN NIFAQI WA SOU 'I AL MANDHARI, WA AL MOUNQA-LABI FI AL MALI WA AL AHLI WA AL WALADI.

ALLAHUMMA INNI AS ALUKA RIDHAKA WA AL JAN-NATA WA A 'AOODHU BIKA MIN SAKHTIKA WA ANNAR.

ALLAHUMMA INNI A 'OODHU BIKA MIN FITNATI AL QUABRI WA A 'OODHU BIKA MIN FITNATI AL MAHIA WAL MAMAT.

O Allah, I seek Thy refuge from doubt, idolatry, schism, hypo-crisy, insincerity, wrong thinking and inversion in respect of property, family and children.

O Allah, I seek Thy pleasure and the bliss of the Garden. I also seek Thy refuge from Thy anger and the torment of the Fire.

O Allah, I also seek Thy refuge from the trial of the grave and also from the ordeals of life and pangs of death.

بسم الله الرحمن الرحيم

وَلِلّٰهِ الأَسْمَاءُ الحُسْنَى فَادْعُوهُ بِهَا

هو الله الذي لا إله إلا هو

الرَّحْمٰن الرَّحِيم الملك القدُّوس السَّلام المؤمن المهيمن
العزيز الجبار المتكبر الخالق البارئ المصور الغفار
القهار الوهاب الرزاق الفتاح العليم القابض الباسط
الخافض الرافع المعز المذل السميع البصير الحكم
العدل اللطيف الخبير الحليم العظيم الغفور الشكور
العلي الكبير الحفيظ المقيت الحسيب الجليل الكريم
الرقيب المجيب الواسع الحكيم الودود المجيد الباعث
الشهيد الحق الوكيل القوي المتين الولي الحميد
المحصي المبدئ المعيد المحيي المميت الحي القيوم
الواجد الماجد الواحد الصمد القادر المقتدر المقدم المؤخر
الأول الآخر الظاهر الباطن الوالي المتعالي
البر التواب المنتقم العفو الرؤوف مالك الملك ذو الجلال والإكرام
المقسط الجامع الغني المغني المانع الضار النافع
النور الهادي البديع الباقي الوارث الرشيد الصبور

جل جلاله وتقدست أسماؤه

Du'a Ashawt Arrabi
(Invocation for the fourth Round)

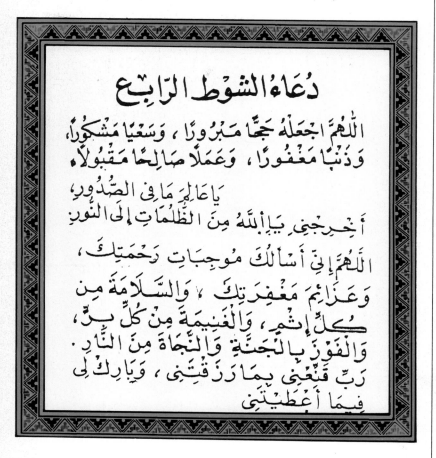

ALLAHUMMA AJ 'ALHU HAJJAN MABRURAN, WA SA 'YAN MACHKURAN, WA DHANBAN MAGHFURAN, WA 'AMALAN SALIHAN MAQBULAN.

YA 'ALIMA MA FI'S'SUDOOR, AKHREJNI MINA ADHU-LUMATI ILA ANNUR.

ALLAHUMMA INNI AS ALUKA MOOJIBATI RAHMA-TIKA, WA 'AZA 'IMA MAGH-FIRATIKA, WA ASSALA-MATA MIN KOLLI ITHMIN, WAL GHANEEMATA MINE KULLI BIRRIN, WA AL FAWZA BIL JANNATI WA AN NAJATA MIN ANNAR.

RABBI QANNI 'NI BIMA RAZAQTANI WA BAREK LI FI MA A 'TAITANI.

Allah, make this for me a righteous pilgrimage and an endeavour acceptable unto Thee and a means of forgiveness of sin, and also an act that is right and fit, and a merchandise that shall not perish.

O Thou who knowest the innermost parts of our hearts. Lead me, O Allah, out of the dark into the light.

O Allah, I implore Thee to grant me Thy mercy and Thy forgiveness, and to save me from every type of sin. And grant me an opportunity to reap all good and success leading to Paradise and deliverance from Hell.

O my Lord, make me such that I ever feel contented with what Thou hast bestowed upon me, and grant Thy bliss in whatever Thou hast given me.

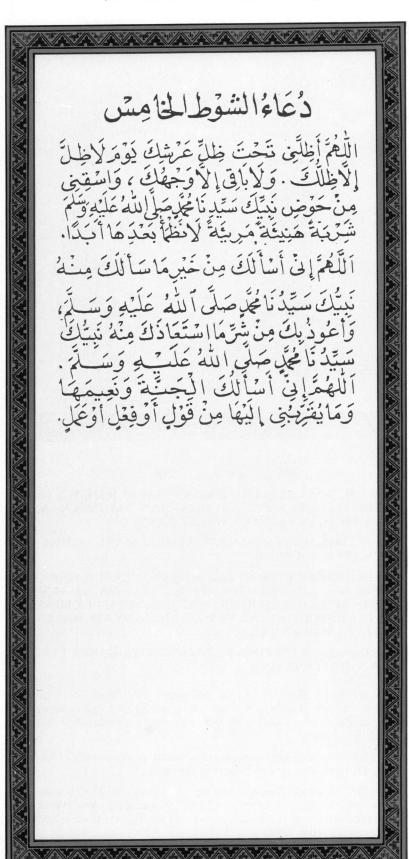

دُعَاءُ الشَّوْطِ الْخَامِس

اللّٰهُمَّ أَظِلَّنِى تَحْتَ ظِلِّ عَرْشِكَ يَوْمَ لَاظِلَّ إِلَّا ظِلُّكَ . وَلَا بَاقِىَ إِلَّا وَجْهُكَ ، وَاسْقِنِى مِنْ حَوْضِ نَبِيِّكَ سَيِّدِنَا مُحَمَّدٍ صَلَّى اللّٰهُ عَلَيْهِ وَسَلَّمَ شَرْبَةً هَنِيئَةً مَرِيئَةً لَا نَظَأُ بَعْدَهَا أَبَدًا. اللّٰهُمَّ إِنِّى أَسْأَلُكَ مِنْ خَيْرِ مَا سَأَلَكَ مِنْهُ نَبِيُّكَ سَيِّدُنَا مُحَمَّدٌ صَلَّى اللّٰهُ عَلَيْهِ وَسَلَّمَ، وَأَعُوذُ بِكَ مِنْ شَرِّ مَا اسْتَعَاذَكَ مِنْهُ نَبِيُّكَ سَيِّدُنَا مُحَمَّدٌ صَلَّى اللّٰهُ عَلَيْهِ وَسَلَّمَ. اللّٰهُمَّ إِنِّى أَسْأَلُكَ الْجَنَّةَ وَنَعِيمَهَا وَمَا يُقَرِّبُنِى إِلَيْهَا مِنْ قَوْلٍ أَوْ فِعْلٍ أَوْ عَمَلٍ.

ALLAHUMMA ADHILLANI TAHTA DHI'-LLI
'ARCHIKA, YAWMA LA DHILLA ILLA DHILLUK, WA
LA BAQI I LLA WAJHUK WA ASQINEEMIN HAWDHI
NABIYYIKA MUHAMMAD, SALLA ALLAHU ALAYHI
WA SALLAM, CHARBATAN HANIATAN MARI'ATAN
LA NADHMU BA'DAHA ABADA.

ALLAHUMMA INNI AS'ALUKA MIN KHAYRI MA
SA'ALAKA MINHU NABIYUKA SAYYIDINA MUHAM-
MAD SALLA ALLAHU ALAYHI WA SALLAM WA
A'OODHU BIKA MIN SHARRI MA ISTA 'ADHAKA
MINHU NABIYYUKA SAYYEDINA MUHAMMED SALLA
ALLAHU ALAYHI WA SALLAM.

ALLAHUMMA AS ALUKA AL JANNATA WA
NA'IMAHA WA MA YOU QARIBUNI ILAYHA MIN
QAWLIN AW FI'LIN AW'AMALIN.

*O Allah, take me under the shade of Thy Throne on the day
when there shall be no shade but Thine, and no survivor but Thy
face. Quench my thirst from the tank of Thy Prophet, our chief
Muhammed, may Allah send blessings and peace upon him, a
pleasant and wholesome draught whereafter I shall never again
feel thirst.*

*O Allah, I ask Thee for the best that Thy Prophet, our chief
Muhammed, asked Thee for. I also seek Thy refuge from evil
that the Prophet, our chief Muhammed, may Allah send blessings and peace on him, hath sought.*

*O Allah, I implore Thee to grant me Paradise and its delights
and all those things - actions, sayings or acts - which can bring
me nearer unto it.*

Du'a Ashawt Assadis
(Invocation for the sixth Round)

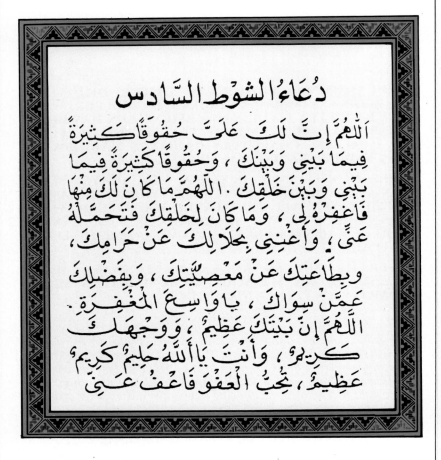

ALLAHUMMA INNA LAKA 'ALAYYA HUQOOQAN KATHEERATAN FIMA BAYNI WA BAYENAK, WA HUQOOQAN KATHEERATAN FI MA BAYNI WA BAYENA KHALQIKA.

ALLAH MA MA KANA LAKA MINHA FAGHFERHU LEE, WA MĀKĀNA LIKHALQIKA FATAHAMHALHU 'ANNI, WAGHINEE BIHALĀLIKA 'AN HARAMIK, WA BITA'ATIKA 'AN MA'SYATIK WA BIFADHLIKA 'AMMAN SIWAKA YA WASSI'A AL MAGHFIRAH.

ALLAHUMMA INNA BAYTAKA 'ADHIM WA WAJHUKA KARIM, WA ANTA YA ALLAHU HALIMUN, KARIMUN, ADHIMUN TUHIHŪ AL'AFWA FA'FOO ANNI.

O Allah, I owe Thee innumerable duties that concern Thee and me, and innumerable duties also that concern Thy creatures and me.

O Allah, acquit me of my debts towards Thee and acquit Thyself on my behalf of my duties towards Thy creatures.

O Allah, grant me that which is lawful and preserve me from the unlawful. Grant me the privilege of obedience unto Thee and save me from disobedience unto Thee. Grant me Thy grace rather than otherwise, O Thou Forgiver of all things.

O Allah, Thy House is great, Thy face is noble and Thou art, O Allah, Forbearing, Noble and Great. Thou who lovest forgiveness, forgive me.

Du'a Ashawt Assabi
(Invocation for the seventh Round)

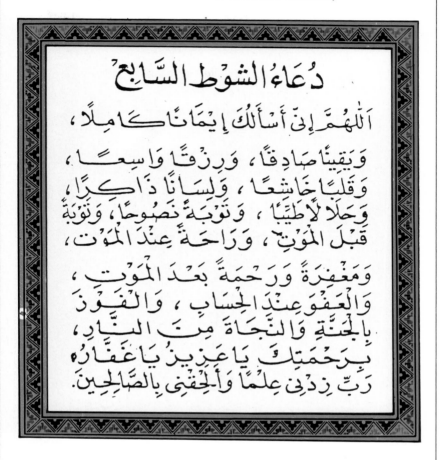

ALLAHUMMA INNI AS ALUKA IMANAN KĀMILAN, WA YAQEENAN SADIQAN, WA RIZQAN WASSI'AN, WA QALBAN KHĀCHI'AN, WA LISSĀNAN DHĀKIRAN, WA HALALAN, TAYEBAN, WA TAWBATAN NASSU-HAN, WA TAW BATAN QABLA AL MAWT, WA MAGH-FIRATAN WA RAHMATAN BA'DA AL MAWT, WA AL LAFWA 'INDA AL HISSAB, WA AL FAWZA BI-L-JANNATI WA ANNAJANATA MIN, ANNAR, BIRAHMA-TIKA YA AZIZ YA GHAFFAR.

RABBI ZIDNI 'ILMAN WA ALHEKNI BISSALIHIN.

O Allah, I implore Thee to bestow on me perfect faith, sincere belief, boundless provision, a humble heart, a tongue wont to mention Thy name, pleasant lawful things, true repentance, an opportunity to express contrition before death and satisfaction at the moment of death, forgiveness and mercy after death, and Thy forgiveness on the Day of Judgment.

O Thou Mighty, O Thou Merciful and Forgiving, grant me Paradise and preserve me from the Fire.

O my Lord, increase knowledge unto me and join me with the righteous.

Du‘a al-Multazam
(At the foot of the wall between
the Black Stone and the door of the Ka‘bah)

دُعَاءُ الْمُلْتَزَم

اَللّٰهُمَّ يَارَبَّ الْبَيْتِ الْعَتِيقِ اعْتِقْ رِقَابَنَا .
وَرِقَابَ آبَائِنَا وَأُمَّهَاتِنَا، وَإِخْوَانِنَا وَأَوْلَادِنَا مِنَ النَّارِ؛
يَاذَا الْجُودِ وَالْكَرَمِ، وَالْفَضْلِ وَالْمَنِّ، وَالْعَطَاءِ
وَالْإِحْسَانِ . اَللّٰهُمَّ أَحْسِنْ عَاقِبَتَنَا فِى الْأُمُورِ كُلِّهَا،
وَأَجِرْنَا مِنْ خِزْىِ الدُّنْيَا وَعَذَابِ الْآخِرَةِ .
اَللّٰهُمَّ إِنِّى عَبْدُكَ وَابْنُ عَبْدِكَ، وَاقِفٌ تَحْتَ بَابِكَ،
مُلْتَزِمٌ بِأَعْتَابِكَ، مُتَذَلِّلٌ بَيْنَ يَدَيْكَ، أَرْجُو
رَحْمَتَكَ وَأَخْشَى عَذَابَكَ يَا قَدِيمَ الْإِحْسَانِ .
اَللّٰهُمَّ إِنِّى أَسْأَلُكَ أَنْ تَرْفَعَ ذِكْرِى، وَتَضَعَ وِزْرِى،
وَتُصْلِحَ أَمْرِى، وَتُطَهِّرَ قَلْبِى، وَتُنَوِّرَ لِى فِى قَبْرِى،
وَتَغْفِرَ لِى ذَنْبِى، وَأَسْأَلُكَ الدَّرَجَاتِ الْعُلَى مِنَ الْجَنَّةِ. آمِينَ

**ALLAHUMMA YA RABBA AL BAYTI AL'ATIQ A 'TIQ
RIGABANA WA RIQĀBA ĀBAANA WA OMMAHATINA
WA IKHWANINA WA AWLADINA MIN AWWAR, YA
DHAL JOUDI WA AL KARAM, WAL FADHLI, WA AL
MANNI, WA AL 'ATA'I WAL IHSAN.**

**ALLAHUMMA ASHEN 'AQIBATANA FIL- OUMOURI
KULLIHA WA AJIRNA MIN KHIZYI ADDUNYA WA
ADHABI AL AKHIRAH.**

*O Allah, O Lord of the ancient House, save us and save our
parents, brothers and children from the Fire. O Thou whose
hospitality, generosity, grace and magnanimity are without
limits.*

*O Allah, make the end of all our affairs noble and grant us
refuge from the worldly disgrace and the torment of the hereafter.*

**ALLAHUMMA INNI 'ABDUKA WA BNU'ABDIKA,
WAQIFUN TAHTA BABIKA, MULTAZIMUN BI'ATA-
BIKA MOUTADHALLILUN BAYNA YADAYKA ARJU
RAHMATAKA, WA AKHSHA ADHABAKA, YA QADIMA
AL IHSAN.**

**ALLAHUMMA INNI AS'ALUKA AN TARFA'A DHIKRI
WA TADHA'A WIZRI WA TOSLIHA AMRI, WA TUTA-
HIRA QALBI WA TUNAWWIRA LI FI QABRI, AS ALUKA
ADDARAJATI AL 'ULA MIN AL JANNAH AMIN.**

*O Allah, I am Thy servant and the son of Thy servant, standing
underneath Thy Gate and holding Thy thresholds with full
humility in Thy presence. I hope to receive Thy mercy and I
dread the torment of Thy chastisement. O Thou art Eternal in
Thy benevolence.*

*O Allah, I implore Thee to raise my mention and to remove
from me my burden, to improve my affair, to purify my heart,
and to illuminate my grave for me, to pardon my sins and to
grant me lofty ranks in the Garden of Paradise. Amen.*

At the station
of Abraham

ALLAHUMMA, INNAKA TA'LAMU SIRRI WA ALA-
NIYATI FAQBAL MA'DHIRATI, WA TA'LAMU HAJATI
FA''TINI SO'ALI WA TA 'LAMU MA FI NAFSI FAGH-
FERLI DHUNOOBI ALLAHUMMA INNI AS'ALUKA IMA-
NAN YUBASHIROU QALBI WA YAQEENAN SADIQAN
HATTA A'LAMU ANNAHU LA YUSSEEBOONI ILLA
MAKATABTA LEE RIDHAN MINKA BIMA QASAMTA
LEE, ANTA WALLIYYI FIDDUNYA WA FIL AKHERAH,
TAWAFFANI MUSLIMAN WA ALHQNI BISSALIHEENA.

*O Allah, Thou knowest all my affairs, both hidden and mani-
fest, wherefore forgive me ! Thou knowest my need, wherefore
grant me that which I beseech. Thou knowest what is in my
innermost heart, wherefore forgive my sins.*

*O Allah, I ask Thee for the faith that shall busy my heart, and
for the sincere belief till I should know that no affliction shall
overtake me except what Thou hast writ for me. I also ask Thee
for contentment whereby I shall readily accept from Thee whatever Thou hast ordained for me. Thou art my Guardian both in
this world and the hereafter. Cause me to die a Muslim and join
me with the righteous.*

ALLAHUMMA LA TADA'LANA FI MAQĀMINA HADHA
DHANBAN ILLA GHAFARTAH, WA LA HAMMAN ILLA
FARRAJTAH, WA LA HAJATAN ILLA QADHAYTAHA
WA YASSERTAHA, FAYASSER OMOORANA, WA
ASH'REH SUDOORANA, WA NAWWER QULOOBANA,
WA'KHTEM BISSALIHATI A'MALANA.

ALLAHUMMA IHYINA MUSLIMEEN WA TAWAFFINA
MUSLIMEEN WA ALHIQUA BISSALIHEEN GHAYRA
KHAZAYA WA LA MAFTUNEEN.

*O Allah, leave not for us in this place of ours any sin but that
Thou hast forgiven it, nor any worry but that Thou hast dispelled it, nor any desire but that Thou hast satisfied it and hast
made its accomplishment easy for us. Make easy our affairs for
us, and enlarge our breasts, illuminate our hearts, and close our
deeds with the best ones.*

*O Lord, cause us to die Muslims, to live Muslims and join us
with the rigtheous - not disgraced and demented.*

At the Hijr Ismael

ALLAHUMMA ANTA RABBI LA ILAHA ANTA KHA-
LAQTANI WA ANA 'ABDUK, WA ANA 'ALA'AHDIKA
WA WA'DIKA MASTATA'TU, A 'UDHU BIKA MIN
SHARRI MA SANA'TU. ABU'OU LAKA BINI'MATIKA
'ALAYYA, WA ABU'OUBIDHANBI FAGHFER LEE, FA
INNAHU LA YAGHFIRU ADH'DHUNOOBA ILLA ANTA.

*O Allah, Thou art my lord. None is worthy of worship but
Thou. Thou hast created me and I am Thy servant, and I shall
keep my pact and covenant to the utmost I can. I seek Thy
refuge from the evil that I may commit. I return unto Thee with
Thy grace on to me and I acknowledge my sin, wherefore forgive me. For none doth forgive sins but Thou.*

ALLAHUMMA INNI AS'ALUKA MIN KHAYRI MA SA'ALAKA BIHI 'IBADUKA ASSALIHOON, WA A'UDHOU BIKA MIN SHARRI MA ISTA'ADHAKA MINHU 'IBADUKA ASSALIHOON.

ALLAHUMMA BI ASMA'IKA AL HUSNA WA SIFATIKA AL'OLYA TAHHIR QULOOBANA MIN KULLI WASFENE YOB'IDUNA 'AN MUSHAHADATIKA WA MAHABBA-TIKA WA AMITNA 'ALA AS'SUNNATI WA AL JAMA'ATI, WA ASH'SHAWQI ILA LIQA'IKA, YA DHA AL JALALI WA AL IKRAM.

O Lord, I ask Thee for the good that Thy righteous servants had asked Thee for. I also seek Thy refuge from evil that Thy pious servants had sought.

O Allah, I invoke Thee by Thy excellent Names and by the Lofty Attributes to purify our hearts from anything that might keep us from Thy vision and Thy love. Cause us to die acting on the practice of the Prophet and on the concensus of the Community, filled with desire to meet Thee, O possessed of Majesty and Glory.

**ALLAHUMA NAWWAR BIL 'ILMI QALBI, WASTA'MIL
BITA'ATIKA BADANI, WA KHALLIS MIN AL FITANI
SIRRI, WASHGHEL BIL I'TIBARI FIKRI WA QINI
SHARRA WASSAWISSI I'SHAYTAN WA AJIRNI MIN-
HUYA RAHMANU HATTA LA YAKUNA LAHU ALAYYA
SOLTAN.**

**RABBANA INNANA AMAN'NA, FAGHFIR LANA DHOU-
NUBANA WA QINA 'ADHABA ANNAR.**

*O Allah, make Thou my heart resplendent with knowledge,
employ Thou my body for Thy obedience, rid Thou my heart
from trials, and occupy Thou my mind with lofty thoughts.
Deliver me Thou from the mischief of devilish whisperers and
grant me refuge from Satan, O Lord, that he shall never have
power over me.*

*O Lord, I believe in Thee. Forgive me my sins and spare me
from the torments of the fire.*

Aŝŝafa du'a
Aŝŝafa invocation

Du'a Aŝŝafā
(Prayer to be recited
on the hill of Aŝ-Ŝafā)

ABDA' U BIMA BADA ALLAḤU WA RASSULUḤU, INNA AŜŜAFĀ WA AL MARWATA MIN SHA'AIRI ILLAḤI, FAMAN HAJJA AL BAÏTA AW I'TAMARA FALA JOU-NAHA ALAYḤI AN YATATAWAFA BIHIMA.

WA MAN TATAWA'A KHAYRAN FA INNA ALLAḤA SHAKIRUN 'ALIM.

I commence where Allah and his Messenger commenced. Verily, Aŝ-Ŝafā and Al-Marwah are rites prescribed by God. Whoso-ever therefore goes on pilgrimage to the House or visiteth it ('Umrah) does well to compass them both.
As for those who do so with a glad heart, they do so for their own good, for Allah is Grateful and All-Knowing.

Niyyat Assa'y
(Declaration of intention to perform the Sa'y)

**ALLAHUMMA INNI ORIDU AN AS'AA MA BAINA AŜ-
ŜAFĀ WA AL MARWATA-SAB'ATA ASHWATIN-SA'YA
AL HAJJ (or AL'UMRAH) LILLAHĪ AZZA WA JALLA,
YA RABBA AL 'ALAMIN.**

**ALLAHU AKBAR, ALLAHU AKBAR, ALLAHU AKBAR,
WA LILLAHI AL HAMD.**

*O Allah, I intend to perform the Sa'y between Aŝ-Ŝafā and Al-
Marwah in seven rounds for the Pilgrimage (or for the 'Umrah,
i.e., the lesser Pilgrimage) for the sake of Allah, who is Great,
Powerful and Mighty. O the Lord of all the worlds.*

The pilgrim then climbs up on the hillock of Aŝ-Ŝafā and says :

*Allah is the greatest, Allah is the greatest of all. Immense praise
is due to Allah. Allah the Great is free from all imperfections.
May He be praised.*

Du‘a Ashawt al-Awwal Min Assa‘y
(First lap of the rush
between Aŝ-Ŝafā and al-Marwah)

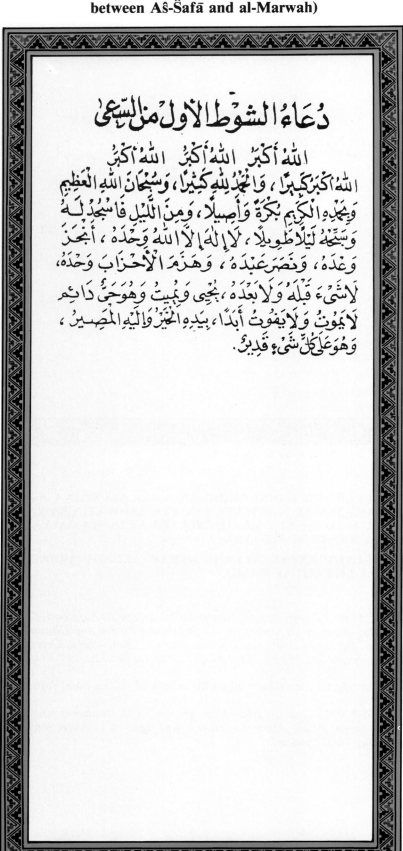

دُعَاءُ الشَّوْطِ الأوّلِ مِنَ السَّعْي

اللهُ أَكْبَرُ اللهُ أَكْبَرُ اللهُ أَكْبَرُ اللهُ أَكْبَرُ كَبِيرًا، وَالْحَمْدُ لِلهِ كَثِيرًا، وَسُبْحَانَ اللهِ الْعَظِيمِ وَبِحَمْدِهِ الْكَرِيمِ بُكْرَةً وَأَصِيلًا، وَمِنَ اللَّيْلِ فَاسْجُدْ لَهُ وَسَبِّحْهُ لَيْلًا طَوِيلًا، لَا إِلَهَ إِلَّا اللهُ وَحْدَهُ، أَنْجَزَ وَعْدَهُ، وَنَصَرَ عَبْدَهُ، وَهَزَمَ الْأَحْزَابَ وَحْدَهُ، لَاشَيْءَ قَبْلَهُ وَلَا بَعْدَهُ، يُحْيِى وَيُمِيتُ وَهُوَ حَيٌّ دَائِمٌ لَا يَمُوتُ وَلَا يَفُوتُ أَبَدًا، بِيَدِهِ الْخَيْرُ وَإِلَيْهِ الْمَصِيرُ، وَهُوَ عَلَى كُلِّ شَيْءٍ قَدِيرٌ.

ALLAHU AKBAR! ALLAHU AKBAR! ALLAHU AKBAR! ALLAHU AKBARU KABIRA, WAL HAMDU LILLAHI KATHIRA, WA SUBHANA ALLAHI AL 'ADHIMI WA BI HAMDIHI AL KARIMI BOKRATAN WA ASSILA, WA MINA AL LAYLI FASJUD LAHU WA SABBIHAHU LAY-LAN TAWEELA.

LA ILAHA ILLA ALLAHU WAHDAH, ANJAZA WA'DAH WA NASSARA 'ABDAH, WA HAZAMA AL AHZABA WAHDAH, LA SHAY'A QABLAH WA LA SHAY'A BA'DAH, YUHYI WA YOUMEET, WAHWA HAY'YUN DA'IMUN LA YAMOOT ABADAN, BIYADIHI AL KHAYRU WA ILAYHI ALMASSEER, WA HUWA 'ALA KULLI SHAI'EN QADEER.

Allah is the Greatest, Allah is the Greatest, Allah is the Greatest!

With praise unto Him who is Noble, both in the morning and in the evening. And during some part of the night, worship Him and glorify Him the livelong night!

None is worthy of worship but Allqh alone. He fulfilled His promise, helped His servant and routed the confederates by Himself.

Nothing existed before Him nor shall anything survive Him. He giveth life, putteth to death. He is the Eternal who does not die.

In His hand is good, and to Him shall come back everything at the last. He hath power over all things.

رَبِّ اغْفِرْ وَارْحَمْ، وَاعْفُ وَتَكَرَّمْ،
وَتَجَاوَزْ عَمَّا تَعْلَمُ، إِنَّكَ تَعْلَمُ مَا لَا نَعْلَمُ، إِنَّكَ أَنْتَ اللهُ الْأَعَزُّ الْأَكْرَمُ،
رَبَّنَا نَجِّنَا مِنَ النَّارِ سَالِمِينَ غَانِمِينَ، فَرِحِينَ مُسْتَبْشِرِينَ.
مَعَ عِبَادِكَ الصَّالِحِينَ، مَعَ الَّذِينَ أَنْعَمَ اللهُ عَلَيْهِمْ
مِنَ النَّبِيِّينَ وَالصِّدِّيقِينَ وَالشُّهَدَاءِ وَالصَّالِحِينَ،
، ذَلِكَ الْفَضْلُ مِنَ اللهِ وَكَفَى بِاللهِ عَلِيمًا.
لَا إِلَهَ إِلَّا اللهُ حَقًّا حَقًّا، لَا إِلَهَ إِلَّا اللهُ تَعَبُّدًا وَرِقًّا، لَا إِلَهَ
إِلَّا اللهُ، وَلَا نَعْبُدُ إِلَّا إِيَّاهُ، مُخْلِصِينَ لَهُ الدِّينَ وَلَوْ كَرِهَ
الْكَافِرُونَ. وَكُلَّمَا قَرُبَ مِنَ الْمَرْوَةِ قَرَأَ: إِنَّ الصَّفَا وَالْمَرْوَةَ
مِنْ شَعَائِرِ اللهِ، فَمَنْ حَجَّ الْبَيْتَ أَوِ اعْتَمَرَ فَلَا جُنَاحَ عَلَيْهِ
أَنْ يَطَّوَّفَ بِهِمَا، وَمَنْ تَطَوَّعَ خَيْرًا فَإِنَّ اللهَ شَاكِرٌ عَلِيمٌ.

RABBI IGHFIR WARHAM WA'FU WA TAKARRAM, WA TAJĀWAZ 'AMMA TA'LAME, INNAKA TA'LAMU MA LÂ NA'LAME, INNAKA ANTA ALLAĦU AL A'AZZOO AL AKRAM.

RABBANA NAJJINA MIN ANNAR, SALIMEENA GHANI-MEENA, FARIHEENA MOSTABSHIREEN MA'A 'IBA-DIKA ASSALIHIN MA'A ALLADHINA NA'AMA ALLAĦU ALAYĦEM MINA ANNABIYYINA WAS'SED-DEEQUEENA WA SHUĦADA'I WA ASSALIHEENA, DHALIKA AL FADHLU MIN ALLAĦI, WA KA FA BIL-LAĦI 'ALIMA.

LA ILAĦA ILLA ALLAĦ HAQ'QAN LA ILAĦA ILLA ALLAĦ TA'ABBUDAN WA RIQ'QAN, LA ILAĦA ILLA ALLAĦ LA NA'BUDU ILLA IYYAĦ MUKHLISSEENA LAĦU AD'DINA WA LAW KARIĦA AL KAFIROON.

Upon arriving at the top of the Al-Marwah hillock, the pilgrim must recite :

INNA ASSAFA WAL MARWATA MIN SHA'A'IR ILLAH FA MAN HAJJA ALBAÏTA AW I'TAMARA FALA JUHANA ALAIĦI AN YATATAWWAFA BIĦIMA WA MAN TATAWWA, A KHAYRAN FA INNA ALLAĦA SHA-KIRUN 'ALIM.

O my Lord, forgive me and have mercy on me, pardon and do good unto me. Pass off my sins of which Thou art aware. Thou art indeed the Most Powerful, the Most noble.

O my Lord, deliver me from the torment of the Fire, granting me the success and the happiness that Thou granteth Thy right-eous servants. Lord, let me be among the number of those that Thou hast fully rewarded, the Prophets, the faithful, the martyrs and the righteous. These are most excellent company. This is the bounty from Allah, and Allah knoweth all things.

There is none worthy of worship except Allah; indeed, only He must be adored. There is none worthy of worship except Allah and we offer sincere worship unto none but Him, though the infidels abdhor it.

Aŝ-Ŝafā and Al-Marwah are rites prescribed by God. He who goes on pilgrimage to the House or visiteth it ('Umrah) does well to compass them both. As for those who do it with a glad heart, they do so for their own good, for Allah is Grateful and All-Knowing.

Du‘a Ashawt ath-Thani Mine Assa‘y
(Second lap of the Sa‘y,
going from Al-Marwah to Aŝ-Ŝafā)

دُعَاءُ الشَّوْطِ الثَّانِى مِنَ السَّعْىِ

اللهُ اكْبَرُ اللهُ اكْبَرُ اللهُ اكْبَرُ وَلِلهِ الْحَمْدُ، لَا اِلهَ اِلَّا اللهُ الْوَاحِدُ الْفَرْدُ الصَّمَدُ، الَّذِى لَمْ يَتَّخِذْ صَاحِبَةً وَلَا وَلَدًا وَلَمْ يَكُنْ لَهُ شَرِيكٌ فِى الْمُلْكِ، وَلَمْ يَكُنْ لَهُ وَلِىٌّ مِنَ الذُّلِّ، وَكَبِّرْهُ تَكْبِيرًا. اللّهُمَّ اِنَّكَ قُلْتَ فِى كِتَابِكَ الْمُنْزَلِ، "ادْعُونِى اسْتَجِبْ لَكُمْ". دَعَوْنَاكَ رَبَّنَا فَاغْفِرْلَنَا كَمَا اَمَرْتَنَا اِنَّكَ لَا تُخْلِفُ الْمِيعَادَ

ALLAHU AKBAR! ALLAHU AKBAR! ALLAHU AKBAR! WA LIL'LAHI AL HAMD, LA ILAHA ILLA ALLAH AL WAHIDU AL FARDU ASSAMADU ALLADHI LAM YAT-TAKHIDH SAHIBATAN WA LA WALADAN, WA LAM YAKON LAHU SHAREEKUN FIL MULK WA LAM YAKUN LAHU WALIYUN MINA ADHOULA, WAKABBI-RHU TAKBIRA.

ALLAHUMMA INNAKA QOLTA FI KITABIKA AL MUNAZZAL "ID UNI ASTAJIB LAKUM". DA AWNAKA RABBANA FAGHFIR LANA KAMA AMARTA NA INNAKA LA TUKHLIFU AL MI'ADE.

There is none worthy of worship except Allah the Solitary, the One, the Single, the eternally-besought of all, who hath taken no spouse, nor hath He begotten any offspring, nor hath any partner in the kingdom of Heaven and Earth, nor hath any to Protect Him from contempt. Magnify Him by pronouncing His greatness.

O Allah, verily Thou hast said in Thy revealed Book: Call upon me - I will harken unto you. We call upon Thee. O our Lord, forgive us then, as Thou hast proclaimed. Verily, Thou wilt not fail Thy promise!

رَبَّنَا إِنَّنَا سَمِعْنَا مُنَادِيًا يُنَادِى لِلْإِيمَانِ أَنْ آمِنُوا بِرَبِّكُمْ فَآمَنَّا، رَبَّنَا فَاغْفِرْ لَنَا ذُنُوبَنَا، وَكَفِّرْ عَنَّا سَيِّئَاتِنَا، وَتَوَفَّنَا مَعَ الْأَبْرَارِ. رَبَّنَا وَآتِنَا مَا وَعَدْتَنَا عَلَى رُسُلِكَ، وَلَا تُخْزِنَا يَوْمَ الْقِيَامَةِ إِنَّكَ لَا تُخْلِفُ الْمِيعَادَ. رَبَّنَا عَلَيْكَ تَوَكَّلْنَا، وَإِلَيْكَ أَنَبْنَا، وَإِلَيْكَ الْمَصِيرُ. رَبَّنَا اغْفِرْ لَنَا وَلِإِخْوَانِنَا الَّذِينَ سَبَقُونَا بِالْإِيمَانِ، وَلَا تَجْعَلْ فِى قُلُوبِنَا غِلًّا لِلَّذِينَ آمَنُوا، رَبَّنَا إِنَّكَ رَءُوفٌ رَحِيمٌ.

RABBANA INNANA SAMI'NA MUNADIYAN YUNADEE LIL EAMAN AN AMINU BIRABBIKUM, FA ĀMANNĀ, RABBANA, FAGH'FER LANA DHUNUBANA, WA KAFFIR 'ANNA SAYYE'ATINA WA TAWAFFANA MA'A AL ABRAR. RABBANA WA Ā'TINA MĀ WA'ADTANA 'ALA RUSSULIKA WA LA TUKHZINA YAWMA AL QIYĀMATI INNAKA LA TUKHLIFU AL MI'AD .

RABBANA 'ALAYKA TAWWAKALNA WA ILAYKA ANABNA, WA ILAYKA AL MASSEER. RABBANA IGHFER LANA WA LI IKHWANINA ALLADHINA SABAQUNA BIL EAMAN, WA LA TAJ'AL FI QULUBINA GHILLAN. LIL'LADHINA AMANU RABANA INNAKA RAOUFUN RAHEEM.

O our Lord, we have indeed heard of a preacher inviting us to the faith: 'Believe on your Lord'. And we have believed; therefore our Lord, forgive us our sins and expiate our evil deeds from us, and cause us to die with the righteous. O our Lord, give us also the reward which Thou hast promised us by Thine Apostles and put us not to shame on the day of resurrection, for Thou art not contrary to the promise.

O our Lord, in Thee do we trust and unto Thee do we turn. And before Thee shall we be assembled hereafter. O our Lord, forgive us and our brethren who have preceded us in the faith, and put not into hearts ill-will against those who believe.

O our Lord, verily Thou art Compassionate and Merciful.

RABBI IGHFER WARHAM, WA'FOU WA TAKARRAM, WA TAJĀWAZ 'AMMA TA'LAM INNAKA TA'LAMU MA LA NA'LAM; INNAKA ANTA ALLAHU AL'AZZU AL AKRAM.

INNA ASSAFA WAL MARWATA MIN CHA'ARI ILLAH FA MAN HAJJA AL BAYTA AW I'TAMARA FA LA JUNAHA ALAYHI AN YATTAWWAFA BIHIMA, WAMAN TATAWWA 'A KHAYRAN FA INNA ALLAHA SHAKIRUN 'ALIM.

O our Lord, make our light perfect and forgive us, for Thou hast power over all things.

Upon reaching the hillock of Aŝ-Ŝafā, the pilgrim says:

Aŝ-Ŝafā and Al-Marwah are rites prescribed by God. Whosoever goes on pilgrimage to the House or visiteth it ('Umrah) does well to compass them both. As for those who do it with a glad heart, they do so for their own good, for Allah is Grateful and All-Knowing.

Du'a Ashawt ath-Thalith
(Third lap of the Sa'y, going from Aŝ-Ŝafā to Al-Marwah)

دُعَاءُ الشَّوْطِ الثَّالِثِ مِنَ السَّعْيِ

اللهُ أَكْبَرُ اللهُ أَكْبَرُ اللهُ أَكْبَرُ وَلِلَّهِ الْحَمْدُ، رَبَّنَا أَتْمِمْ لَنَا نُورَنَا، وَاغْفِرْ لَنَا إِنَّكَ عَلَى كُلِّ شَيْءٍ قَدِيرٌ، اللَّهُمَّ إِنِّي أَسْأَلُكَ الْخَيْرَ كُلَّهُ، عَاجِلَهُ وَآجِلَهُ، وَأَسْتَغْفِرُكَ لِذَنْبِي، وَأَسْأَلُكَ رَحْمَتَكَ يَا أَرْحَمَ الرَّاحِمِينَ رَبِّ اغْفِرْ وَارْحَمْ، وَاعْفُ وَتَكَرَّمْ، وَتَجَاوَزْ عَمَّا تَعْلَمُ، إِنَّكَ تَعْلَمُ مَا لَا نَعْلَمُ، إِنَّكَ أَنْتَ اللهُ الْأَعَزُّ الْأَكْرَمُ.

ALLAĦU AKBAR, ALLAĦU AKBAR ALLAĦU AKBAR. WA LILLAĦI AL HAMD.

RABBANA ATMIM LANA NOYRANA, WA AGHFER LANA INNAKA ALA KULLI SHAYINE QADEER. ALLAĦUMMA INNI ASALOUKA AL KHAYRA KULLAHU ĀJILAĦU WA ĀJILAĦU, WA AS TAGHFIRUKA LIDHANBI, WA AS ALUKA RAHMATAKA YA ARHAMA ARRAHIMEEN.

RABBI IGHFIR WAR HAM WA 'FOU WA TAKARRAM WA TAJĀWAZ 'AMMA TA LAM, INNAKA TA'LAMU MALA NA 'LAM, INNAKA ANTA ALLAĦU AL A 'AZZU AL AKRAM.

Allah is the Greatest, Allah is the Greatest, Allah is the Greatest. Praises be unto Allah.

O Lord, show us the way and forgive us. Thou art the All-Powerful!

O Allah, I beg of Thee all good that may come soon or late. I also seek Thy refuge from all evil, imploring Thy forgiveness and beseeching Thy mercy.

O my Lord forgive us and grant us Thy indulgence, Thy grace. Be Thou generous and forgive us all which Thou knowest. O Thou who knowest that which we know not. For verily Thou art the All-Powerful and He who giveth.

رَبِّ زِدْنِي عِلْمًا ،
وَلَا تُزِغْ قَلْبِي بَعْدَ إِذْ هَدَيْتَنِي . وَهَبْ لِي مِنْ لَدُنْكَ رَحْمَةً
إِنَّكَ أَنْتَ الْوَهَّابُ . اَللَّهُمَّ عَافِنِي فِي سَمْعِي وَبَصَرِي ،
لَا إِلٰهَ إِلَّا أَنْتَ . اَللَّهُمَّ إِنِّي أَعُوذُ بِكَ مِنْ عَذَابِ الْقَبْرِ .
لَا إِلٰهَ إِلَّا أَنْتَ سُبْحَانَكَ إِنِّي كُنْتُ مِنَ الظَّالِمِينَ . اَللَّهُمَّ إِنِّي
أَعُوذُ بِكَ مِنَ الْكُفْرِ وَالْفَقْرِ . اَللَّهُمَّ إِنِّي أَعُوذُ بِرِضَاكَ
مِنْ سَخَطِكَ ، وَبِمُعَافَاتِكَ مِنْ عُقُوبَتِكَ ،

**RABBI ZIDNI 'ILMAN WA LA TUZIGH QALBI BA'DA
IDH HADAYTANI, WA HABLI MIN LADUNKA RAHMA-
TAN INNAKA ANTA AL WAHAB.
ALLAHUMMA A 'FINI FI SAM'I WA FI BASSARI, LA
ILAHA ILLA ANTA.
ALLAHUMMA INNI A ODHU BIKA MIN LADHABIL
QABRI. LA ILAHA ILLA ANTA SOBHANA KA INNI
KUNTU MIN ADH DHALIMEENE.
ALLAHUMMA INNI A ODHU BIKA MIN AL KUFRI WAL
FAQR.
ALLAHUMMA INNI A ODHU BIRIDHAKA MIN SAKH-
TIKA WA BIMU 'AFATIKA MIN KUBATIKA.**

*O Lord! Increase my knowledge, and do not cause my heart to
go astray once Thou hast guided me. Bestow upon me a grace
issued from Thee, for Thou art verily the dispenser of all good
things.*

*O Lord! Protect my hearing and my sight. There is no other God
than Thou.*

*O Lord! I seek refuge in Thee against the punishment of the
tomb. There is no divinity save Thyself, be Thou exalted! For
verily I have been among the unjust.*

O Lord! I seek refuge in Thee against loss of faith and property.

*O Lord! I seek refuge in Thee and Thy satisfaction, and against
Thy wrath, in Thy indulgence and against Thy punishment.*

INNA ASSAFA WA AL MARWATA MIN SHA ARI
ALLAH. FAMAN HAJJA AL BAITA AW I 'TAMARA
FALA JUNAHA ALAYHI AN YATAWWAFA BIHIMA,
WA MANE TATAWA A KHAYRANE FA INNA ALLAHA
SHAKIRUN ALIM.

Verily aŝ-Ŝafā and Al-Marwah are rites prescribed by God.
Whosoever goes on pilgrimage to the House or visiteth it
(Ùmrah) does well to compass them both. As for those who do it
for their own good, Allah is Grateful and All-Knowing.

Ashawt ar-Rabi'
(Fourth lap of the Sa'y,
going from Al-Marwah to Aŝ-Ŝafā)

ALLAĦU AKBAR, ALLAĦU AKBAR, ALLAĦU AKBAR, WA LILLAĦI AL HAMD.

ALLAĦUMMA INNI AS ALUKA MIN KHAYRI MA TA'LAMU, WA ALODHU BIKA MIN SHARRI MA TA'LAM. WAS TAGHFIRUKA MIN KULLI MA TA'LAM, INNAKA 'ALLAMU AL GHUYUB.

LA ILAĦA ILLA ALLAĦ, AL MALIKU AL HAQUAL MOUBIN MUHAMMADUN RASSULUL LAHI ASSIDIKU AL WA'DI AL'AMIN.

ALLAĦUMMA INNI AS ALUKA KAMA ĦADAYTANI LIL ISLAM ALLA TANZA'AHU MINNI HATTA TATAWWA-FANI WA ANA MUSLIM.

Allah is the Greatest, Allah is the Greatest, Allah is the Greatest. Praises unto Allah.

O Allah, only Thou knowest the future. Grant me the best of that which Thou knowest. I seek in Thee a refuge against the worst which Thou knowest. I ask Thy forgiveness.

There is no other god than Allah! The Unique, the All-Powerful. Muhammed the sincere, the faithful, is His Messenger.

O Allah, I beseech Thee not to tear off from me the faith of Islam as Thou hast guided me unto it, till Thou causest me to die a Muslim.

ALLAHUMMA IJ'AL FI QALBI NOORAN, WA FI SAM'I NOORAN WA FI BASSARI NOORAN.

ALLAHUMMA ISHRAH LI SADRI WA YASSER LI AMRI WA A'ODHU BIKA MIN SHARRI WASSAWISSI AS SADRI WA SHATATI AL AMRI WA FITNATI AL QABRI. QABRI.

SOBHANAKA MA 'ABADNAKA HAQQA 'IBADATIKA YA ALLAH, SOBHANAKA MA DHAKARNAKA HAQQA DHIKRIKA YA ALLAH.

O Allah, cast in my heart a light, in my ear a light and in my eyes a light. O Allah, enlarge my breast and make my task easier for me.

I betake myself for refuge to Thee against the mischief of the temptations of the heart and against the trials of the grave.

Glory be unto Thee, O Lord. We have not been able to worship Thee in a manner worthy of Thy worship, O Allah, nor have we glorified Thee as Thou deservest.

RABBI IGHFIR WARHAM WA'FU WATAKARRAM WA
TAJĀWAZ. 'AMMA TA'LAM, INNAKA TA'LAMU MA
LA NA'LAM. INNAKA ANTA AL A'ZZU AL AKRAMU.

INNA ASSAFA WAL MARWATA MIN SHA'AIRI ILLAH
FA MAN HAJJA AL BAITA AW I'TAMARA FALA
JUNAHA ALAYHI AN YATATAWWAFA BIHIMA, WA
MAN TATAWWA 'A KHAYRRAN FA INNA ALLAHA
SHAKIRUN 'ALIM.

*O Lord, forgive us and be indulgent unto us. Grant us Thy grace
and be Thou generous. Forgive us all that Thou knowest, Thou
who knowest all that we know not. Thou art the All-Powerful
and the most Generous.*

*Aŝ-Ŝafā and Al-Marwah are rites prescribed by God. Whoso-
ever makes a pilgrimage to the House or visiteth it ('Umrah)
does well to compass them both. As for those who do it with a
glad heart, they do so for their own good, for Allah is Grateful
and All-Knowing.*

Du'a Ashawt al-Khamis
(Invocation of the fifth lap from Aŝ-Ŝafā to al-Marwah)

ALLAĤU AKBAR, ALLAĤU AKBAR, ALLAĤU AKBAR, WA LILLAĤI L'HAMMD.

SOBHANAKA MA SHAKARNAKA HAQQA SHUUKRIKA YA ALLAĤ SOBHANAKA MA A 'LA SHA'NAKA YA ALLAĤ.

ALLAĤUMMA HABBIB ILAYNA AL EAMANA WA ZAYYENHU FI QULUBINA WA KARRE Ĥ ILAYNA AL KUFRA WAL FUSSUQA WAL 'ISYAN, WAJ 'ALNA MINA ARRACHIDEEN.

Allah is Great, Allah is Great, Allah is Great, Glory be to Allah.

O Lord, we have not been able to worship Thee in a manner worthy of Thy worship, O Allah. Glory be unto Thee.

O Allah, make the faith amiable unto us and prepare the same in our hearts, and render infidelity, iniquity and disobedience hateful unto us, and thereby reckon us among those Thou hast enlightened.

RABBI IGHFIR WARHAM, WA 'FU WA TAKRRAM WA TAJĀWAZ 'AMMA TA 'LAM INNAKA TA 'LAMU MA LA NA 'LAM, INNAKA ANTA ALLAḤU AL A'AZZU AL AKRAM.

ALLAḤUMMA QINEE ADHABAKA YAWMA TAB'ATHU IBADAKA.

ALLAḤUMMA IḤDINI BIL HOUDA, WA NAQQINEE BITTAQWA, WAGHFIRLEE FIL'AKHIRA WAL ULA.

ALLAḤUMMA IBSIT ALAYNA MIN BARAKĀTIKA, WA RAHMATIKA WA FADHLIKA, WA RIZQIKA.

ALLAḤUMMA INNEE AS'ALUKA ANNA 'IMA AL MUKEEMA ALLADHI LA YAHULU WA LA YAZULU ABADAN.

O Lord, forgive us and be Thou indulgent. Grant us Thy grace and be Thou generous. Forgive us all that Thou knowest, Thou who knowest that which we know not.

Thou art the most Powerful and the most Generous.

O Allah, deliver us from Thy punishment on the day when Thou shalt resurrect Thy servants. O Allah, may the faith guide me. Cleanse my soul by virtue of the faith and forgive me in this world and the next.

O Allah, I beg of Thee Thy blessing, Thy mercy, Thy grace and Thy generosity.

O Allah, I ask of Thee eternal and infinite bliss.

ALLAHUMMA IJ'AL FEE QALBEE NURAN WA FE NAF-SEE NURAN. RABBI ISHRAH LEE SADREE, WA YASSER LEE AMREE.

INNA ASSAFA WAL MARWATA MIN SHA 'ARI LLAH, FA MAN HAJJA AL BAÏTA AW I'TAMARA FALA JUNAHA ALAYHI AN YATATAWWAFA BIHIMA WA MAN TATAWWA'A KHAYRAN FA INNA ALLAHA SHA-KIRUN 'ALEEM.

O Allah, illuminate my heart, my soul and all my being. O Lord, relieve my heart and make my task easier.

Aṣ-Ṣafā and Al-Marwah are rites prescribed by God. He who goes on a pilgrimage to the House or visiteth it (makes 'Umrah) does well to compass them both. He who does so with a glad heart is acting for his own good, for God is Grateful and All-Knowing.

Du'a Ashawt As-Sadis
(Invocation of the sixth lap
from Al-Marwah to As-Safā)

دُعَاءُ الشَّوْطِ السَّادِسِ مِنَ السَّعْيِ

اللهُ أَكْبَرُ اللهُ أَكْبَرُ اللهُ أَكْبَرُ وَلِلّٰهِ الْحَمْدُ . لَا إِلٰهَ إِلَّا اللهُ وَحْدَهُ ، صَدَقَ وَعْدَهُ ، وَنَصَرَ عَبْدَهُ ، وَهَزَمَ الْأَحْزَابَ وَحْدَهُ ، لَا إِلٰهَ إِلَّا اللهُ ، وَلَا نَعْبُدُ إِلَّا إِيَّاهُ ، مُخْلِصِينَ لَهُ الدِّينَ وَلَوْ كَرِهَ الْكَافِرُونَ ، اللّٰهُمَّ إِنِّي أَسْأَلُكَ الْهُدَى وَالتُّقَى ، وَالْعَفَافَ وَالْغِنَى . اللّٰهُمَّ لَكَ الْحَمْدُ كَالَّذِي نَقُولُ ، وَخَيْرًا مِمَّا نَقُولُ .

ALLAHU AKBAR, ALLAHU AKBAR, ALLAHU AKBAR, WA LILLAHI AL HAMD.

LA ILAHA ILLA ALLAH WAHDHAH. SADAQA WA'DAH, WA NASSARA 'ABDAH, WA HAZAMA AL AHZABA WAHDAH. LA ILAHA ILLA ALLAH WA LA NA 'BUDU ILLA IYYAH MUKHLISEENA LAHU EDDEENA WA LAW KARIHA AL KAFIRUN.

ALLAHUMMA INNEE AS 'AL UKA AL HODA WA ATTUQA, WAL 'AFAFA WAL GHINA.

ALLAHUMMA LAKA AL HAMDU KALLADHI NAQUL, WA KHAYRAN MIMMA NAQUL.

Allah is the Greatest, Allah is the Greatest, Allah is the Greatest. Praises be unto God.

Allah is the Only God. He has been true to His promise. He has helped His servant and given strength to his troops, and routed the Confederates Himself.

There is none worthy of worship save Allah. He hath no partner. We worship Him with a sincere faith, despite the miscreants.

O Allah, I ask Thee for faith, piety, purity and opulence. All praises be unto Thee and more besides.

ALLAHUMMA INNEE AS'ALUKA RIDHAKA WAL JAN-NAH, WA A'ODHU BIKA MIN SAKHTIKA WA ANNARI, WA MA YUQARRIBUNEE ILAYHA MIN QAWLIN AW FI'LIN AW'AMALIN.

ALLAHUMMA BI NURIKA IHTADAYNA WA BI FADH-LIKA ISTAGHNAYNA, WA FI KANAFIKA, WA IN'AMIKA, WA 'ATA-IKA, WA ISHANIKA, AS'BAHNA WA AMSAYNA. ANTA AL AWWALU FALA QABLAKA SHAY'ON, WAL AKHIRU FALA BA'DAKA SHAY'ON, WA ADHA'HIRU FALA SHAY'A FAWQAK, WAL BATINU FALA SHAY'A DUNAK. NA 'ODHU BIKA MIN AL FALASSI, WAL KASSALI, WA 'ADHABA AL QABRI, WA FITNATA AL GHINA WA NAS'ALUKA AL FAWZA BIL JANNAH.

O Allah, truly I seek Thy satisfaction as I seek Paradise. I seek refuge in Thee from Thy Wrath and Thy Fire, and from whatever draweth me nearer to it whether by word, deed or action.

O Allah, Thy light guides us. Thy generosity, Thy gifts and Thy grace are showered upon us night and day. We need naught other than Thou alone.

Thou art He whom nothing precedes and after which nothing succedes. Thou art the known beyond whom there is nothing, and the hidden without whom nothing can be accomplished.

We seek in Thee a refuge against failure, against sloth, against vanity and the trial of the grave.

We implore Thee to grant us Paradise.

RABBI IGHFIR WARHAM, WA 'FU WA TAKARRAM, WA TAJĀWAZ 'AMMA TA 'LAM, INNAKA TA 'LAMU MA LA NA 'LAM, INNAKA ANTA AL A'AZU AL AKRAM.

INNA ASSAFĀ WAL MARWATA MIN SHA'ARI ILLAĤ, FA MAN HAJJA AL BAYTA AW I'TAMARA FALA JUNAHA ALAYĤI AN YATATAWWAFA BIĤIMA, WA MAN TATAWWA'A KHAYRAN FA INNA ALLAĤA SHA-KIRUN 'ALEEM.

Our Lord, forgive us and be Thou indulgent. Grant us Thy grace and be Thou generous. Forgive us that which Thou knowest, Thou who knowest all that which is hidden. Thou art the All-Powerful and the most Generous.

Aŝ-Ŝafā and Al-Marwah are rites prescribed by God. He who goes on a pilgrimage to the House or visiteth it (make 'Umrah) does well to compass them both.

He who does so with a glad heart is acting for his own good, for God is Grateful and All-Knowing.

Du'a Ashawt As-Sabi 'Wal Akhir
(Invocation of the seventh and the last lap from Aŝ-Ŝafā to Al-Marwah)

ALLAĦU AKBAR, ALLAĦU AKBAR, ALLAĦU AKA-BARU KABIRA, WAL HAMDU LI LLAĦI KATHIRA.

ALLAĦUMMA HABBIB ILAYNA AL EAMANE WA ZAYYENĦOU FI QULUBINA, WA KARREH ILAYNA AL KOFRA WA FUSUKA WA 'ISYAN, WAJ'ALNI MIN ARRACHIDEEN.

RABBI IGHFIR WARHAM, WA 'FU WA TAKARRAM, WA TAJAWAZ 'AMMA TA'LAM, INNAKA TA'LAM MA LA NA'LAM.
INNAKA ANTA ALLAĦU AL A'AZOU AL AKRAM.

Allah is the Greatest, Allah is the Greatest, Allah is the Greatest, all praises unto Him.

O Allah, make us love our faith and cause us to magnify it in our hearts. Make us hate godlessness, debauchery and disobedience. Guide us on the right path.

Our Lord, forgive us and be Thou indulgent, grant us Thy grace and be Thou magnanimous. Forgive us that which Thou knowest, Thou who knowest that which is hidden from us.

Thou art the All-Powerful and the most Generous.

ALLAĦUMMA IKHTIM BIL KHAYRATI ĀJĀLANA, WA HAQQIQ BI FADHLIKA MALANA, WA SAĦĦIL LIBU-LUGHI RIDHAKA SUBWALANA, 'WA HASIN FI JAMEE'I AL AHWALI Ā MALANA, YA MUNQIDHA AL GHARQA, YA MUNJJIYA AL HALKA YA HÂĦIDA KOLLI SHAKWA YA QADEEMA AL ISHAN YA DAIMA AL MA'ROUF, YA MAN LA GHINA BISHAY 'EN 'ANĦ WA LĀBUDDA LI KULLI SHAY'EN MINĦU YA MAN RIZQU KULLI SHAY'EN ALAYHI, WA MASIRU KULLI SHAY'EN ILAYĦI.

O Allah, give Thou a happy ending to my existence. Grant that my hopes be fulfilled by Thy grace. Ease Thou for me the path that leadeth to Thy satisfaction. Improve my actions in all circumstances.

O Thou who savest the drowning man and all those who are in peril.

O Thou witness of all secrets, I turn unto Thee from whence cometh all comfort, Thou whose generosity is eternal, whose favour is infinite.

Thou art the Irreplaceable, the Indispensable. All things depend on Thy will and all destinies are accountable unto Thee.

ALLAHUMMA INNEE 'AIDHUN BIKA MIN SHARRI MA
A'TAYTANA, WA MIN SHARRI MA MANA'TANA.

ALLAHUMMA TAWAFFANA MUSLIMEENA WA
ALHIQNA BISSALIHEEN GHAYRA KHAZAYA WA LA
MAFTUNEEN RABBI YASSER WA LA TU'ASSIR, RABBI
ATMIM BILLKHAYR.

INNA ASSAFA WAL MARWATA MIN SHA'AIRILLAHI
FA MAN HAJJA AL BAITA AW I'TAMARA FA LA
JUNAHA ALAYHI AN YATATAWWAFA BIHIMA, WA
MAN TATAWWA'A KHAYRAN FA INNA ALLAHA
SHAKIRUN 'ALEEM.

*O Allah, I seek refuge with Thee from affliction and from all
that Thou forbids us.*

*O Allah, grant that I shall die a Muslim and shall join the
righteous - not disgraced and demented.*

*O my Lord, make this easy for me, and make it turn out as it
should.*

*Verily Aṣ-Ṣafā and Al-Marwah are rites prescribed by God.
Whosoever goeth on pilgrimage to the House or visiteth (for
'Umrah) does well to compass them both. As for him who does
it with a glad heart, he does himself good for God is Grateful
and All-Knowing.*

Du'a Taman Assa'y
(Invocation to be recited
at the close of the deambulation)

دُعَاءٌ بَعْدَ تَمَامِ السَّعْيِ

رَبَّنَا تَقَبَّلْ مِنَّا ، وَعَافِنَا وَاعْفُ عَنَّا ،
وَعَلَى طَاعَتِكَ وَشُكْرِكَ أَعِنَّا ،

وَعَلَى غَيْرِكَ لَا تَكِلْنَا ، وَعَلَى الْإِيمَانِ
وَالْإِسْلَامِ الْكَامِلِ جَمِيعًا نَوِّفْنَا وَأَنْتَ
رَاضٍ عَنَّا . اللَّهُمَّ ارْحَمْنِي بِتَرْكِ الْمَعَاصِي

مَا أَبْقَيْتَنِي ، وَارْحَمْنِي أَنْ أَتَكَلَّفَ
مَا لَا يَعْنِينِي ، وَارْزُقْنِي حُسْنَ النَّظَرِ ،
فِيمَا يُرْضِيكَ عَنِّي يَا أَرْحَمَ الرَّاحِمِينَ .

RABBANA TAQABBAL MINNA WA 'AFFINA, WA
A'FU'ANNA, WA 'ALA TAA'ATIKA WA SHUKRIKA
A'INNA, WA ALA GHAYRIKA, LA TAKELNA WA 'ALA
AL EAMANI, WAL ISLAMI AL KĀMILI JAMEE'AN
TAWWAFA WA ANTA RADHIN 'ANNA.
ALLAĤUMMA, IRHAMNI BI TARKI AL MA'ASEA MA
ABQAYETANI WA ARHMANI AN ATAKALLAFA MA LA
YA'NEANI WA ARZUQNEE HUSNA ANNADHARI,
FEEMA YORDHEAKA 'ANNI YA ARHAMA ARRAHI-
MEEN.

*O our Lord, accept this from us, and preserve us, and forgive
us. Grant us Thy aid for obedience and gratefulness unto Thee.
Entrust us not to anyone other than Thyself. Cause us to die
believers and perfect Muslims so that Thou art happy with us.*

*O Allah, grace me with power to shun sin for all the time that
Thou keepest me living. Grace me with power so that I do not
strive for what concerneth me not. Grant me an optimistic view
whereby Thou shalt be pleased with me, O Thou Most Merciful
of all who show mercy.*

Ad'iya Al-Wuqūf bi 'Arafāt
(At the standing on 'Arafāt
on the 9th Thu-l-Hijjah)

These invocations are recited after the prayers of *Az-Zuhr* (noon) and of *Al-'Asr* (mid-afternoon), until the moment of departure from 'Arafāt shortly after sunset.

LA ILAHA ILLA LLAHU WAHDAHU LA SHAREEKA LAHU, LAHU, LAHU-L-MULKU WA LAHU-L-HAMDU, YOUHYE WA YUMEETU, WA HUWWA HAYUN LA YAMOOTU, BIYADIHI AL KHAYRU WA HUWWA 'ALA KULLI SHAY'EN KADEER.

There is none worthy of worship but Allah alone. He hath no partner. To him belongeth the sovereignty, and unto Him is all praise due.

He giveth life, He putteth to death. He is living and is never to die. In His hand is good. He hath power over all things.

اللَّهُمَّ إِلَيْكَ خَرَجْنَا، وَبِفِنَائِكَ أَنَخْنَا، وَإِيَّاكَ أَمَّلْنَا، وَمَا عِنْدَكَ طَلَبْنَا، وَلِإِحْسَانِكَ تَعَرَّضْنَا، وَلِرَحْمَتِكَ رَجَوْنَا، وَمِنْ عَذَابِكَ أَشْفَقْنَا، وَلِبَيْتِكَ الْحَرَامِ حَجَجْنَا، يَا مَنْ يَمْلِكُ حَوَائِجَ السَّائِلِينَ، وَيَعْلَمُ ضَمَائِرَ الصَّامِتِينَ، يَا مَنْ لَيْسَ مَعَهُ رَبٌّ يُدْعَى، وَلَا إِلَهٌ يُرْجَى، وَلَا فَوْقَهُ خَالِقٌ يُخْشَى، وَلَا وَزِيرٌ يُؤْتَى، وَلَا حَاجِبٌ يُرْشَى. يَا مَنْ لَا يَزْدَادُ عَلَى السُّؤَالِ إِلَّا كَرَمًا وَجُودًا،

وَعَلَى كَثْرَةِ الْحَوَائِجِ إِلَّا تَفَضُّلًا وَإِحْسَانًا. يَا مَنْ ضَجَّتْ بَيْنَ يَدَيْهِ الْأَصْوَاتُ بِلُغَاتٍ مُتَخَالِفَاتٍ، يَسْأَلُونَكَ الْحَاجَاتِ، وَسُكِبَتِ الدُّمُوعُ بِالْعَبَرَاتِ،

مُلِحِّينَ بِالدَّعَوَاتِ. فَحَاجَتِي إِلَيْكَ يَا رَبِّ مَغْفِرَتُكَ، وَرِضًى مِنْكَ عَنِّي لَا سُخْطَ بَعْدَهُ، وَهُدًى لَا ضَلَالَ بَعْدَهُ، وَعِلْمٌ لَا أَجْهَلُ بَعْدَهُ، وَحُسْنُ الْخَاتِمَةِ، وَالْعِتْقُ مِنَ النَّارِ، وَالْفَوْزُ بِالْجَنَّةِ، وَأَنْ تَذْكُرَنِي عِنْدَ الْبَلَاءِ إِذَا نَسِيَنِي أَهْلُ الدُّنْيَا، وَوَارَانِي التُّرَابُ، وَانْقَطَعَ عَنِّي الْأَحْبَابُ، وَتَقَطَّعَتْ بِيَ الْأَسْبَابُ، يَا عَزِيزُ يَا وَهَّابُ، يَا أَرْحَمَ الرَّاحِمِينَ.

ALLAHUMMA ILAYKA KHARAJNA WA BIFINAIKA ANAKHANA, WA IYYAKA'AMMALNA, WA MA 'INDAKA TALABNA, WA LI ISHANIKA TA'ARRADHNA, WA LIRAHMATIKA RAJAWNA, WA MIN 'ADHABIKA ASHFAQNA, WA LI BAYTIKA AL HARAMI HAJAJNA.

YA MAN YAMLIKU HAWA'IJA ASSA'ILEEN, WA YA'LAMU DHAMA'IRA ASSAMITEEN, YA MAN LAYSSA MA' 'AHU RABBON YUD'A, WA LĀ ILAHUN YURJA, WA LĀ FAWQAHU KHALIQUN YUKHSHA, WA LĀ WAZEARUN YU'ETA, WA LĀ HABIJUN YURSHA, YA MAN LĀ, YAZDADU 'ALA S' SU'ALI ILLA KARA-MAN WA JODAN, WA'ALA KATHRATI AL HAWAI'JI ILLA TAFADHULAN WA IHSANAN. YA MAN DHAJJAT BAYNA YADAYHI AL ASWATU BILUGHATIN MUKH-TALIFATIN YAS'ALUNAKA AL HĀJATI, WA SUKIBATI ADDUMU 'U BIL 'ABARATI, MULEHHINA BI D'DA'AWATI.

FAHAJATI ILAYKA YA RABBI MAGHFIRATUKA, WA RIDHAN MINKA'ANNI, LA SUKHTA BA'DAHU WA HODAN LA DHALALA BA'DAHU, WA 'ILMON LA JAHLA BA 'DAHU, WĀ HOSNU AL KHATIMATI WAL'ITQU, MINA ANNAR, WA AL FAWZU BIL JAN-NATI, WA AN HADHKURANI 'INDA AL BALA I IDHA NASIYANEE AHLOU D'DUNYA, WA WĀRANEE ATTU-RAB, WA INQATA 'A 'ANNI' L' AHBĀB. WA TAQATTA 'AT BIYA AL ASBĀB, YA 'AZIZU YA WAHHAB, YA ARHAMA ARRAHIMEEN.

O Allah, to Thee we have set out, in Thy courtyard have we made a halt, in Thee do we hope, Thy favours do we seek, at Thy grace do we snatch for. Thy mercy do we hope for, Thy chastisement do we fear and Thy Sacred House do we visit.

O Thou the Master of the needs of all seekers and Thou Knower of the conscience of those who keep peace.

O Thou who hath no lord beside Him to invoke, nor any one worthy of worship to beseech, nor any creator above Him to fear, nor any vizier under Him to visit, nor any chamberlain with Him to bribe. Thy bounty is infinite. The more we have need of Thou, the greater Thy benevolence and Thy generosity.

O Thou before whom clamours in different languages accumu-late, all seeking Thy succour in their importuning with prayers. My sole demand, O Lord, is Thy pleasure unto me not to be fol-lowed by Thy anger, and guidance not to be followed by error, and knowledge not to be followed by ignorance, and happy con-clusion leading to Paradise, and deliverance from the Fire.

I beseech Thee to remember me in time of affliction when the people of this world shall have forgotten me, after I am buried and my friends in this world are lost unto me. O the Powerful, O the Bountiful, O the Merciful of those who shew mercy.

اللَّهُمَّ إِنِّى أَسْأَلُكَ الْهُدَى وَالتُّقَى، وَالْعَفَافَ وَالْغِنَى، اللَّهُمَّ لَكَ الْحَمْدُ كَالَّذِى نَقُولُ، وَخَيْرًا مِمَّا نَقُولُ. اللَّهُمَّ إِنِّى أَسْأَلُكَ رِضَاكَ وَالْجَنَّةَ، وَأَعُوذُ بِكَ مِنْ سَخَطِكَ وَالنَّارِ، وَمَا يُقَرِّبُنِى إِلَيْهَا مِنْ قَوْلٍ أَوْ فِعْلٍ أَوْ عَمَلٍ. اللَّهُمَّ اجْعَلْهُ حَجًّا مَبْرُورًا، وَذَنْبًا مَغْفُورًا، وَعَمَلًا صَالِحًا مَقْبُولًا، رَبَّنَا آتِنَا فِى الدُّنْيَا حَسَنَةً، وَفِى الْآخِرَةِ حَسَنَةً، وَقِنَا عَذَابَ النَّارِ.

ALLAHUMMA INNI AS'ALUKA AL HUDA, WA ATTUQA, WAL'AFAFA WAL GHINA, ALLAHUMMA LAKA AL HAMDU KALLADHI NAQOOLU, WA KHAY-RAN MIMMA NAQOOLU.

ALLAHUMMA INNI AS'ALUKA RIDHAKA WAL JAN-NAH WA A'ODHU BIKA MIN SOKHTIKA WAN'NAR, WA MA YUQARRIBUNI ILAYHA MIN QAWLIN AW FI'LIN AW'AMALIN.

ALLAHUMMA IJ'ALHU HAJJAN MABRURAN, WA DHAN'BAN MAGHFURAN, WA'AMALAN SALIHAN MAQBULAN.

RABBANA ATINA FI D'DUNYA HASANATAN WA FIL AKHIRATI HASANATAN WA QUINA'ADHABA ANNAR.

O Allah, I implore Thee to grant me guidance, piety, continence and satisfaction in this world.

O Allah, to Thee is all praise due, as we praise Thee and better still.

O Allah, I beg of Thee Thy pleasure, and thereby the Garden, and I seek Thy refuge from Thy anger, from the Fire and from all those things - sayings, actions and deeds - that should bring me near unto it.

O Allah, make this for me a righteous pilgrimage and a means of forgiveness of sin and also an act that is righteous and accept-able unto Thee.

O our Lord, give us good in this world and also good in the hereafter, and deliver us from the torment.

ILAHI, LĀ QUWATA LI'ALA SAKHTIK, WA LĀ SABRA LI 'ALĀ ADHABIK, WA LĀ QUWATA LI ALĀ L'BALA'I WA LA TAQATA LI ALĀ AL JAHD, A 'ODHU BIRI-DHAKA MIN SAKHTIK, WA MIN FOUJ'ATI NIQMATIK, YA AMALI WA YA RAJA'I, YA KHAYRA MUSTAGHA-THEN, WA YA AJWADA ALMU 'TEEN, YA MAN SABA-QAT RAHMATAHU HU GHADHABAH, YA SAYYIDI WA YĀ MAWLAYE, YĀ THIQATI WA YĀ RAJA'I WA MU'TAMADI.

O Allah, I have no power to defend myself from Thy anger, nor patience to endure Thy chastisement. There is no satisfaction for me without Thy mercy, nor any power against that trial, nor even power to exert it. I seek refuge with Thy pleasure from Thy anger and from Thy terrible punishment. O my hope, O my great expectation, O Thou the best one implored.

O Thou the most liberal of those who give. Thou art my Lord and my Master and my only Saviour.

ALLAHUMMA YĀ MAN LA YASHGHALUHU SAM'UN
'AN SAM'IN, WA LA TASHTABIHU 'ALAYHI AL
ASWĀT, YĀ MAN LA TASHTABIHU, 'ALAYHI
MASA'ILU YĀ MAN LA YUBRIMUHU IL' HAHU AL
MULEHHEEN WA LA TU'AJJIZZUHU MAS'ALATA
ASSA'ILEEN, ADHIQNA BARDA AFWIK, WA HALA-
WATA MAGHFIRATIK. YA ARHAMA ARRAHIMEEN.

*O Allah, O Thou whose attention is not to be distracted by one
hearing from another, and is not to be confused by the different
invocations : O Thou who is not annoyed by the importunings
of those who implore Thee. Thou who can satisfy all their needs,
give us to taste Thy satisfying forgiveness and Thy sweet remis-
sion of our sins. O most Merciful of those who shew mercy.*

اللّٰهُمَّ يَا عَالِمَ الْخَفِيَّاتِ، وَيَا سَامِعَ
الْأَصْوَاتِ، يَا بَاعِثَ الْأَمْوَاتِ، يَا مُجِيبَ الدَّعَوَاتِ،
يَا قَاضِيَ الْحَاجَاتِ، يَا خَالِقَ الْأَرْضِ وَالسَّمَوَاتِ،
أَنْتَ اللّٰهُ الَّذِي لَا إِلٰهَ إِلَّا أَنْتَ، الْوَاحِدُ الْأَحَدُ، الْفَرْدُ
الصَّمَدُ، الْوَهَّابُ الَّذِي لَا يَبْخَلُ، وَالْحَلِيمُ الَّذِي
لَا يَعْجَلُ. لَا رَادَّ لِأَمْرِكَ، وَلَا مُعَقِّبَ لِحُكْمِكَ،
رَبُّ كُلِّ شَيْءٍ، وَمَلِيكُ كُلِّ شَيْءٍ، وَمُقَدِّرُ كُلِّ شَيْءٍ. أَسْأَلُكَ
أَنْ تَرْزُقَنِي عِلْمًا نَافِعًا، وَعَمَلًا زَكِيًّا، وَإِيمَانًا خَالِصًا،
وَهَبْ لَنَا إِنَابَةَ الْمُخْلِصِينَ، وَخُشُوعَ الْمُخْبِتِينَ،
وَأَعْمَالَ الصَّالِحِينَ، وَيَقِينَ الصَّادِقِينَ، وَسَعَادَةَ
الْمُتَّقِينَ، وَدَرَجَاتِ الْفَائِزِينَ، يَا أَفْضَلَ مَنْ قُصِدَ،
وَأَكْرَمَ مَنْ سُئِلَ، وَأَحْلَمَ مَنْ أَعْطَى.

**ALLAḤUMMA YA 'ALIMA AL KHAFIYYAT, WA YA
SĀMI'A AL AṢWĀT, YA BAA'ITHA AL AMWAT, YA
MUJEABA ADDA'AWAT, YA ǪADHIYA AL HĀJAĀT,
YA KHALIQA AL ARDHI WAS' SAMĀWĀT, ANTA
ALLAḤ ALLADHI LA ILAḤA ILLA ANTA, AL WĀHIDU
AL AHAD, AL FARDU, ASSAMAD; AL WAḤḤABU
ALLADHI LA YABKHAL, AL HALIMU ALLADHI LA YA
'JAL.**

**LA RADDA LI AMRIKA, WA LA MU'AQQIBA LI HUK-
MIKA, RABBU KULLI SHAY'EN, WA MALEEKU KULLI
SHA'YEN, WA MU'QADDIRU KULLA SHAY'EN,
AS'ALUKA AN TARZUQANEE 'ILMAN NĀFI'AN, WA
'AMALAN ZAKIYYAN, WA EEAMANAN KHALISAN.**

**WA ḤAB LANA INABATA, AL MUKHLISEEN WA KHUS-
HOO'A AL MUKHLISEEN WA KHUSHOO'A AL MUKH-
BITEEN WA 'AMALA ASALIHEEN, WA YAQEENA
ASSADIQEEN, WA SA 'ADATA AL MUTTAQEEN, WA
DAJARĀTI-L-FA'IZEEN, YA AFDHALA MAN QUSID WA
AKRAMA MAN SU'IL WA AHLAMA MAN A'TAA.**

*O Allah, O Thou who knowest even the obscure things. O Thou
who hearest the clamours. O thou who shall quicken the dead. O
Thou who listeneth to the invocations.O Thou who fulfilleth the
needs. O the Creator of the earth and the heaven.*

*Thou art Allah, who alone is worthy of worship. Thou art the
One, the Single, the Unique, the only One who is resorted to, the
Liberal-giver who is never niggardly, and the Forbearing who
hasteneth not in inflincting punishment. There is none to repel
Thy order, nor any one to reverse Thy command. Thou art the
Lord of all things and Thou ordainth everything.*

*I implore Thee to grant me useful knowledge, vast and bound-
less provisions, a humble heart, a tongue wont to mention Thy
name, righteous acts and sincere belief.*

*Grant us penitence of the sincere, humility of the humble, acts
of the righteous, belief of the sincere, bliss of the fearing and
ranks of the successful.*

*O Thou the Best of those who are resorted to, the Noblest of
those who are invoked and the most Forbearing of those who
are disobeyed.*

مَا أَحْلَمَكَ

عَلَى مَنْ عَصَاكَ ، وَأَقْرَبَكَ إِلَى مَنْ دَعَاكَ ، وَأَعْطَفَكَ
عَلَى مَنْ سَأَلَكَ . لَا مَهْدِيَ إِلَّا مَنْ هَدَيْتَ ، وَلَا ضَالَّ
إِلَّا مَنْ أَضْلَلْتَ ، وَلَا غَنِيَ إِلَّا مَنْ أَغْنَيْتَ ، وَلَا فَقِيرَ
إِلَّا مَنْ أَفْقَرْتَ ، وَلَا مَعْصُومَ إِلَّا مَنْ عَصَمْتَ ،
وَلَا مَسْتُورَ إِلَّا مَنْ سَتَرْتَ . أَسْأَلُكَ أَنْ تَهَبَ لَنَا
جَزِيلَ عَطَائِكَ ، وَالسَّعَادَةَ بِلِقَائِكَ ، وَالْمَزِيدَ
مِنْ نِعَمِكَ ، وَأَنْ تَجْعَلَ لَنَا نُورًا فِي حَيَاتِنَا ،
وَنُورًا فِي حَشْرِنَا ، وَنُورًا فِي قِمَانِنَا ، وَنُورًا فِي قُبُورِنَا ،
وَنُورًا نَتَوَسَّلُ بِهِ إِلَيْكَ ، وَنُورًا نَفُوزُ بِهِ لَدَيْكَ .
فَإِنَّا بِبَابِكَ سَائِلُونَ ، وَبِنَوَالِكَ مُعْتَرِفُونَ ،
وَلِلِقَائِكَ رَاجُونَ .

MA AHLAMAKA 'ALA MAN 'ASSAKA, WA AQRABAKA
'ILA MAN DA'ĀKA, WA A'TAFAKA'ALA MAN
SA'ALAK, LĀ MAHDI YA ILLA MAN HADAYTA, WA LA
GHANIA ILLA MAN WA DHALLA ILLA MAN ADLATA.
AGH'NAITA, WA LĀ FAQEERA ILLA MAN AFQARTA,
WA LĀ MA SUMA ILLA MAN 'ASAMTA WA LA MAS-
TURA ILLA MAN SATARTA. AS'ALUKA AN TAHABA
LANA JAZEELA 'ATA'IK. WAS'SA'ADATA BILIQA'IK,
WAL MAZEEDA MIN NI'AMEK, WA AN TAJ'ALA LANA
NOORAN FEE HAYATINA, WA NOORAN FEE HASH-
RINA, WA NOORAN FEE MAMĀTINA, WA NOORAN
FEE QUBOORINA, WA NOORAN NATAWASSALU BIHI
ILAYK, WA NOORAN NAFOOZU BIHI LADAYK, FA
INNA BIBĀBIKA SA'ILUN, WA BI NAWALIKA MU'TARI-
FOON, WA LILIQA'IKA RAA'JOON.

*How forbearing art Thou unto him who disobeys Thee! How
nigh Thou art unto him who implores Thee! How attentive art
Thou unto him that calls out to Thee!*

*Guided is he whom Thou hast directed; astray is he whom Thou
hath caused to err; satisfied is he to whom Thou hath granted
satisfaction; poor is he whom Thou hath made poor; flawless is
he whom Thou hath saved from sins; veiled is he whose shortcomings hath Thou overlooked.*

*I implore Thee to grant us the best of Thy benevolence and the
bliss of Thy meeting and excess of Thy favours and bounties,
and to cast for us in our life a light, and also in our assembly,
and in our death, and a light in our graves, and a light whereby
we may approach Thee, and a light whereby we may gain Thy
grace.*

*O Lord, we are at Thy door earnestly imploring Thee, acknow-
ledging Thy bounty and hoping to meet Thee.*

ALLAḤUMMA' J'AL KHAYRA 'OMRI AKHIRAH, WA KHAYRA 'AMALI KHAWĀTIMAH, WA KHAYRA AYYA-MEE YAWMA LIQA'IK.

O Allah, make for me the last part of my life the best part of my life, make the end of my acts the best of my acts, and make for me the day of my meeting Thee the best of my days.

**ALLAHUMMA THABBITNI BI AMRIK, WA AYYEDNI BI
NASRIK, WARZUQNEE MIN FADHLEK, WA NAJJINEE
MIN ADHABEK YAWMA TAB'ATHU'IBADAK, FA QAD
ATAYTUKA LIRAHMATIKA RAJIYAN, WA 'AN WATA-
NEA NA'IYAN, WA LI NUSUKEE MU ADDIYAN, WA LI
FARA'IDHIKA QADHIYAN, WA LI KATIBIKA
TALIYAN, WA LAKA DA'IYAN, WA LI QASWATI QAL-
BEE SHAKIYAN WA MIN DHANEBI KHASHIYAN, WA
LI NAFSEE DHALIMAN.**

*O Allah, help me to follow Thy command and support me with
Thy assistance, and grant me of Thy grace, and deliver me from
Thy chastiment on the day Thou shalt ressurect Thy servants.*

*For I have come to Thee in hope to receive Thy mercy,
performing my devotion, accomplishing Thy ordinances, rect-
ting Thy Book, imploring Thee, repenting for the hardness of
my heart, showing humility on account of my sins.*

DU‘A’A MAN JUMI‘AT ‘UYOOBUḤ, WA KATHURAT
DHUNOOBUḤ, WATASARRAMAT ÂMĀLUḤ WA
BAQIYAT ATHAMUH WA N’SAKABAT DAM‘ATUḤ
W’AN‘QATA‘AT MUDDATUḤ, DU‘A’A MAN LA YAJIDU
LINAFSIḤI GHAFIRAN GAYRAK, WA LĀ LI MA’E’
MULIHI MIN AL KHAYRATI M’TIYAN SIWAK, WA LA
LIKASRIHI JABIRAN ILLA ANTA YA ARHAMA ARRA-
HIMEEN, WA LA HAWLA WA LA QUWWATA ILLA
BILLAH AL ‘ALLIYYE AL ADHEEM.

*This is the prayer of one whose vices have accumulated and
whose sins have multiplied, but whose hopes are cut off, whose
sins still survive, whose tears are pouring and whose life is drawing to an end. I implore Thee like one who findeth no pardoner
of his sins except Thee, nor doth he find anyone to grant him the
expected gifts except Thee, O the most Merciful!*

*There is no might, no power but from Allah, the High, the
Great.*

سورة البقرة مدنية مائتان وست وثمانون آية

بِسْمِ اللَّهِ الرَّحْمَنِ الرَّحِيمِ

الٓمٓ ۞ ذَٰلِكَ الْكِتَٰبُ لَا رَيْبَ فِيهِ

هُدًى لِّلْمُتَّقِينَ ۞ الَّذِينَ يُؤْمِنُونَ

بِالْغَيْبِ وَيُقِيمُونَ الصَّلَوٰةَ وَمِمَّا

رَزَقْنَٰهُمْ يُنفِقُونَ ۞ وَالَّذِينَ يُؤْمِنُونَ

اللّٰهُمَّ لَا تُقَدِّمْنِي لِعَذَابِكَ، وَلَا تُؤَخِّرْنِي لِشَيْءٍ مِنَ
الْفِتَنِ. مَوْلَايَ هَا أَنَا أَدْعُوكَ رَاغِبًا، وَأَنْصِبُ
إِلَيْكَ وَجْهِي طَالِبًا، وَأَضَعُ لَكَ خَدِّي مَهِينًا
رَاهِبًا، فَتَقَبَّلْ دُعَائِي، وَأَصْلِحِ الْفَاسِدَ مِنْ أَمْرِي،
وَاقْطَعْ مِنَ الدُّنْيَا هَمِّي وَحَاجَتِي، وَاجْعَلْ فِيمَا
عِنْدَكَ رَغْبَتِي، وَاقْلِبْنِي مُنْقَلَبَ الْمَذْكُورِينَ عِنْدَكَ،
الْمَقْبُولِ دُعَاؤُهُمُ، الْقَائِمَةِ حُجَّتُهُمُ، الْمَغْفُورِ ذَنْبُهُمُ،
الْمَبْرُورِ حَجُّهُمُ   الْمَمْحُوَّةِ
سَيِّئَاتُهُمُ، الرَّاشِدِ أَمْرُهُمْ، مُنْقَلَبَ مَنْ لَا يَعْصِي لَكَ
أَمْرًا، وَلَا يَأْتِي بَعْدَهُ مَأْثَمًا، وَلَا يَحْمِلُ بَعْدَهُ وِزْرًا.
مُنْقَلَبَ مَنْ عَزَّزْتَ بِذِكْرِكَ لِسَانَهُ، وَطَهَّرْتَ
مِنَ الْأَدْنَاسِ بَدَنَهُ، وَاسْتَوْدَعْتَ الْهُدَى قَلْبَهُ،

وَشَرَحْتَ بِالْإِسْلَامِ صَدْرَهُ، وَأَقْرَرْتَ بِرِضَاكَ
وَعَفْوِكَ قَبْلَ الْمَمَاتِ عَيْنَهُ، وَعَفَفْتَ عَنِ الْمَأْثَمِ
بَصَرَهُ، وَاسْتَعْمَلْتَ فِي سَبِيلِكَ نَفْسَهُ، وَأَسْأَلُكَ
أَنْ لَا تَجْعَلَنِي أَشْقَى خَلْقِكَ الْمُذْنِبِينَ عِنْدَكَ، وَلَا
أَخْيَبَ الرَّاجِينَ لَدَيْكَ، وَلَا أَحْرَمَ الْآمِلِينَ لِرَحْمَتِكَ،
وَلَا أَخْسَرَ الْمُنْقَلِبِينَ مِنْ هَذَا الْمَوْقِفِ الْعَظِيمِ.
مَوْلَايَ رَبَّ الْعَالَمِينَ،

ALLAḤUMMA LA TUQADDIMNEE LI ADHABIKA, WA LA TUAKHERNEE LI SHAY'EN MINAL FITAN.

MAWLAYA, ḤA ANA AD'OUKA RAGHIBAN, WA ANSIBU ILAYKA WAJ'ḤEE TĀLIBAN, WA ADHA'OO LAKA KHADDI MUHEENAN, RAḤIBAN, FA TAQABBAL DU'A'I, WA ASLIH'IL FASIDA MIN AMRI, WAQTA' MINA ADDONYA ḤAMMI WA HAJATI, WAJ'AL FEE MA 'INDAKA RAGHBATI WA AQLIBNI MUNQALABA AL MADḤKUREENA INDAK, AL MAQBOOLI DU'A 'OḤUM AL QA'IMATI HUJJATUḤUM AL MAGFOORI DHANBUḤUM, AL MABROORI HAJJUHUM, AL MAM'HUWATI SAYYI'ATIḤEM ARRAHIDI AMRUḤUM MUNQALABA MAN LA YA'SSI LAKA AMRAN WA LA YA'ETI BA'DAḤU MA'ETHAMAN WA LA YAMILHU BA'DAHU WIZRAN, MONQALABA MAN'AZZAZTA BI DHIKRIKA LISANAH, WA TAHHARTA MINA AL ADNASI BADANAH, WA STAWDA'TA AL HUDA QAL-BAH. WA SHARAHTA BIL ISLAMI SADRAH, WA AQKARTA BIRIDHAKA, WA AFOUIKA QABLA AL MAMATI'AYNAH WA AFAFTA'AN EL ETHMI BASSA-RAḤ WAS TA'MALTA FI SABILIKA NAFSAH, WA AS'ALUKA AN LA TAJ'ALANI ASHQĀ KHALQIKA, AL MUDHNIBEENA 'INDAK, WA LA AKHIABA ARRA-JEENA LADAYKA, WA LA AHRAMA AL AMILEENA LI RAHMATIK, WA LA AKHSARA AL MUN'QALABEENA MIN ḤADHA AL MAWQIFI AL'ADHEEM, MAWLAYA RABBA AL ALAMEEN.

O Allah, I beg Thee not to punish me readily, nor try me with ordeals as a last affair of my life. O my Master, here I implore Thee with supplication, I direct my face unto Thee with requests. I humbly place my forehead to the ground. Therefore accept my prayer, correct my failings, rid me of the worries and the needs of this world.

Grant me love for what is with Thee. Change me into those who are favourably mentioned before Thee, those whose prayers are accepted, those whose pleas are established, whose sins are pardoned, and whose pilgrimage is accepted.

Change me into those who do not disobey Thy command and do not commit any sin thereafter, whose tongues hast Thou made meritorious by Thy mention, whose bodies hast Thou cleansed from impurities and whose breasts hast Thou opened to receive the faith of Islam.

I implore Thee not to place me among those who are in Thy sight the wretched of Thy sinning creatures, nor among those who are according to Thee the unsuccessful of those who hope, nor among those who hold hopes for Thy mercy, but are deprived of it, nor among the most losing of those who return from this grand muster, O my Master, O the Lord of the worlds.

اَللّٰهُمَّ وَقَدْ دَعَوْتُكَ بِالدُّعَاءِ الَّذِي عَلَّمْتَنِيهِ، فَلَا تَحْرِمْنِي مِنَ الرَّجَاءِ الَّذِي عَرَّفْتَنِيهِ، يَا مَنْ لَا تَنْفَعُهُ الطَّاعَةُ وَلَا تَضُرُّهُ الْمَعْصِيَةُ. وَمَا أَعْطَيْتَنِي مِمَّا أُحِبُّ فَاجْعَلْهُ لِي عَوْنًا فِيمَا تُحِبُّ، وَاجْعَلْهُ لِي خَيْرًا، وَحَبِّبْ طَاعَتَكَ لِي وَالْعَمَلَ بِهَا، كَمَا حَبَّبْتَهَا إِلَى أَوْلِيَائِكَ حَتَّى رَأَوْا ثَوَابَهَا، وَكَمَا هَدَيْتَنِي لِلْإِسْلَامِ فَلَا تَنْزِعْهُ مِنِّي، حَتَّى تَقْبِضَنِي إِلَيْكَ وَأَنَا عَلَيْهِ.

ALLAHUMMA WA QAD DA 'AWTUKA BI D'DU 'A'I-L-LADHI ALHAMTANIH, FA LA TAHRIMNI MINA ARRJA'I-L-LADHI 'ARRAFTANIH, YA MAN LA TAN'FA'HU ATTA'ATU, WA LĀ TADHURUHU AL MA 'SIYATU.

WA MA A 'TAYTANI MIMMA OHIBU, FAJ'ALHU LEE'AWNAN FEE MA TUHIBU, WA AJ'ALHU LEE KHAYRAN, WA HABBIB TAA'ATAKA LEE WAL 'AMALA BIHA, KAMA HABBABTAHĀ LI AWLIYAIKA, HATTA RA'AW THAWABAHA, WA KAMA HADAY-TANI LIL ISLAMI FA LA TANZA'HU MINNI HATTA TAQBIDHNI ILAYKA, WA ANA ALAYHI.

O Allah, I have called upon Thee with the invocation that Thou hast taught me. Therefore disallow me not the hope that Thou hast caused me to recognize, O Thou to whom obedience can do no profit, nor to whom disobedience can do any harm.

Cause me to love Thy obedience and to act accordingly as Thou hast done with Thy friends till they could see for themselves the reward for it.

As Thou hast directed me unto Islam, cause me not to draw away from it till Thou snatchest away my soul unto Thee.

ALLAḤUMMA INNA NA 'ODHU BIKA MIN JAHDI AL BALA'I, WA DARAKI SH'SHAQA'I WA SHAMATATI AL A'DA'I WA SU'I L'MANDHARI WAL MUNQALABI FI AL AḤLI, WAL MALI, WAL WALADI.

O Allah, we fly to Thy refuge from the efforts of calamity, from the approach of wretchedness, from the rejoicing of foes on our affliction, from wrong-thinking, and from inversion in respect of the family, our children and our property.

ALLAHUMMA LĀ TADA' FEE MAQĀMINA HADHA
DHANBAN ILLA GHAFARTAH, WA LĀ HAMMAN ILLA
FARRAJTAH, WA LĀ GHĀ'IBAN ILLA RDADTAH, WA
LA KARBAN ILLA CHAFAITAH WA LA DAYNAN ILLA
QADHAYTAH, WA LĀ ADUWWAN ILLA KAFAYTAH,
WA LA FASADAN ILLA ASLAHTAH, WA LA MAREE-
DHAN ILLA 'ĀFAYTAH WA LĀ KHALLATAN ILLA
SADADTAHA, WA LĀ HAJATAN MIN HAWAÏJI
ADDONYA WAL AKHIRAH, LAKA FIHA RIDHAN WA
LANA FIHA SALAHON ILLA QADHAYTAHA FA
INNAKA TAHDI ASSABEEL WA TUBIRU AL KASEER,
WA TUGNI AL FAQEER.

*O Allah, leave not for us here in this muster, any of our sins but
that Thou hast forgiven it, nor any of our worries but that Thou
hast repelled it, nor any loss of ours but that Thou hast retrieved
it, nor any grief but that Thou hast dispelled it, nor any debt but
that Thou hast arranged to pay it, nor any of our patients but
that Thou hast granted him recovery, nor any snag but that
Thou hast smoothed it.*

*O Lord, leave not for us any desire of this world and of the
hereafter but that Thou hast satisfied it to Thy pleasure and to
our advantage.*

*For verily Thou directest on the right path, Thou settest broken
bones and Thou grantest wealth to the poor.*

ALLAHUMMA LA BUDDA LANA MIN LIQA'IKA, FAJ'AL ODHRANA INDAKA MAQBULAN, WA DHANBANA MAGHFURAN, WA ILMANA MAWFURAN WA SA'YANA MASHKURAN.

ASBAHA WAJHI ALFANEE MUSTAJEERAN BI WAJHIKA AL BAQEE AL QAYOUM, DHIL IZZATI WAL JABARUT.

O Allah, verily we have inevitably to meet Thee. Therefore make unto Thee our excuses accepted and our sins forgiven, our knowledge ample and our endeavour acceptable.

May my perishable face find refuge in Thy surviving face, self-subsisting and possessed of honour and might.

ALLAḤUMMA, LĀ YAMNA' UNI MINKA AHADON IDHA ARADTANEE, WA LĀ YO'TEENI AHADON IDHA HARAMTANI, FALĀTAHRIMNEE BIQILLATI SHUK-REE, WA LĀ TAKHDHOLNEE, IJ'AL BIQILLATI SABREE.

ALLAḤUMMA AL MAWTA KAYRA GHAYBEN NANTA-DHIRUḤU, WAL QABRA, KHAYRA BAYTIN NA'MURUḤU, WAJ'AL MA BA'DAHOU KHAYRON LANA MINHU.

RABBI IGHFIR LEE, WA LI WALIDAYYA, WA LI IKH-WANEE WA LI AHLI BAYTI, WA DHURRIYATI, WA LIL MO'EMINEENA, WAL MU'EMINATI, WAL MUSLI-MEENA WAL MUSLIMATI, AL AHYAE'A MINHUM WAL AMWATI.

O Allah, let not anyone stop me from Thee when Thou wilt it, and let not anyone give me when Thou wilt it not. Deprive me not of Thy graces on account of my remiss in thanking Thee, and desert me not for lack of patience on my part.

O Allah, make death for me the best of the hidden things which we await, and the grave the best of the dwellings which we should inhabit, and make for us what follows it better than that.

O my Lord, forgive me and forgive my parents, my children and my brothers, and forgive my wife and the believing men and the believing women, and all Muslims, both the living and the dead.

ALLAHUMMA INNI AS'ALUKA EEMANAN YUBA-
SHIRU QALBI WA YAQEENAN SADIQAN HATTA
A'LAMA ANNAHU LA YUSIBUNEE ILLA MA KATABTA
LEE, WA RADH'DHINI BI QADHA'ILKA WA A'IN'NEE
'ALA ADDUNIA BIL 'IFFATI WAL QANA'ATI WA 'ALA
D'DEENI BITTA 'AH, WA TAHHIR LISANEE MINAL
KADHIB, WA QALBEE MINA ANNIFAQ, WA 'AMALI
MINA R'RIYA'I. WA BASARI MINAL KHIYANAH, FA
INNAKA TA'LAMU KHIYANATA AL A'YUN, WA MA
TAKHFEE S'SUDOOR.

*O Allah, I implore Thee for the faith that shall busy my heart,
and for the sincere belief till I should know that no favour or affliction shall overtake me except what Thou hast writ for me.*

*Content me with Thy irreversible decree and help me to struggle
against the world with continence and contentment, and help me
in matters of faith and obedience to Thee.*

*Cleanse my tongue from ostentation and show, and my sight
from dishonesty, for Thou knowest the dishonesty of the eye
and what men's breasts conceal.*

ALLAHUMMA IRHAM GHURBATI FID'DUNIA, WA
MASRA'I 'INDA AL MAWT, WA WAHSHATI FIL
QABREF, WA MAQAMI BAYNA YADAYK. ALLA-
HUMMA ANTA ASSALAM, WA MINKA ASSALAM,
TABARAKTA YA DHAL JALALI WAL IKRĀM.

*O Allah, Thy mercy for my remoteness in this world, for my
overthrow at the time of death, for my disquietude in my grave,
and for my presence before Thee.*

*O Allah, Thou art peace, and from Thee is peace and salvation.
Blessed art Thou, and exalted is Thy majesty, O Thou possessed
of glory and honour.*

ALLAHUMMA ANTA AL MALIK LA ILAHA ALLA ANTA, WA ANA 'ABDUK, DHALAMTU NAFSEE WA A'TARAFTU BIDHANBI, FAGHFER LI DHUNUBEE FA INNAHU LA YAGHFIRU DH'DHUNOOBA ILLA ANTA, WAHDINEE LI AHSANI AL AKHLAQI, FALA YAHDI LI AHSANIHA ILLA ANTA, WAS'REF 'ANNEE SAYYI'AHA, FA INNAHU LA YASRIFU SAYYI'AHA ILLA ANTA.

LABBAYKA WA SA'DAIKA WAL KHAYRU KULLUHU BI YADAYKA ; ASTAGHFIRUKA WA ATUBU ILAYKA.

O Allah, Thou art the King. There is none worthy of worship except Thee, and I am Thy servant. I have acted wrongly to myself and I confess my sins. Forgive me my sins, for none shall forgive the sins but Thee.

Direct me towards better conduct, for none shall be able to direct me so except Thee.

Divert me from vice, for none shall be able to divert me from vice save Thee.

Mayest Thou be happy and aided. All good is in Thy hands. I turn to Thee, repenting of my sins.

ALLAHUMMA AHYINEE MA 'ALIMTA AL HAYATA
KHAYRAN LEE, WA TAWWAFANEE, IDHA 'ALIMTA
AL WAFATA KHAYRAN LEE, WAHDINI LI ARCHADI
AMRI. ALLAHUMMA AHSEN AQIBATANA. FIL OMURI
KULLIHA, WA AJJIRNA MIN KHIZYI-D-DUNIA WA
'ADHABI AL AKHIRAH, WARHAM GHURBATI FI-D-
DUNIA, WA TADHARU 'I 'INDA AL MAWTI, WA WAH-
DATI FIL QABRI, WA MAQAMEE BAYNA YADAYKA.

*O Allah, keep me alive as long as in Thy knowledge my living is
good and worthy, and cause me to die when Thou knowest that
death is better for me. Lead me so that I should set my affairs
right. Grant me refuge from the mischief of my soul.*

*O Allah, make the end of all our affairs noble, and grant us
refuge from worldly disgrace and the torment of the hereafter.
Thy mercy for my remoteness in this world, for my humble en-
treaties at the time of death, for my solitude in the grave, for my
presence before Thee on the Day of Judgment.*

ALLAHUMMA INNEE AS'ALUKA BISMIKA ATTAYIBI
ATTAHIRI AL MUBĀRAKI AL AHABBI ILAYK, ALLA-
DHI IDHA DU'ITA BIHI AJABTA WA IDHA ISTA-
RHAMTA BIHI RAHIMTA, WA IDHA ISTAFRAJTA BIHI
FARRAJTA, AN TU 'IDHANI MINAL KUFRI WAL
FAQRI, WAL QILLATI WA 'DHILLATI, WAL'ILLATI
WA KAFFATI AL AMRADHI WAL A'RADHI, WA SAIRI
AL ASQAMI WAL ĀLAMI WA AS'ALUKA FAWATIHA
AL KHAYRI, WA KHAWATIMAHU WA JAWAMI 'AHU
WA AWWALAHU WA ĀKHIRAHU WA DHAHIRAHU
WA BATINAHU WA ADDARAJATJ AL 'ULA.

*O Allah, I implore Thee in Thy pure, clean and blessed name
which pleaseth Thee most when Thou art invoked.*

*By that name, when Thou art asked to grant relief, Thou
grantest it. Grant me refuge from incredulity, poverty, in-
digence, humiliation, ailment and all types of diseases and
needs, and all other shortcomings and griefs.*

*I implore Thee for all good, its beginnings and its endings, its
whole, its first and its last, that which can be seen and that which
is invisible.*

ALLAHUMMA INNEE AS'ALUKA FARAJAN QAREE-BAN, WA NASRAN AZEEZAN, WA SABRAN JAMEE-LAN, WA FAT'HAN MUBEENAN, WA 'ILMAN KATHEE-RAN NAFI 'AN WA RIZQAN WASI 'AN MUBARAKAN FI 'ĀFIYATIN BILĀ BĀLA'IN. WA AS'ALUKA AL AFIYATA MIN KULLI BALIYYATIN, WA AS'ALUKA TAMAMA AL ĀFIYATI WA ASHUKRI 'ALA AL AFIYATI.

O Allah, I implore Thee to grant me early relief, powerful assistance, becoming patience, clean victory, vast, useful knowledge and ample, blessed provision in preservation without any affliction, as well as the ability to offer Thee infinite thanks for this preservation.

ALLAHUMMA AQSIM LEE MIN KHASHYATIKA MA TAHULOO BIHI BAYNI WA BAYNA MA 'ASSEEKA, WA MIN TAA 'ATIKA, MA TUBALLIGHUNEE BIHI JANNATAK, WA MIN AL YAQEENI MA TAHUNU BIHI ALAYA MASSA. IBA ADDUNIA, WA MATTE 'NI ALLAHUMMA BI SAM'I, WA BASARI, WA DEENEE WAJ'ALHA AL WARITHA MINNEE, WAJ'AL THA'ERI 'ALA MAN DHALAMANEE WANSURNI 'ALA MAN 'ADANEE, WA LA TAJ'AL IDD NIA AKBARA HAMMEE WA LA MABLAGHA 'ILMEE, WA LA ILA ANNACI MASEEREE.

O Allah, grant unto me a share of Thy fear that I may never disobey Thee. Inspire in me that obedience towards Thyself that shall lead me unto Thy Paradise. Bestow upon me the faith that shall make it easy for me to firmly bear the troubles of this world.

O Allah, let me enjoy my hearing and my sight and my faith as long as I live. I seek in Thee a refuge against those that oppress me. Grant me assistance against my enemies. Make not the affairs of the world my foremost aim, nor my ultimate goal, and let me not depend upon Thy creatures.

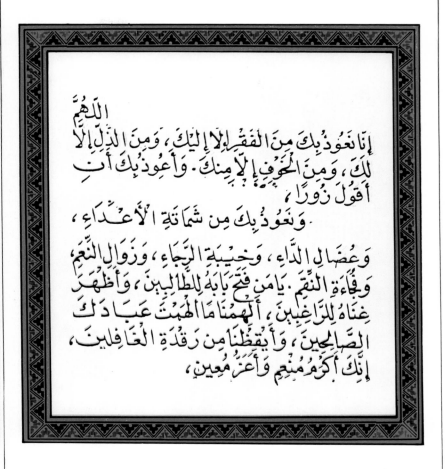

اللَّهُمَّ
إِنَّا نَعُوذُ بِكَ مِنَ الْفَقْرِ إِلاَّ إِلَيْكَ، وَمِنَ الذُّلِّ إِلاَّ
لَكَ، وَمِنَ الْخَوْفِ إِلاَّ مِنكَ. وَأَعُوذُ بِكَ أَنْ
أَقُولَ زُورًا
. وَنَعُوذُ بِكَ مِن شَمَاتَةِ الْأَعْدَاءِ،
وَعُضَالِ الدَّاءِ، وَخَيْبَةِ الرَّجَاءِ، وَزَوَالِ النِّعَمِ،
وَفُجَاءَةِ النِّقَمِ .يَا مَن فَتَحَ بَابَهُ لِلطَّالِبِينَ، وَأَظْهَرَ
غِنَاهُ لِلرَّاغِبِينَ، أَلْهِمْنَا مَا أَلْهَمْتَ عِبَادَكَ
الصَّالِحِينَ، وَأَيْقِظْنَا مِن رَقْدَةِ الْغَافِلِينَ،
إِنَّكَ أَكْرَمُ مُنْعِمٍ وَأَعَزُّ مُعِينٍ،

ALLAHUMMA INNEE 'A'ODHU BIKA MINA AL FAQRI
ILLA ILAYK, WA MINA ADH'DHULLI ILLA LAK, WA
MINAL KHAWFI ILLA MINK WA A'ODHU BIKA AN
AQULA ZOORAN, WA NA'ODHU BIKA MIN SHAMATI
AL A'DAI, WA 'ODHALI ID'DA'I, WA KHAIBATI
ARRAJA'I, WA ZAWALIN INNI'AM, WA FUJA'ATI
INNIQAM YA MAN FATAHA BABAHU LITTALIBEEN,
WA ADH'HARA GHINA'AHU LIRRAGHIBEEN,
ALHIMNA MA ALHAMTA IBADAKA ASSALIHEEN WA
AYQEDHNA MIN RAQDATILA GHAFILEEN, INNAKA
AKRAMU MUN'IM, WA AZZU MU'IN.

*O Allah, preserve me from having need of aught but Thee,
preserve me from humbling myself to any but Thee, from
having any fear save that of Thee. I seek in Thee a refuge from
all falsehood.*

*We seek a refuge in Thee from the rejoicing of our enemies over
our loss, from incurable diseases, from the frustation of hopes,
from the absence of bliss and from anger.*

*O Allah, Thou who hast opened Thy gate for the seekers, who
hast granted eloquence to those who are short of it, inspire us
with what Thou hast inspired Thy righteous servants and awake
us from the slumber of the negligent.*

*Thou art the Noble Giver, the Mighty Helper whose aid is never
bestowed in vain.*

اللّهُمَّ إِنَّ عُيُوبَنَا لَا يَسْتُرُهَا إِلَّا مَحَاسِنُ عَطْفِكَ، وَذُنُوبَنَا لَا يَغْفِرُهَا إِلَّا وَاسِعُ إِحْسَانِكَ، وَعَفْوُكَ . وَاجْعَلْنَا مِنَ الْمُتَّقِينَ الْأَبْرَارِ، وَاسْلُكْ بِنَا سَبِيلَ عِبَادِكَ الْأَخْيَارِ، وَأَلْهِمْنَا رُشْدَنَا، وَأَجْزِلْ مِنْ رِضْوَانِكَ حَظَّنَا، وَلَا تَحْرِمْنَا بِذُنُوبِنَا، وَلَا تَطُرْ ذَنْبًا بِعُيُوبِنَا، وَلَا تَقْطَعْنَا مِنْ بِرِّكَ، وَلَا تُنْسِنَا ذِكْرَكَ، وَلَا نَهِّتِكْ عَنَّا سِتْرَكَ، وَاغْفِرْلَنَا

مَا اقْتَرَفْنَاهُ مِنْ ذُنُوبِنَا، وَاعْفُ عَنْ تَقْصِيرِنَا فِي طَاعَتِكَ وَشُكْرِكَ، وَأَدِمْ لَنَا لُزُومَ الطَّرِيقِ إِلَيْكَ، وَهَبْ لَنَا نُورًا نَهْتَدِي بِهِ إِلَيْكَ، وَارْزُقْنَا حَلَاوَةَ مُنَاجَاتِكَ، وَاسْلُكْ بِنَا سَبِيلَ مَرْضَاتِكَ، وَاقْطَعْ عَنَّا كُلَّ مَا يُبْعِدُنَا عَنْ خِدْمَتِكَ وَطَاعَتِكَ، وَأَنْقِذْنَا مِنْ دَرَكَاتِنَا وَغَفَلَاتِنَا،

وَحَقِّقْ فِيكَ قَصْدَنَا، وَاسْتُرْنَا فِي دُنْيَانَا وَآخِرَتِنَا، وَاحْشُرْنَا فِي زُمْرَةِ الْمُتَّقِينَ، وَأَلْحِقْنَا بِعِبَادِكَ الصَّالِحِينَ .

ALLAHUMMA INNA 'OYUBANA LA YASTURUHA ILLA MAHASINU 'ATFIK, WA DHUNUBANA LA YAGHFI-RUHA ILLA WASI'U IHSANEK, WA AFWIK. WA IJ'ALWA MIN AL MUTTAQEEN AL ABRAR, WASLUK BINA SABEELA 'IBADIKAL AKHYAR WA ALHIMNA RUSHDANA, WAJ'ZEL MIN RIDHWANIKA HADHANA, WA LA TAHRIMNA BI DHUNUBINA, WA LA TATRUDNA DI 'OYUBINA WA LA TAQTA'NA MIN BIR-RIKA WA LA TUN'SINA DHIKRAK, WA LA TAHTIK 'ANNA SATRAK, WAGHFER LANA MA QTARAFANHU MIN DHUNUBINA. WA'FU 'AN TAQSEERINA FI TA'ATIKA, WA SHUKRIKA, WA'ADIM LANA LUZU-MAT TAREEQI ILAYKA, WA HAB LANA NURAN NAH-TADEE BIHI ILAYKA, WAR'ZUQNA HALAWATA MUNAJATIKA, WAS'LUK BINA SABEELA MARDHA-TIKA, WAQ'TA'ANNA KULLA MA YUB'IDUNA 'AN KHIDMATIKA WA TA'ATIK WA ANQIDHNA MIN DARAKATINA WA GHAFALATINA, WALIHIMNA RUSHDANA, WA HAQ'QEQ FEEKA QASDANA, WAS'TURNA FEE DUNYANA WA FI AKHIRATINA, WAHSHURNA FEE ZUMRATI AL MUTTAQEEN, WAL'HEQNA BI'IBADIKA ASSALIHEEN.

O Allah, nothing shall hide our vices but Thy gracious turning. Nothing shall forgive our sins except Thy unlimited kindness and forgiveness. Place us among those who fear Thee and are pious. Cause us to follow the path of Thy servants who are the best of people. Inspire us with our right direction and grant us a share of what pleaseth Thee. Despair us not on account of our sins and cast us not away on account of our vices. Sever us not from Thy piety and cause us not to forget Thy mention.

Forgive us our sins and pardon us for any of our remiss in Thy obedience or in thanking Thee. Grant us light whereby we may find true direction unto Thee. Provide us with the sweet and pleasant taste of speaking in secret discourse unto Thee. Cause us to follow the path leading to Thy pleasure and sever from us all that should take us away from doing service unto Thee, and from Thy obedience. Save us from our pitfalls and follies. Inspire us with our right direction. Make true our expectations concerning Thee. Hide our failings in this world and in the Hereafter. Raise us along the group of those who fear Thee. Join us with Thy servants who are righteous.

ALLAHUMMA IJ'ALNA MIN'AL AYEMMATIL ABRAR,
WAS KIN'NA MA'AHUM FEE DARIL QARAR, WA LA
TAJ'ALNA MIN'AL MUKHALIFEENA AL FUJJAR, WA
WAFFEQNA LI HUSNIL IQ BALI 'ALAYKA, WAL
ISGHA'I I LAYKA, WAL MU BA DARATI ILA KHIDMA-
TIK, WA HUSNIL ADABI FEE MU'AMALATIK,
WAT'TASLEEMI LI AMREK, WA ARRIDHA'A BI
QADHA'EK WA ASSABRI 'ALA BALAEK, WA ASH'
SHUKRI. LI NA'A' MA-IKA, WA A'IDHNA MIN AHWALI
ASHAQA'I WA WAFFEQNA LI A'MALI AH'LI T'TUQA,
WAR'ZUQNA AL ISTI'DADA LI YAMI ALLIQA. YA
MAN'ALAÏKA AL I'TIMADU WA AL MUTAKKAL.

*O Allah, place us among the noble leaders and cause us to dwell
with them in the mansion that abideth, and place us not among
those who oppose Thy commands and are wicked. Grace us with
the good entrance unto Thy presence, with Thy audience, with
alacrity to serve Thee, with the best of manners that we should
observe in dealing with Thee, with submission to Thy command,
with contentment in respect of Thy irreversible decree, with patience to bear the trial from Thee, with gratitude to Thee for Thy
favour.*

*Grant us refuge from great misfortune, grant us power to act
like the pious, grant us also the power to stand the Day of Thy
meeting. O Thou on whom is reliance and who is trusted.*

ALLAHUMMA LĀ TAJ'AL HADHA AKHIRA 'AHDI MIN
HADHA AL MAWQIFI AL'ADHEEM, WAR'ZUQNEE
ARRUJU'A ILAYHI MARRATIN KATHIRAH BI LUF-
TIKA AL'AMEEM, WAJ'ALNI MUFLIHAN MUSTAJĀBA
ADDU'A'I, FA'IZAN BIL QABOOLI WAR'RIDHWANI,
WAT'TAJĀWUZI WAL GHUFRANI, WAR'RIZQI AL
HALALI AL WASI'I, WA BARIK LEE FEE JAMEE'I
OMURI, WA MĀ ARJI'O ILAYHI MIN AHLEE WA
MALEE WA AWLADEE.

*O Allah, make not this visit my last visit to this grand muster,
and deal out to me return to this holy place several times by Thy
immense grace, and thereby make me a person who prospereth
and who enjoyeth Thy mercy.*

*O Lord, make me a person whose invocation has been answe-
red and who has succeeded in obtaining divine acceptance, pleasure of Allah, connivance and forgiveness, and ample lawful
provision.*

*Grant me blessing in all my affairs and also in those to whom
I shall shortly return - my family, my children and all whom
I shall see once more.*

RABBANA ĀTINA FID'UNIA HASANATAN WA
FIL'AKHIRATI HASANATAN, WA QINA 'ADHABA
ANNAR, WA AGHFIR LANA WA LIWALIDAYNA WA
DHORRIYATINA, WA IKHWANINA WA AHLINA, WAL
HADHIREENA WA GHA'IBEENA MIN AL MUSLI-
MEENA AJMA'IN BI RAHMATIKA YA ARHAMA ARRA-
HIMEEN, WA SALLA L'LAHU 'ALA SAYIDINA WA
MAWLANA MUHAMMAD, WA'ALA ĀLIHI WA SAH-
BIHI AJMA'EEN.

*O our Lord, give us good in this world and also good in the next
world, and deliver us from the torment of Hell-Fire. Forgive us
and our parents, our posterity, our brothers and our families.
Forgive also those Muslims who are present and those who are
absent. Save us all with Thy mercy, O the Most Merciful of
those who shew mercy.*

*May Allah send blessings on Muhammed and his posterity and
all his companions.*

Ad'iyat-al-Madinah
(Invocations at Medinah)

Invocation to be recited before the Prophet's tomb at Medinah

السَّلَامُ عَلَى رَسُولِ اللهِ صَلَّى اللهُ عَلَيْهِ وَسَلَّمَ،
السَّلَامُ عَلَيْكَ أَيُّهَا النَّبِيُّ وَرَحْمَةُ اللهِ وَبَرَكَاتُهُ،
الصَّلَاةُ وَالسَّلَامُ عَلَيْكَ يَاسَيِّدِنَا يَارَسُولَ اللهِ،
الصَّلَاةُ وَالسَّلَامُ عَلَيْكَ يَانَبِيَّ اللهِ، الصَّلَاةُ
وَالسَّلَامُ عَلَيْكَ يَاخَيْرَخَلْقِ اللهِ، الصَّلَاةُ

ASSALAMU 'ALA RASULIL LAHI SALLA ALLAHU
ALAYHI WA SALLAM, ASSALAMU ALAYKA AYYUHA
AN NABIYOU WA RAHMATU L'LAHI WA BARAKA-
TUH, ASSALATU WAS SALAMU ALAYKA YA SAYYI-
DANA YA RASULALAH, ASSALATU WAS SALAMU
ALAYKA YA NABI YA 'ALLAH, ASSALATU WAS
SALAMU 'ALAYKA YA KHAYRA KHALQ 'IL'LAH.

Peace be on thee, O Prophet, and also the Mercy of Allah and His blessings. Blessings and peace on thee, O Prophet of Allah. Blessings and peace be on thee, O beloved of Allah.

Peace and blessings be on thee, O the best of Allah's creation.

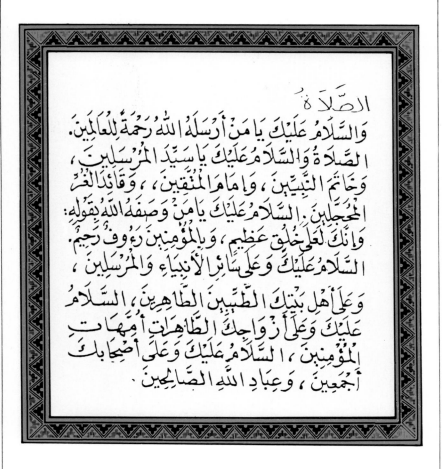

**ASSALATU WAS SALAMU ALAYKA YA SAYYIDAL'
MURSALEEN, WA KHATIMA ANNABIYYEEN, WA IMA-
MAL' MUTTAQEEN.**

**ASSALUMU ALAYKA YA MAN WASAFAHU L'LAHU
BIQAWLIHI : WA INNAKA LA 'ALA KHULUQIN
ADHEEM, WA BIL MU'EMINEENA RAOUFUN RAHEEM
ASSALAMU ALAYKA WA 'ALA SA'IRI AL ANBIYA'I
WAL MURSALEEM, WA 'ALA AHLI BAYTIKA
ATTAYYIBEEN, ATTAHIREEN, ASSALAMU 'ALAYKA
WA 'ALA AZWAJIKA ATTAHIRATI OMMAHATIL
MU'EMINEEN, ASSALAMU 'ALAYKA WA 'ALA ASHA-
BIKA AJMA'EEN, WA 'IBAD ALLAHI ASSALIHEEN.**

*Peace and blessings be on thee, O the intercessor of sinners with
Allah. Peace and blessings be on thee, O thou whom Allah hath
sent as mercy for the worlds. Peace and blessings be on thee, O
the chief of the messenger and the last of all the Prophets, and
the leader of the pious.*

*Peace and blessings be on thee, whom God hath so described :
"Thou art a noble nature, and compassionate and full of mercy
for believers."*

*Peace and blessings be on thee and the people of thy family who
are pure. Peace and blessings be on thee and on thy wives who
are pure and who are the mothers of believers. Peace and blessings be on thee and all thy companions and on the rest of the
prophets and messengers and also on the pious servants of
Allah.*

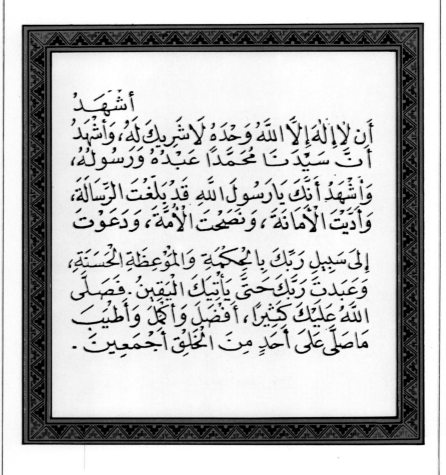

ASH'HADU ANNA LA ILAHA ILLA ALLAH WA
ASH'HADU ANNA SAYYIDINA MUHAMMADAN
'ABDUHH WA RASULUH WA ASH'HADU ANNAKA YA
RASUL ALLAH QAD BALLAGHTA AR RISALAH. WA
ADDAYTAL AMANAH WA NASAHTAL'OMMAH, WA
DA 'AWTA ILA SABEELI RABBIKA BIL HIKMATI WAL
MAW 'IDHATI AL HASANATI, WA ABADTA RABBAKA
HATTA YA'ETIYAKA AL YAQEEN, FA SALLA ALLAHU
ALAYKA KATHEERAN, AFDHALA WA AKMALA WA
ATYABA MA SALLA 'ALA AHADIN MIN AL KHALQI
AJMA 'EEN.

*I bear witness to the fact that there is none worthy of worship
except Allah, who is alone and hath no partner. I also testify that
Muhammed is His servant and His Prophet. I also testify that
thou, O Messenger of Allah, hast communicated the message of
the Lord to the people, and that thou, O Messenger of Allah,
hast been sincere to thy community, and that thou hast called
them to the path of thy Lord with wisdom and good admoni-
tions, and that thou hast worshipped thy Lord till the truth came
unto thee.*

*May Allah send innumerable blessings on thee - the most ex-
cellent, fullest and purest of blessings which Allah hath sent on
any of His creations.*

ALLAHUMMA AJZI 'ANNA NABIYYANA AFDHALA MĀ JAZAYTA AHADAN MIN ANNABIYYINA WAL MURSALEEN.

ALLAHUMMA ATIHI L'WASEELATA WAL FADHI-LATA, WAB' 'ATH'HU MAQAMAN MAHMUDAN ALLA-DHI WA'AD'TAHU.

ALLAHUMMA SALLI 'ALA MUHAMMADIN KAMA SALLAYTA 'ALA IBRAHEEM WA 'ALA ALI IBRAHEEM, INNAKA HAMEEDUN, MAJEED RABBANA AMAN'NA BIMA ANZALTA WAT TABA'NA ARRASULA FAK-TUBNA MA'A ASH SHAHIDEEN, WAL HAMDU LIL-LAHI RABBI L''ALAMEEN.

O Allah, grant our Prophet on our behalf the excellent reward that Thou hast ever granted to any of the Prophets and Messengers.

O Allah, grant him union with Thyself and excellence, and raise him to the glorious station which Thou hast promised him.

O Allah, send peace on Muhammed and on his posterity as hast Thou done on Abraham and his posterity. Verily praise and glory are Thy due !

O Allah, send blessings on Muhammed and on his posterity, for we have believed in what Thou hast revealed to Muhammed and have followed Thy Messenger. May we be associated to the righteous witnesses.

Verily, Praise and Glory are Thy due, Master of the worlds.

Salutations to be recited
at the tomb
of Abu Bakr Aŝ-Ŝiddiq

ثُمَّ يَنْتَقِلُ إِلَى يَمِينِهِ قَدْرَ ذِرَاعٍ، وَيُسَلِّمُ عَلَى أَبِي بَكْرٍ الصِّدِّيقِ رَضِيَ اللهُ عَنْهُ وَيَقُولُ:

السَّلَامُ عَلَيْكَ يَا خَلِيفَةَ رَسُولِ اللهِ أَبَا بَكْرٍ الصِّدِّيقِ، السَّلَامُ عَلَيْكَ يَا مَنْ قَالَ فِي حَقِّكَ رَسُولُ اللهِ صَلَّى اللهُ عَلَيْهِ وَسَلَّمَ: يَا أَبَا بَكْرٍ أَنْتَ عَتِيقُ اللهِ مِنَ النَّارِ. السَّلَامُ عَلَيْكَ يَا صَاحِبَ رَسُولِ اللهِ وَثَانِيَ اثْنَيْنِ إِذْ هُمَا فِي الْغَارِ ... السَّلَامُ عَلَيْكَ يَا مَنْ أَنْفَقَ مَالَهُ كُلَّهُ فِي حُبِّ اللهِ وَحُبِّ رَسُولِهِ، حَتَّى تَخَلَّلَ بِالْعَبَاءِ. جَزَاكَ اللهُ عَنْ أُمَّةِ رَسُولِ اللهِ خَيْرَ الْجَزَاءِ. اللَّهُمَّ ارْضَ عَنْهُ، وَارْفَعْ دَرَجَتَهُ، وَأَكْرِمْ مَقَامَهُ، وَأَجْزِلْ ثَوَابَهُ، بِفَضْلِكَ وَكَرَمِكَ آمِينَ.

ثُمَّ يَنْتَقِلُ إِلَى يَمِينِهِ قَدْرَ ذِرَاعٍ، وَيُسَلِّمُ عَلَى عُمَرَ بْنِ الْخَطَّابِ رَضِيَ اللهُ عَنْهُ وَيَقُولُ:

السَّلَامُ عَلَيْكَ أَمِيرَ الْمُؤْمِنِينَ عُمَرَ بْنَ الْخَطَّابِ، السَّلَامُ عَلَيْكَ يَا مَنْ قَالَ فِي حَقِّكَ رَسُولُ اللهِ صَلَّى اللهُ عَلَيْهِ وَسَلَّمَ: عُمَرُ بْنُ الْخَطَّابِ سِرَاجُ أَهْلِ الْجَنَّةِ، وَقَالَ أَيْضًا: وَمَا طَلَعَتِ الشَّمْسُ عَلَى رَجُلٍ خَيْرٍ مِنْ عُمَرَ. السَّلَامُ عَلَيْكَ يَا نَاطِقًا بِالْعَدْلِ وَالصَّوَابِ، السَّلَامُ عَلَيْكَ يَا أَبَا الْفُقَرَاءِ وَالضُّعَفَاءِ وَالْأَرَامِلِ وَالْأَيْتَامِ، جَزَاكَ اللهُ عَنْ أُمَّةِ رَسُولِ اللهِ خَيْرَ الْجَزَاءِ. اللَّهُمَّ ارْضَ عَنْهُ، وَارْفَعْ دَرَجَتَهُ، وَأَكْرِمْ مَقَامَهُ، وَأَجْزِلْ ثَوَابَهُ، بِفَضْلِكَ وَكَرَمِكَ آمِينَ.

ASSALAMU'ALAYKA YA KHALIFATA RASULI L'LAHI ABA BAKRIN AŜŜIDDIQ, ASSALAMU'ALAYKA YA MAN QĀLA FEE HAQQIKA RASULUL LAĦI SALLA ALLAĦU ALAYHI WA SALLAM : YA ABA BAKR ANTA ATEEQU'L'LAĦI MINA N'NAR.

ASSALAMU ALYKA YA SAHIBA RASULI LAĦI, WA THANI YA ITHNAYNI IDH ĦUMA FIL GHĀR... ASSA-LAMU ALAYKA YA MAN ANFAQA MALAĦU KUL-LAĦU FEE HUBBI L'LAĦ WA HUBBI RASULIĦI HATTA TAKHALLALA BIL ABA'I, JAZAKA ALLAĦU 'AN OMMATI RASULI'L'LAH KHAYRA JAZA'E.

ALLAĦUMMA IRDHA 'ANĦU, WARFA' DARAJATAĦH WAKRIM MAQAMAĦU, WAJZIL'THAWBAĦ BIFADH-LIKA, WA KARAMIKA, AMEEN.

The pilgrim then walks a yard to the right of the tomb of the Prophet to greet that of Abu Bakr Aŝ-Ŝiddiq (the first Caliph) in the following terms :

Peace be on thee, O Abu Bakr the truthful. Peace be on thee, O the true Caliph of the Messenger of Allah. Peace be on thee, O the companion of the Messenger of Allah and the Second of the Two when they two were in the cave*.

Peace be on thee, O thou who hath spent all his property in love for Allah and in love for His Messenger, till he retired apart with his cloak.

May Allah grant thee the best of reward on behalf of the community of the Messenger of Allah.

May Allah be pleased with thee and may He grant thee the best of contentment and make the Garden thy abode and resort. Peace be on thee and also the mercy of Allah and His blessings. Amen.

(*) Reference to the grotto in which the Prophet and Abu Bakr hid for three days, after flee-ing Mecca, thanks to which they were able to avoid being discovered by their Qureishite pur-suers, and thus managed to reach Yathrib (later called Medinah) safe and sòund. The Hira (the emigration) dates from this moment and spells the beginning of the Muslim era (622 A.D.).

ASSALAMU'ALAYKA YA AMIRA L'MU'EMINEEN 'UMAR IBNA L'KHATTAB, ASSALAMU ALAYKA YA MAN QALA FEE HAQQIKA RASULUL'LAHI SALLA ALLAHU ALAYHI WA SALLAM :

'UMARU IBNUL KHATTAB SIRAJU AHLI L'JANNAH, WA QALA AYDHAN WA MA TALA'AT ISH SHAMSU 'ALA RAJULIN KHAYRUN MIN 'UMAR.

ASSALAMU ALAYKA YA NATIQAN BIL 'ADL WAS'SAWAB. ASSALAMU ALAYKA YA ABAL FUQARA'I WA DH'DHU 'AFA'I, WAL ARAMILI WAL AYTAM, JAZAKA ALLAHU 'AN UMMATI RASULI'L'LAHI KHAYRA JAZA'E.

ALLAHUMMA IRDHA 'ANHU, WARFA 'DARAJATAHU WAKREEM MAQAMAHU, WAJZILTHAWABAHU BI FADHLIKA WA KARAMIKA, AMEEN.

The pilgrim then moves one yard to the right of tomb of Abu Bakr to face that of 'Umar Ibn al-Khattab (the second Caliph) greeting it in the following terms :

Peace be on thee, O the Commander of those who believe, thou of whom the Prophet said :

" 'Umar Ibn al-Khattab, peace be on thee who spoke just and fit. The sun has never risen on a better man than 'Umar."

Peace be upon thee, O just man !Peace be upon thee, O the patron of the needy, of the weak, of the widows and of the orphans !

May Allah be pleased with thee and may He grant thee the best of contentment and make the Garden thy abode and place of resort.

O Allah, be pleased with him and raise his rank and make noble his position and grant him full reward. Amen.

glossary

A

'Abd al-Muttalib Ibn Hashim : Grandfather of the Prophet. Rediscovered the Zamzam well.

Abraham : See **Ibraheem el-Khalil.**

Abu Bakr aṣ-Ṣiddiq : One of the first converts to Islam. Born around 573 AD, died in 13/H (634). Accompanied the Prophet during the *Hijrah.* First caliph of Islam. Buried close to the Prophet.

Abu Hanifah : Founder of the Hanifite school. Born in 80/H (699 AD), died in 150/H (767 AD).

Abbu Qubays : Hill overlooking Mecca.

Abu Sufian Mu'awid : The most eminent Qureishite leader and originally an enemy of the Prophet. Became converted to Islam when Mecca was taken. Died in 30/H (652 AD). His son, Mu'awid, was the founder of the Umayyad dynasty. One of the subtlest political leaders in Arab history. Died in 61/H (680 AD).

Ahzāb (sing. **Hizb**) : Parties or factions. Title of the XXXIIIth surah of the Koran. Coalition formed against the Prophet by the Jews of Medinah in the year 5 of the Hijrah.

'Ali Ibn Abi Ṭālib : Fourth of the orthodox caliphs (600-661). Cousin and son-in-law of the Prophet. His courage, physical strength and warrior's skill, as well as his asceticism, his wisdom and his tremendous juridical expertise, have made of him a legendary figure. Muslims all over the world and at all times have regarded him as one of the major figures of Islam, irrespective of the sect or school to which they belonged. The Shi'ites in particular (Iraqi and Iranian) — notably the Imam Khumayni) look upon 'Ali Ibn Abi Ṭālib as the prototype — after the Prophet — of the enlightened, fair-minded and disinterested sovereign. His tomb at Najaf (Iraq) is a place of veneration second only to that of the Prophet.

'Aleem : Omniscient. One of the 99 sublime epithets of God.

Al-Marwah : See **Aṣ-Ṣafā.**

Ansār : Medinan allies of the Prophet, who persuaded them to officially fraternize with the *Muhajireen* (immigrants) of Mecca.

'Arafāt (or **'Arafa**) : Valley situated approximately 25 kilometres from Mecca where the *Hajj* pilgrims must perform the rite of standing *(Wuqūf)* on the 9th Thu-l-Hijjah.

Asma Allah al-Husna : The most beautiful names for God, the most sublime epithets for God.

Ayat (sing. **Ahah**) : Signs, miracles, proofs and especially verses from the Koran.

'Ayesha : Daughter of Abu Bakr and wife of the Prophet. famous for her extensive knowledge of juridical and religious matters. Died in 58/H (678).

Ayyam at-Tashreeq : Literally, days of dissection and drying in the sun of the flesh of sacrificial animals. Days spent at Minā by the pilgrims after the Day of Sacrifice (*Yawm an-Na'hr*).

Ayyam Ma'Loumāt : Known days.

B

Bab (plural, **Abwab**) : Gate.

Badana : Animal destined for the sacrifice.

Bairam : Name given by the Turks to the *Eid al Ad'hā*, Feast of the Sacrifice of the animals at Minā and in all other parts of the Muslim world on the 10th Thu-l-Hijjah.

Bakkah : Ancient name of Makkah (Mecca).

Baqara : Cow, or heifer. Name of the second surah of the Koran, which is also the longest : 286 verses.

Bayt (plural, **Bouyout**) : House, temple.

Bilal : Black African born into slavery. He was one of the first to accept Islam. Emancipated by Abu Bakr, he later became the first Islamic muezzin. The "Black Muslims" of the United States have now changed their name to "Bilalians" in his honour.

C

Caliph : See **Khalifah.**

Chaf' : Pair, supererogatory prayer of two *Raka'at* to be accomplished at night after the compulsory *'Ishā* prayer.

Chay'e : Thing.

Coalesced : See **Ahzāb.**

D - E

Dayne : Debt.

Dhan'b : Sin.

Dine : Cult, religion, confession.

Du'ā (plural, **Ad'iya**) : Invocation.

Eid al-Fitr : First day of the month of Shawwal, marks the end of the fast of Ramadān.

F

Fadilah : Quality, merit, virtue.

Fahichah : Turpitude, abomination, adultery.

Fajj : Defile, far-away place.

Fajr : Dawn. First prayer of the day, supererogatory, recommended but non-compulsory (two *Raka'at*) recited inaudibly.

Falak : Celestial sphere, orbit.

Falaq : Beginning of dawn, sunrise.

Fana' : Obliteration, annihilation.

Fani : Perishable.

Fara'id (plural of **Farida**) : Divine prescriptions, religious obligations, canonical rites.

Fard (plural, **Fourod**) : Prescription in the Koran, religious obligation.

Fasiq : Perverse, harmful, debauched, adulterous.

Fat'h : Opening, conquest, victory.

Fātihah : Beginning, introduction. First surah in the Koran.

Fatwa : Decision. Anwer given to a juridical or theological enquiry.

Fidyah : Atonement for an omission by an expiatory giving of alms. Sacrifice.

Fiq'h : Jurisprudence, law, knowledge in general.

Fitnah : confusion, trial, revolt, seduction, discord, riot, war, civil war.

Fuqaha' (plural of **Faqih**) : Legal experts, men of law.

Fuqara' : Indigents.

G

Ghadab : Wrath, anger.

Ghayb : Absence, mystery of the world, invisible (substantive).

Ghazawat (plural of **Ghazwah**) : Military expeditions or skirmishes in which the Prophet participated personally, such as those of Badr, Uhud, al-Khanaq (the ditch), Khaybar, Mecca, Hunayn and Tabuk, as opposed to those in which he did not participate directly though he commanded them, which are called *Saraya* (plural of *Sariyyah*).

Ghosl : Toilet, major ablutions, washing, bath.

H

Hadeeth Shareef : Sayings (of the Prophet).

Hadi : He who indicates the right path. Guide.

Had'y : Offering, oblation (during the pilgrimage). Animals immolated at Mecca.

Hājir (also known as **Agar**) : Coptic wife of the Prophet Abraham, mother of Ismāeel.

Hajj : Pilgrimage taking place at a set time of the year (first half of the month of Thu-l-Hijjah).

Hakeem : Wise. One of the sublime epithets of God.

Halq : Shaving of the hair or of the beard.

Hamzah : Son of 'Abd al-Muttalib. Uncle of the Prophet, scarcely older than his nephew. Celebrated warrior, known as "the Lion of God". With 'Ali, was the hero of the battles of Badr and Uhud, in which he found death at the hands of an Abyssinian slave called Wahshi, whose mistress, Hind, wife of the Qureishi leader Abu Sufian, had promised him his freedom in return for killing Hamzah (see page 83, for the battle of Mount Uhud and Hind, daughter of Utba).

Hanīf : Pre-Islamic devout monotheist. A moralist searching for the ancient religion of Abraham, thus by extension a Muslim ; Islam also is named : *Al-Hanīfiyyah.*

Hanifites : Adepts of the Imam Abu Hanifa.

Haqq : Truth, when preceded by the definite article — *al-Haqq* — becomes one of the sublime epithets of God.

Haram or **Harām** : Sacred, inviolable, forbidden, sacro-saint.

Al-Haram al-Madani : Territory of Medinah, forbidden to all non-Muslims.

Al-Harām an-Nabawee : Mosque of the Prophet at Medinah, which houses the tomb of God's Messenger, as well as that of the first two Caliphs, Abu Bakr and 'Umar.

Al-Harām ash-Shareef : Sacred mosque of Mecca, at the centre of which is the Ka'bah. The entire territory of Mecca is *Harām*, which means that it is forbidden to all non-Muslims.

Hashr : Assembly or gathering (particularly for the Last Judgement).

Hassanah : Good deed or action.

Hayd : Menstruation, menses, period.

Hijrah (or **Hegira**) : Emigration of the Prophet from Mecca to Medinah. Beginning of the Muslim era (622 AD).

Hissab : Account. **Yawm al-Hissab** : day of reckoning or accounting, eg : day of the Last Judgement.

Huda : Right direction. Islam (when one adds the definite article *Al*).

I

Ibadah : Adoration. Devotion. Cult.

Ibraheem El-Khalil : Abraham (in the Bible). Prophet. Father of Jewish and Arab monotheism, builder of the Ka'bah. *Al-Khalil* means "intimate friend" (of God).

Ifādah : Etymologically : "unfurling", "flow" or "movement", departure of the pilgrims from 'Arafāt after the *Wuqūf* (standing).

Ifrād : The intention of accomplishing the pilgrimage ; it is part of the rites of entry into the sacred state.

Ihrām: Sacralization. Also the clothing donned by pilgrims upon entering this state.

Ihsan: Meritorious action, embellishment, seemly behaviour, improvement, striving after perfection.

Ikhlās: Sincerity. Consecration of a pure cult to God. Name of the 112th surah in the Koran.

Ikrah: Constraint.

Ikram: Generous treatment, mark of respect.

Ilhad: Atheism.

I'lm: Science, knowledge.

Imān: Faith.

In Sha Allah: Please God. If God wishes it.

Iqab: Sanction. Punishment.

'Ishā (Sālāt al): Canonical prayer recited as soon as night has fallen completety. It consists of four *Raka'at* (the first two spoken audibly, the final two under one's breath).

Ithm: Sin, danger, inconvenience, naiveté.

I'tiraf: Confession, gratitude.

Izar: Length of cloth covering the loins down to the knees, seamless garb which the pilgrim wraps around his waist when he enters the sacred state of *Ihrām*.

J

Jamrat (singular, **Jamra**): Pillars or steles symbolizing Satan which pilgrims stone at Minā. The pebbles used for the stoning are also called *Jamarat*.

Jannah: Garden, paradise.

Jihad: Effort, struggle, fight (chiefly for the defense of Islamic ideals and of Muslim interests). In the West, the Jihad has come to be known as a "holy war", which is generally incorrect except when it refers to the war-effort of the Muslims to repel European invaders from their lands at the time of the Crusades and in the 19th Century.

Jumada-I-Ūlā: 5th month of the Muslim lunar calendar. In its masculine form, it is sometimes referred to as **Jumad al-Awal.**

Jumada-th-Thani: 6th month of the Muslim or Hegiran lunar calendar. Sometimes called, in the masculine form, **Jumad at-Thani.**

Jumu'ah: Friday. Etymologically: day of reunion or gathering.

K

Kafara: To disbelieve, abjure, forwear or blaspheme.

Kaffarah: Expiation.

Kafir: Miscreant, unbeliever.

Kalimah: Word.

Karamh: Generosity.

Khalifah (plural **Khulafa**): Successor, vicar, lieutenant (the term, "caliph" in the European languages).

Khalil: Close friend, confident. Name given to Abraham (with the addition of the definite article *Al*).

Khatam al-Anbiya: Seal of the prophets.

Khati'a: Fault, sin.

Khatim al-Anbiya: The last of the prophets to date.

Khayr: The good.

L

Labbayka: "Here I am!". See **Talbiyah.**

La'nat: Malediction, curse.

Layalin 'Ashr: The first ten nights of Thu-l-Hijjah.

Lutf: Grace, benevolence, sollicitude, clemence, compassion.

M

Macir: Becoming, walk, course, destiny of the world.

Mafrud: Prescribed, imposed.

Maghrib: Sunset, West, fourth canonical prayer consisting of three *Raka'at*, the first two of which are spoken aloud, the last inaudibly.

Makr: Perfidy.

Mal: Wealth. Belongings.

Mala'ika: (plural of **Mal'ak** and **Malak**): Angels.

Maqām Ibraheem: Station of Abraham. Sanctuary located a few feet away from the Ka'bah, indicating the spot where the patriarch Abraham would stand when calling the faithful to prayer, and where he prayed in summer, the Ka'bah itself being reserved for winter prayers.

Ma'ruf: Well known, good deed appropriate.

Mash'ar: Place destined for fulfilment of a rite.

Mashi'a: Will-power.

Ma'siyya: Disobedience, sin.

Masjid: Place of prayer (place where one prosternates oneself), mosque.

Mathab: Etymologically, a passage. Juridical and theological school and its concept of the application of rites.

Meeqāt: Place and time where and when the pilgrim must enter the sacred state of *Ihrām*.

Mihrab: Hollow in the wall of a mosque indicating the direction of Mecca (*Qiblah*).

Minā: A place located 6 kilometres east of Mecca, on the road to 'Arafāt, in a valley of the same name.

Miskeen: Indigent, poor.

Mithaq: Pact, agreement.

Mufti: Jurisconsult.

Muharrām: First month of the Muslim or Hegiran lunar calendar, and first sacred month.

Mu'mine: Believer.

Munafiqun (plural of **Munafiq**): Hypocrite.

Munawwarah: Illustrious, illuminated, haloed. Epithet applied to the town of the Prophet (Medinah).

Munkar: Outcast, abominable, reprehensible.

Muqarrabun: Close to God, archangels, angels.

Mus'haf: Copy of the Koran.

Mushrik: Idolater, pagan.

Muslim (or **Moslem**): Showing submission to God. Belonging to the Muslim faith.

Mutawwif (plural **Mutawwifeen**): He who guides and lodges foreign pilgrims during their stay at Mecca. Literally, he who makes the pilgrims circumambulate around the Ka'bah.

Muttaqun: Pious, fearing God, virtuous.

Muzawwir (plural **Muzawwiren**): He who shows around, the Medinan equivalent of the Meccan *Mutawwif*.

Muzdalifah: Hill located halfway between Minā and 'Arafāt, where pilgrims spend the nights of 9th and 10th Thu-l-Hijjah after the departure from 'Arafat.

N

Nabi: Prophet.

Nafilah: Prayer, supererogatory.

Nafs: Breath, soul.

Na'hr: Immolation. Sacrifice of livestock (camel, cow, sheep or goat).

Nah'y: Reprobation, disapprobation, warning.

Na'im: Well-being, comfort, felicity.

Najas: Impurity, stain.

Na'l: Sandals.
Nar: Fire Hell.
Ni'mah: Good deed, favour.
Niqmah: Revenge, evil.
Niyah: Intention.
Nur: Light. God.
Nussuk: Oblations, devotions, rites.

P - Q

Prayer: See Ŝalāt.
Qadar: Destiny, determinism.
Qaddassa: To santify.
Qanata: To adore, to worship (particularly during the final third of the night), to pray assiduously.
Qawl: Word.
Qawm: People, persons.
Qayyum: Existing, extant. One of the sublime epithets of God.
Quiblah: Direction of prayer (in other words, direction of the Ka'bah).
Qiran: Jurisdiction of the *'Umrah* (individual pilgrimage) and the *Hajj* (great pilgrimage), which are undertaken together.
Qisas: Talion (retaliation).
Qunot: Despair (in God).

R

Rabb: Master, God.
Rabi 'al-Awwal: Third month of the Muslim, or Hegiran lunar calendar.
Rabi' ath-Thani: Fourth month of the Muslim, or Hegiran lunar calendar.
Raheem: Very compassionate. All-merciful. One of the sublime epithets of God.
Rahmah: Mercy, clemency.
Rahman: All-merciful. One of the sublim epithets of God.
Raja: Hope.
Rajab: Seventh month of the Muslim, or Hegiran lunar calendar. Second of the sacred months and the only one of the four sacred months to stand on its own, in other words to be neither preceded nor followed by another sacred month, the other three being in succession.
Rajama: To lapidate, to stone.
Rajeem: He who is stoned (Satan).
Raka'ah: Prayer unit made up of various gestures and positions, among them the inclination (*Roukou'*). The five (compulsory) canonical prayers consist of seventeen *Raka'at*. The longest prayers (*Zuhr, 'Asr* and *'Ishā*) each contain four, the *Maghrib* three and the *Sob'h* two. The shortest prayer (*Witr*) contains only one, but is supererogatory.
Ramadan: The ninth month of the Muslim, or Hegiran lunar calendar month. Month of fasting, during which the Revelation of the Koran started. The Revelation was to go on for another twenty-three years, until the death of the Prophet. This is why Ramadan is the holiest and the best-observed of the four sacred months.
Rassul: Envoy, messenger.
Ridā: Length of unsewn cloth which the pilgrim drapes around his torso, leaving only the right shoulder uncovered, when he enters the sacred state of Ihrām.
Rissalah: Message.
Ruchd: Majority, right direction, maturity.
Ruh: Spirit, soul, breath.

S

Sabil Allah: Path of God, cause of God.
Sabr: Patience
Sadaqah: Alms.
Aŝ-Ŝafā and Al-Marwah: Two hillocks not far from the Ka'bah, between which both *Hajj* and *'Umrah* pilgrims must walk or run no less than seven times.
Ŝafar: Second month in the Muslim, or Hegiran lunar calendar month.
Saheeh: Genuine.
Sahifah: Page, parchment, vellum.
Sa'iqa: Thunderbolt, thunderclap, deafening, apocalyptic noise.
Sakhkhara: To favour, to facilitate, to submit.
Sakht: Irritation, curse.
Sakinah: Quietude.
Salam: Peace, salvation, salutation.
Ŝalat (plural, Ŝalawat): Canonical prayer (prescribed or supererogatory).
Salih (plural, Saliheem): Virtuous, just, holy, useful.
Salihat: Good actions.
Sallata: To subject, force, constrain.
Ŝarraf: Money-changer.
Sa'y: Rapid walk, ritual running between Aŝ-Ŝafā and Al-Marwah.
Sayd: Fishing. Hunting.
Sayf: Saber.
Sayyid: Leader, lord, sir.
Sha'a'ir (sing. Sha'irah): Rites.
Sha'b (plural, Shou'oub): People.
Sha'ban: 8th month of the Muslim or Hegiran lunar calendar.
Shaeed (plural, Shouhda): Martyr, witness.
Shafa 'a: Intercession.
Shafe'ites: Adepts of the Imam Ashshafi'i.
Shahada: (substantive noun). Profession of faith expressed in the formula: "There is no God but Allah and Muhammed is His Prophet" or "Muhammed is His Messenger".
Shahr-ol-Harām (plural, Ash'hur Hurum): Sacred month. There are four of these in the year: Muharrām (lst), Rajab (7th), Thu-l-Qa'dah (11th), and Thu-l-Hijjah (12th).
Shatat: Terrible lie, excess of words.
Shawwal: 10th month of the Muslim, or Hegiran lunar calendar.
Shaykh: Old man, master, spiritual leader.
Shaytan (plural, Shayatin): Satan, diabolical being, demon.
Shi'a: Doctrine of the legitimacy, *Alide* which holds that 'Ali (Ibn) Ali Ṭalib (the fourth of the Orthodox Caliphs) was the true spiritual and political heir of the Prophet. The Shi'ite doctrine predominates in Iraq, and even more so in Iran.
Shi'b: Valley, path in the mountain. District of Mecca.
Shifa: Healing.
Shirk: Polytheism, idolatry, paganism, association of two faiths.
Sidq: Sincerity.
Sifa: Attribute, quality.
Sirat: Path, way.
Sirr: Mystery, secret.
Siyam: Fast.
Sodor: Chests, hearts. Etymologically-speaking: path, way, and by extension custom, tradition, fate, destiny, divine immutability.
Ŝsayf: Summer.
Su'e: Evil, ill intention.
Sunnah: Tradition of the Prophet, covering the body of his words, his gestures, his attitudes and his silences. The *Sunnah* makes up the second foundation of Islam and its jurisprudence after the Koran, which is why its practice is highly recommended. The plural *Sunnan* means the compilations of the Tradition of the Prophet by different authors.

T

Ta'a: Obedience.
Ta'addi: Overstepping the limits, excess, infractions.
Ta'akhi: Fraternization, brotherhood.
Ta'am: Food.
Ṭāfa: To circle or turn around, to accomplish one circumambulation.
Tahallul: Desacralization.
Ṭaharah: Cleanliness, purity.
Tahiyyah: Greetings, salutations.
Tahluka: Peril.
Tahreem: Prohibition.
Tajalli: Brightness, dazzling light, radiance.
Tajweed: Perfect diction of the Koran. Psalmody.
Talbiyah: Acquiescence. Answer to the divine summons, "I am here".
Tamattu': Enjoyment. Sacred state of the pilgrim who performs the *'Umrah* (individual pilgrimage) alone.
Tanzeel: Descent, revelation.
Taqbeel al-Hajar al-Aswad: The act of kissing the Black Stone.
Taqwa: Extreme fear of God.
Tarawih: Supererogatory night prayers, recited only during Ramadan.
Tariqa: Spiritual doctrine or method or way.
Tartil: Perfect pronunciation of the Koran (see **Tajweed**).
Tarwiyah: Making provisions of water. Yawm Attarwiyah, 8th Thu-l-Hijjah, or day preceding the standing at 'Arāfat.
Tasdeeq: To add faith to, to regard as the truth.
Tashreeq: The act of cutting up and drying in the sun the flesh of sacrificed animals. **Ayyam at-Tashreeq:** days of the 11th,

12th and 13th Thu-l-Hijjah, which the pilgrims spend at Minā.

Tasmiya: To name, to recite the formula *"Bismi L-Lāhi Ar-Rahmāni Ar-Raheem"* (in the name of God the all-Merciful, the all-Compassionate).

Taṭawwu': Obedience, benevolent action, voluntary act.

Ṭawaf: Circumambulation.

Tawaffa: God calls to him, makes him die (see **Tuwuffiya**).

Tawakkul: To place oneself in God's hands.

Tawheed: Recognition of the oneness of God. Monotheism. **Ilm at-Tawheed:** theology.

Ṭayyib: Agreeable.

Tazakkā: To give alms, to acquit oneself of a tax, to purify oneself morally.

Thu-l-Hijjah: 12th month of the Muslim or Hegiran lunar calendar.

Thu-l-Qa'dah: 11th month of the Muslim or Hegiran lunar calendar.

Tuwuffiya: To be called to God, to die.

U

Ulema (singular, **Alem**): Scholars, theologians.

'Umar Ibn al-Khattab: Second Caliph. Was itinerant ambassador for the Qureishites before Islam. Famous for his conquest of Iraq, Persia, Syria and Egypt. Became converted to Islam all of a sudden and unexpectedly after having vowed to kill the Prophet. Exceedingly ascetic, he also had the reputation of being completely fair (581-644).

'Ummah: Community, nation.

Ummahatu al-Muminine: Mother of believers. Wives of the Prophet.

'Umrah: Pilgrimage to Mecca of an individual nature, which can be carried out at any time, known as the lesser or minor pilgrimage.

W

Wa'd: Promise.

Wah'y: Revelation, divine inspiration.

Wajib: Duty.

Wakeel (plural **Wuhala'**): Curator, mandatory, authorized agent.

Walad: Son.

Waqfa: See **Wuqūf**.

Wassawiss ash-Shaytan: Suggestions by Satan.

Wassi': Powerful, rich, vast. One of the sublime epithets of God.

Wayl: Misfortune, punishment.

Wudhu: Ablutions.

Wuquf: The rite of standing in a holy place.

Y

Ya'issa: To despair.

Yamin: Oath.

Yawma O'ddine: Day of the Last Judgement. Resurrection.

Z

Zawal: Decline of the sun as soon as it drops below the zenith.

Zikr: Memories, reminiscences, collection of *Ad'iya* (invocations), moral edification, another name for the Koran and for the Pentateuque (Torah).

Ziyyarah: Visit.

Zuhr: Midday, and especially beginning of the afternoon.

Ṣalāt az-Zuhr: canonical prayer of four *Raka'at* spoken under one's breath between one o'clock and three o'clock in the afternoon, according to the season.

Zzur: False testimony.

47 colour photographs pages (sud-editions) 11 maps and charts

LETTERS AND CONVENTIONAL SIGNS EMPLOYED FOR TRANSCRIPTION

■ *In order to complete letters whose phonetic equivalents exist in Latin characters, the authors have adopted the following latin and signs for the transcription of letters and sounds that do not exist in English.*

CONSONANTS

DJ	for DJABAL (mountain)	as in "adjective"
TH	for THALATHA (three)	as in "the"
H	for HADITH	aspirate "h" - does not exist in English
KH	for KHAWF	Spanish jota and German "ch" with A/O/U
DH	for DHANB	like "the" in English
Ḏ	for ḌOḤA	emphatic "d"
DḤ	for DOḤR	does not exist in English
Ṭ	for ṬALIB	emphatic "t"
C		does not exist in English
GH	for GHOUSL	"Gh" pronounced like a double "rr" in English
Q	for QOURAYCH	does not exist in English (stronger than the K)
K	for KITAB	"k" like in "kitten"
H	for HIDJRAH	aspirate "h"
W	for WAṬANE	like "w" in "water"
Y	for YOUSR	"y" like in youth
Ṣ	for ṢABR	emphatic "s".

VOWELS

In Arabic, vocals are indicated by means of signs which are placed (or omitted from) above letters. Phonetically, these signs do not quite correspond to English vowels. We have adopted the following to render the corresponding arabic pronunciation.

Short vowels		Long vowels	
A	as in KATABA	Ā	as in QĀLA
I	as in KOUTIBA	Ī	as in QĪLA
OU	as in KOUTIBA	OŪ	as in YAQOŪL

Mecca and Medinah today

series: jean hureau
photographs: sud-editions except when otherwise credited
translated by Marianne Sinclair

in the same series

by jean hureau	■ iran today *2nd edition*
	■ egypt today
	■ syria today
	■ corsica today
	■ morocco today
	■ tunisia today
	■ provence and the french riviera today
by raymond morineau	■ lebanon today
by mylène rémy	■ ivory coast *3nd edition*
	■ senegal today
	■ ghana today
	■ gabon today
by jacques-louis delpal	■ paris today
	■ the valley of the loire today
by jacques legros	■ scandinavia today
by siradiou diallo	■ zaïre today
by louis doucet	■ the caribbean today
by anne debel	■ cameroon today
by george oor	■ yugoslavia today
by maurice piraux	■ togo today
by clarisse desiles	■ japan today
by william skyvington	■ great britain today
by sennen andriamirado	■ madagascar today
by marie-ange donzé and claude sauvageot	■ china today

¦¦¦ les éditions j.a.

3 rue Roquépine 75008 paris

© 1980 - all rights reserved
printed in holland
printing completed 4 th quarter 1980
legal copy deposited 4 th quarter 1980
publisher's n° 1237/1 ISBN 2-85258-214.7